THE *IDEA* OF
MAN

books by Floyd W. Matson

THE IDEA OF MAN
THE BROKEN IMAGE
PREJUDICE, WAR, AND THE CONSTITUTION
(with Jacobus tenBroek and Edward N. Barnhart)
HOPE DEFERRED (with Jacobus tenBroek)
THE HUMAN DIALOGUE (Co-editor with Ashley Montagu)
WITHOUT/WITHIN (Editor)
BEING, BECOMING, AND BEHAVIOR (Editor)
VOICES OF CRISIS (Editor)

THE IDEA OF MAN

FLOYD W. MATSON

 Delacorte Press / New York

Grateful acknowledgment is made for permission to reprint the following material.

Abridgment from pp. 172, 174, 176–7 in PATHOS OF POWER by Kenneth B. Clark: Copyright © 1974 by Kenneth B. Clark. Reprinted by permission of Harper & Row, Publishers, Inc.

From CIVILIZATION AND ITS DISCONTENTS by Sigmund Freud: Translated and Edited by James Strachey. By permission of W. W. Norton & Company, Inc. Copyright © 1961 by James Strachey. From Volume XXI of THE STANDARD EDITION OF THE COMPLETE PSYCHOLOGICAL WORKS OF SIGMUND FREUD, revised and edited by James Strachey, used by permission of Sigmund Freud Copyrights Ltd., The Institute of Psycho-Analysis and The Hogarth Press Ltd.

"The Very Idea of Man" by F. W. Matson: In B. Marshall (Ed.), EXPERIENCES IN BEING. Copyright © 1971 by Wadsworth Publishing Company, Inc. Reprinted by permission of the publishers, Brooks/Cole Publishing Company, Monterey, California.

From pp. 139–140 in RADICAL MONOTHEISM IN WESTERN CULTURE by H. Richard Niebuhr: Reprinted by permission of Harper & Row, Publishers, Inc.

Library of Congress Cataloging in Publication Data

Matson, Floyd W.
The idea of man.

Includes bibliographical references and index.
1. Man.   I. Title.
BD450.M29   128′,3   76-6146
ISBN 0-440-04038-8

TO LEWIS MUMFORD

ACKNOWLEDGMENTS

During the several years of reading, writing, and redacting that have gone into the making of this book, I have accumulated a large number of intellectual debts which it is a pleasure as well as a duty to acknowledge. Some of these, to be sure, such as the continuous dialogues over ten years with students and colleagues of the Department of American Studies at the University of Hawaii, are too numerous and diffuse to specify; but certain others are direct and crucial. There might have been no book at all without the early encouragement and sustained support of Willis W. Harman, director of the Center for the Study of Social Policy at Stanford Research Institute, who—together with Oliver W. Markley of the Center—provided a forum for the experimental development of many of the ideas and arguments which appear in these pages. A further opportunity to try out various of the themes of the book (specifically of Parts One and Two) was made available to me in the form of the 1972 Salvatori Lectures of Claremont Men's College, for which I am especially indebted to Ward Elliott and to George C. S. Benson, director of the Henry Salvatori Center for the Study of Individual Freedom in the Modern World. I am also grateful to Joseph R. Royce, director of the Center for the Study of Theoretical Psychology of the University of Alberta, for a fruitful week of discussions with an interdisciplinary group of faculty and students in the fall of 1972. An earlier version of Chapter 6 was presented as a lecture at the California Institute of Technology in May, 1973; and partial drafts of Chapters 4, 8, and 10 appeared in two lectures given at the University of Oklahoma, in mid-1974 and early 1975, through the kind initiative of J. Clayton Feaver. The Preface, "The Very Idea of Man," was published in slightly altered form as a chapter in *Experiences of Being*, edited by Bernice Marshall (Copyright © 1971 by Wadsworth Publishing Company, Inc.), and is reprinted by permission of the publisher, Brooks/Cole Publishing Company, Monterey, California.

F.W.M.

CONTENTS

PREFACE THE VERY IDEA OF MAN:
A Personal Prologue   xiii

INTRODUCTION   1

PART I.   MAN AS KILLER:
The Natural History of a Myth

CHAPTER 1   DARWINISM:
The Biologizing of Social Thought   19

CHAPTER 2   FREUD:
Thoughts for the Times on War and Death   36

CHAPTER 3   LORENZ, ARDREY, AND COMPANY:
The Ethics of Ethology   55

PART II.   MAN AS MACHINE:
The Inhuman Uses of Human Beings

CHAPTER 4   TECHNOLOGICAL REVOLUTION:
The Paradox of Power   71

CHAPTER 5   BIOLOGICAL REVOLUTION:
The Nurture of Nature   84

CHAPTER 6   PSYCHOLOGICAL REVOLUTION:
The Rise of Psychotechnocracy   110

PART III.   MAN AS MAN:
The Revival of Humanism

CHAPTER 7   DEMOCRATIC MAN:
The Human Image in the American Creed   137

CHAPTER 8 THE ACADEMIC COUNTERCULTURE:
Toward a Radical Humanism 154

CHAPTER 9 MAN IN HISTORY:
Beyond Consensus 164

CHAPTER 10 MAN IN SOCIETY:
Beyond Utopia 181

CHAPTER 11 MAN IN PSYCHOLOGY:
Beyond Determinism 196

NOTES 211

INDEX 239

THE VERY IDEA OF MAN:
A Personal Prologue

"What is man, that thou art mindful of him?"

That ancient question, asked by the psalmist twenty-five hundred years ago, has had no lack of answers. Here are a few:

"Man is a noble animal" (Sir Thomas Browne) . . . "a mere insect" (Francis Church) . . . "a reasoning animal" (Seneca) . . . "but a beast" (Thomas Percy) . . . "great and strong and wise" (Louis Untermeyer) . . . "small potatoes" (Kipling) . . . "Man is born free" (Rousseau) . . . "is a prisoner" (Plato) . . . "master of his fate" (Tennyson) . . . "certainly stark mad" (Montaigne).

We could go on, piling up the contrasts and compounding the confusion. But that should be enough to make the point. The definition of man—or, more exactly, the *identity* of man—is an open question, a live issue, up for grabs. It has never been settled or agreed upon; possibly it never can be.

But the question keeps coming up. Indeed, it is likely that no other question has been more often pondered, debated, wondered at, worried over, and rhapsodized about. The reason is simple: It is not such an abstract matter as it sounds at first; the question of man's identity is the most personal of questions. The alternative form of the query "What is man?" is *"Who am I?"* It is not just "the others out there" but ourselves we are seeking to know when we raise that overwhelming question.

Man is the only creature that is a problem to itself. In Abraham Maslow's words, "The trouble is that the human species is the only species which finds it hard to be a species." For a cat, there seems to be no problem about being a cat—no complexes or "identity crises." Man alone is the *self-conscious* animal, the one for whom (as Socrates liked to say) the unexamined life is not worth living.

There is a good old saying, attributed to a devout Christian, that man is but an idea in the mind of God. And there is another saying (not quite so old and perhaps not quite so good) that God is but an idea in the mind of man. Take your choice. I prefer a third variation on the theme: *that man is an idea in the mind of man.* I don't mean, of course, that man is *only* an idea—that he is not also a material reality, a physical fact, a palpable presence in the world. What I do suggest is that the meaning of "man" to man—the definition of the term, the explanation of the fact, the answer to the question— depends crucially upon the ideas we hold.

For example, here are three ideas of man, three different images of human nature, that have persisted over a long period of time and give every appearance of persisting for a longer time to come. They are
   —the creature model: man as a *beast*;
   —the robot model: man as a *machine*;
   —the creator model: man as a *free agent*.
Logically speaking, these three ideas are incompatible with one another; if one of them is "true," then the others must be "false." Psychologically speaking, however, they may all be true—which is to say that any of them may be *experienced* as reality. Take the extreme case, that of

the robot model. Is it possible to *feel* like a machine, to regard oneself as merely an assemblage of mechanical parts—in effect, to deny "humanness"?

As for myself, the answer is yes. I often have that feeling—at least in moderate form—whenever I find myself "going through the motions" of some habitual or routine activity without much conscious purpose, performing like a mechanical toy or an automatic pilot. I suspect that most of us feel that way now and then but are able to shake off the illusion before it takes hold seriously. For many emotionally disturbed persons, however, faced with the stresses and distresses of our mechanized and overorganized society, the illusion may become the reality.

Such a person was Joey, the "mechanical boy" whose remarkable case history has been related by the psychiatrist Bruno Bettelheim. "He functioned as if by remote control, run by machines of his own powerfully creative fantasy. Not only did he himself believe that he was a machine but, more remarkably, he created this impression in others."[1] Joey was a schizophrenic nine-year-old who "chose the machine and froze himself in its image," in fierce if unconscious rejection of the human world, which had apparently rejected him. His mechanical existence was elaborately constructed and maintained. Entering the dining room at the hospital, he would string an imaginary wire to his electric outlet—his "energy source"—insulating himself with paper napkins and carefully plugging himself in. Only then, with the "current" turned on, could Joey eat or show any signs of life.

What is especially striking about this case study of a "mechanical boy" is that Joey's performance was so convincing that the doctors and staff found themselves involuntarily responding to him as a machine rather than as a human being—being careful, for example, not to step on his "wires," and failing even to notice him during the long, silent intervals when he was "turned off." It was not Joey alone who believed in his mechanical nature; he also made believers (at least momentarily) of those who encountered him. By *living* his illusion, Joey made it real to himself and others.

But then, why should that surprise us? Not only is the urban environment of modern man filled with the sights and sounds of machines, it is dominated by their images. Machines—from clocks to cars, from toasters to television sets—are the idols and icons of our technological society; their efficiency and productivity, their freedom from fatigue and fever, their great gifts of calculation and coordination, make them vastly superior to mere human beings in the very enterprises that have counted most to our economy and society. Why shouldn't we fashion our-selves in the image of the Great Machine?

There is another, even more forceful, reason for regard-ing man generally (and ourselves in particular) in me-chanical terms: Science *tells* us to do so, and the voice of science is authoritative above all others in our culture. Ever since the apple fell on Newton, three hundred years ago, we have been inclined to view all nature—including human nature—through the cold eye of the physicist. "Let us conclude boldly then," said a French Newtonian of the eighteenth century (La Mettrie), "that man is a machine." To which an American psychologist of our own century (J. B. Watson) has added that man is "an organic machine, ready to run."[2]

This should be enough to show that the robot model of man comes highly recommended. It is not, however, the only popular model in the marketplace of ideas; at least equally well accepted is what I have called the "creature model"—the idea of man as an animal. This alternative way of defining human nature and explaining human conduct is often described as the biological analogy. Just as the robot model was the product of the emergence of modern physics, some three centuries ago, so the creature model is the product of the rise of modern biology, one century ago. It is probable that this animal-centered approach to man will become even more persuasive in the years to come, under the impact of the new developments in genetics and other sciences which have come to be known as the "biological revolution."

What does it mean, in subjective terms, to embrace this biological image of man? What does it feel like to experience oneself as a beast? Two aspects of the inner experience seem to stand out above most others. One (shared with the robot model) is the total absence of consciousness and choice, the disappearance of the realm of *freedom*. The other is what might be termed the "call-of-the-wild" syndrome: the heightened awareness of the "jungle" instincts of aggression and competition. Just as Joey felt himself to be a kind of electric circuit through which the energetic currents passed (never the catalyst or active agent, just the conductor or field), so the felt experience of the self as a creature is dominated by the sensation of blind vital forces welling up through the circulatory system and clamoring for release.

Although it is not precisely illustrative of the point I am making, here is one version of the experience of oneself as a creature, as imagined by Franz Kafka in his story "The Metamorphosis":

As Gregor Samsa awoke one morning from uneasy dreams he found himself transformed in his bed into a gigantic insect. He was lying on his hard, as it were armor-plated, back and when he lifted his head a little he could see his dome-like brown belly divided into stiff arched segments on top of which the bed quilt could hardly be kept in position and was about to slide off completely. His numerous legs, which were pitifully thin compared to the rest of his bulk, waved helplessly before his eyes.[3]

To feel oneself a creature, it would seem, is never to feel oneself a *creator*; rather, it may very well be to feel oneself a *destroyer*—that is, a beast of prey, a killer. At least since Darwin, whose theory of evolution presented a struggle for survival in the animal kingdom in which the strong and cunning prevail over the weak and peaceful, we have cultivated a concept of "nature red in tooth and claw"—an image of the beasts as "beastly" and of animal society as a "jungle." Then we have proceeded, through the doctrine known as Social Darwinism, to extend that unflattering image to human nature and society. Despite overwhelming evidence to the contrary —evidence establishing the essential role of cooperation and mutual aid everywhere in nature (and correcting the false notion that predators are "killers" rather than simply hunters without malice toward the hunted)—the bestial model of man and the jungle model of society flourish more than ever among us.

And why not, given the conflict and confusion of the world we live in? In much the same way that the technological environment shapes our language and thought and makes the machine a convincing model of man, the wars and riots and violent episodes of our century seem to support the idea of man as a creature of murderous impulses—impulses that might be briefly checked or turned aside but can never be "unlearned" or permanently erased. In recent decades a host of theories has been advanced—in biology, ethology, psychology, and elsewhere—claiming to document the inherently aggressive nature of human nature. After Darwin there came the dark forebodings of Sigmund Freud, the father of psychoanalysis, who bequeathed to us a concept of the "death instinct" forever at war with the "life instinct" in the heart of man. What Freud meant by the death instinct was nothing less than a hostile drive, innate and inextinguishable, aimed at harming others as well as oneself— in a word, the "killer instinct." Man, he said forthrightly, is forever a wolf to man; who can deny it, in the face of our bloody human history? We are, according to Freud, our own predators—our own worst enemies.

Perhaps. But is that all there is to human history? Possibly the meaning of history (like the secret of beauty) is in the eye of the beholder. There is, after all, not only a history of war but a history of peace, a recollection of tranquillity and harmony, a chronicle of cooperation and concern, a legendry of love. Our perception of the past, like our perception of the world around us, is surely selective; when we seek to reconstruct the past (to paraphrase a line of Lytton Strachey's), we row out over that great ocean of material and lower down into it, here and there, a little bucket. In an age when things are going rather well—as in that long, relatively peaceful and productive era in American history running from the Civil War to World War I—the study of history tends to mirror our general confidence and complacency. In an age of anxiety, alienation and anger such as our own, it should not be surprising that we tend to find in history a reflection of our pain and pessimism.

To be specific, it might be more than mere coincidence that Freud came upon his gloomy theory of the aggression instinct in the aftermath of World War I, which devastated Europe (Freud lived in Vienna) and was followed by a wave of riots and rebellions. It must surely have seemed only natural then, to see the source of all that manifest evil in the very nature of man. Not only *then*; it has also seemed natural to a great many sensitive students of man and society in the sixties—the decade of Vietnam and Watts, of intracity bombings and intercontinental missiles, and of revolutions among youth, among minorities, and among the new and old nations of the "Third World." That man is not only a beast but a beast of prey—and that, unique among animals, his prey is his own kind—is so familiar a thesis that it has taken on almost the character of a truism, an obvious and elementary "fact of life."

Well, not quite. There is still another model of man available—that which views him as a free agent, a creative actor on the world stage—which is not only distinct from the bestial and mechanical models but profoundly opposed to both. The central point of the creator model is that man is *free*, in a sense and to a degree unknown to animal, vegetable, or mineral. To be more definite about it, the claim is that human existence is open-ended rather than predetermined, that it is characterized primarily by choice and contingency and chance rather than by compulsion. Man, as the existentialist philosopher Jean-Paul Sartre has put it, is "condemned to be free."

What does it mean to accept this idea of man—to experience oneself as a free agent, as fully human? I am tempted to answer: "It means everything." For with that experience, and through it, there emerges an awareness of the self (that is, of *one*self) as active rather than as reactive or passive—and from that healthy shock of recognition arises all that elevates the human condition beyond subhuman existence. It is the basis for self-respect, for the sense of personal responsibility, and for what one perceptive student of man (Ernest G. Schachtel) has called the "open encounter of the total person with the world."[4] That is the real difference of man (to echo Mortimer J. Adler) and the difference it makes.

Another aspect of this third idea of man sets it apart from the other two. Both the bestial and the mechanical models conceive of the human being as a "closed system" —predetermined rather than self-determining, reflexive rather than resourceful. "Freedom" is regarded as an irrelevant sentimentality, out of place in such a scientific analysis. (Thus, one influential psychologist of the present day, B. F. Skinner, has declared: "The hypothesis that man is *not free* is essential to the application of scientific method to the study of human behavior."⁵) On this view, the best that man can do is to discover the forces that rule him and surrender decently to them: "The moving finger writes; and having writ moves on; nor all your piety nor wit shall lure it back to cancel half a line." But the model of man as a free agent cancels more than half a line, for the moving finger is seen as man's, not Fate's. And man, in this liberating perspective, is not compelled to write any particular line, or even to write at all! What is distinctive about man is the power to choose, the freedom to say yes or no to the universe; man alone, in the face of all the forces and constraints of time and circumstance, has the power to make what the philosopher Herbert Marcuse calls the Great Refusal—or, one might add, to undertake an even greater *affirmation*.

What is characteristic of the animal is its will to survive, to maintain its existence; but what is characteristic of man is the need to go beyond survival, to risk his own existence, to "follow all of his days something that he cannot name"—to climb the next mountain, to fly to the moon, to dare the universe, to defy the gods. This is what it means to be a creator: to act upon the world rather than to be acted on, to take chances and to make changes. It is not enough, then, to talk of survival, as William Faulkner advised us more than a quarter-century ago in a Nobel Prize address:

> It is easy enough to say that man is immortal simply because he will endure; that when the last ding-dong of doom has clanged and faded from the last worthless rock hanging lifeless in the last red and dying sunset, that even then there will still be

one more sound: that of his puny inexhaustible voice, still talking. I refuse to accept this. I believe that man will not merely endure, he will prevail. He is immortal, not because he alone among creatures has an inexhaustible voice, but because he has a soul, a spirit, capable of compassion and sacrifice and honor. . . . Machines endure and animals survive; but only man can prevail.[6]

That, in brief, is the difference between the creator model of man on the one hand and the bestial and mechanical models on the other.

Take your choice. It is for each of us to decide which of these ideas of man is most persuasive and plausible. But remember this while you are considering the options: Only the *creator* model, the image of man as a free agent, grants you the right to make such a choice and the power to convince the world of its truth.

F. W. M.

Honolulu, Hawaii
September 1975

> The history of the theory of human nature—of men's ideas about man—therefore is, or should be, one of the major fields of investigation for the student of the history of ideas. . . . We have many works, under various titles, on the history of the idea of God, but none that I can recall on the history of the idea of man.[1]

That was the judgment of the dean of intellectual historians, Arthur O. Lovejoy, in his *Reflections on Human Nature*, composed a generation ago. Lovejoy's sense of the importance of "men's ideas about man" was not limited to the perception that such self-definitions are an essential element in the general history of ideas—although he was emphatic in his recognition that the images of man projected or smuggled into the literature of an age furnish an indispensable clue to its inner character and outer behavior. Beyond that, Lovejoy argued that these underlying assumptions about human nature, however tacit or unexamined, "are important phenomena in the history of the human mind, interacting with and often powerfully influencing other phenomena—most evidently of all, political movements and political constitutions."[2]

To know what man has made of man, in short, is largely to know what man has made of his world—and why.

To be sure, this is not altogether a novel insight. On the level of the individual human being, at least, it is something of a staple of philosophy and folklore. In the *Bhagavad Gita* it is written: "Man is made by his belief . . . as he believes, so he is." And the Bible (Proverbs 23:7) tells us in much the same words that "As man thinketh in his heart, so he is." But this intuition of the ancients, with its implicit affirmation of human freedom and human responsibility, was confounded by the cosmic determinism of systematic theology. And the revival of the old intuition in modern times has been overwhelmed by the no less cosmic determinism of the new theology— that of Science. Against the successive claims of classical physics, biology, and psychology the notion that human thoughts and beliefs, ideas and images, may have an active life of their own and an impact upon the objective world was, until only yesterday, summarily dismissed by the court of respectable opinion. It was customary to explain the nature of ideas by explaining them away— by seeking their hard-edged "causes" in the material world as one rummages for gems on a littered shore or needles in a haystack—thereby reducing *res cogitans*, the things of the mind, to the ethereal dimensions of epiphenomena, or noumena, or simply illusion. (To Thomas Hobbes, ideas were "animal motions"; to Ludwig Gumplowicz, they were "delusions"; to A. F. Bentley, they were "spooks"; and to John B. Watson, they were as irrelevant and incompetent as they were immaterial.[3]) Thus tamed and trivialized, the inner life of man was turned over to the departments of arts and letters—the incorrigible "humanities"—while the scientists, natural and social, got on with the serious business of the real world out there.

That is, of course, not quite the state of things today

in the sciences of nature and man. The cosmological law and order of classical physics—what Ernst Cassirer called the "iron ring of necessity" that enclosed our every thought and action—has been thoroughly subverted by the succession of revolutions within physics itself; and the traditional fixed boundary between Subjectivity and Objectivity, between Appearance and Reality, has been so often penetrated and overrun as to be virtually undefended if not indefensible: the Maginot Line of the old order. In field after field—not only physics but biology, not only psychology but sociology, anthropology, and political science—the distance between the observer and the observed, between the scientist-subject and the scientific object, has become progressively obscured, ambiguous, and problematic. If the observer is also a participant, then it follows that he should observe his own participation; he is found to be included within his own equation and field of vision, and if he is to know his field he must come to know himself. "The true physics," said Teilhard de Chardin, "is that which will, one day, achieve the inclusion of man in his wholeness in a coherent picture of the world."[4]

It is ironic that this insight—the recognition (in P. W. Bridgman's phrase) of an inescapable human presence in every act of observation—should have come earliest and most forcefully from the physical sciences, where that presence is least conspicuous, rather than from the human sciences, where its very obviousness has rendered it suspect. The orthodox disposition of the unsettling issue of "subjectivity" in the social studies has been to regard it as a kind of virus to which even scientists are not wholly immune but against which various preventatives and prophylactics may be therapeutically effective. Thus, a few years ago a scientific psychologist (H. J. Eysenck) could observe that while he might have ethical compunctions about what he was doing as a scientist, "such

feelings are irrelevant and must be prevented from con-
taminating a purely factual and objective study."[5] Another
behavioral scientist (Clark L. Hull) headed his discussion
of the problem: "A Suggested Prophylactic Against Anthropomorphic Subjectivism."[6] And the first selection of
a book of readings for the introductory sociology student
was entitled "Undermining the Student's Faith in the
Validity of Personal Experience."[7]

In a seminal exposition of the "sociology of sociology,"
published in 1970, Robert W. Friedrichs called attention
to the "vast body of evidence supporting the view that
mid-twentieth-century man seeks to flee from the self."[8]
Remarking on the disappearance of man as subject and
his reappearance as object throughout the behavioral
sciences, Friedrichs took note of the frequent occurrence
of "such not completely lighthearted observations as the
one in which man is described as 'a ten-cycle computer
in a one-tenth ton chassis with a one-tenth horse power
motor,' followed by the only appropriate conclusion: 'Get
rid of him.' " And he added: "In point of fact one may
not have to get rid of him. Characterized in such terms,
he has already disappeared."[9] The moral and psychic
consequences of this methodological suicide are illuminated in a passage which Friedrichs cites from the historian H. Richard Niebuhr:

> Our western morality is built on the recognition
> that nothing is more important, more to be served
> and honored, apart from God himself, than human
> I's and Thou's—the selves we are and the selves
> among whom we live. But the morality of personal
> worth maintains itself in our subconscious minds
> like an alien in a strange country where no one
> understands and few acknowledge his presence.
> These selves among selves are required to direct

their attention to things, to impersonal powers, forces, relations, and concepts. They are the knowers, but only the known is acknowledged and honored; they devote themselves to the cause of knowledge, but only the publicly, generally present is accorded the recognition of being real and valuable. These selves are true and false to themselves and to one another, but only the truth and falsity of their statements about things assumed to be objective is considered important. They live in the intense subjectivity of decision, of anxiety about meaning, of commitment to their causes. They live in faithfulness and in treason. They must deal in their isolation with the questions of life and death, of being or not being. They must enact the dramas of devotion to great and little causes, suffer the spiritual pains of betrayal and being betrayed, of reconciliation to life and of revolt.

But as selves they are epiphenomena in the dominant world view of our society. Poetry and religion may portray them, but poetry and faith are officially regarded as dealing with the mythical. What alone is acknowledged, accepted and actual, is the object. So far as selves can be made objects—set before the mind as projected, eternal realities—they have their place. But then they are no longer selves; they are not I's and Thou's but It's.

So we live in a depersonalized and disenchanted world in which we are taught to doubt the primary realities that we experience—the self and its companion selves—and in which we are taught to flee from the knowledge which lies near the beginning of wisdom—the knowledge of ourselves . . . the world in which all selves become objects for objective knowledge on the one hand, for objective manipulation in the market and the political arena on the

other, is not a world in which the morality of personal value can flourish. . . .[10]

Niebuhr's admonition of 1960 is still pertinent and
compelling. But, increasingly of late, the ritual incanta-
tions of the priestly exorcists seeking to banish Anthropomorphic Subjectivism from the sacred grove begin to take
on a plaintive, not to say comic, note; they lack assurance
and authority, and come to be seen as desperate efforts
to shore up fallen ramparts against the ruins of an
obsolete world view. Perhaps they still bespeak the conventional wisdom, the ruling paradigm, of the behavioral-
science orthodoxy; but over the past generation the
current has been moving, gradually but unmistakably, in
the opposite direction. A cumulative series of theoretical
developments, notably in the psychology of science and
the sociology of knowledge, has compelled attention to
the intrinsic and irreducible role performed in all human
activities by the thoughts, beliefs, and values—in a word,
the *presence*—of the human actors. Indeed, the term
"actor" (rather than "reactor" or simply "object") has
reappeared in the lexicon: Man has returned to the stage
of his own science.

If his presence on the stage has not yet been noticed
by all members of the academic audience, and if the significance of his new role remains widely misunderstood,
that is not only because of the organized perceptual
defenses and selective inattention of the old guard. The
contribution to the new understanding of the human actor
by the sociology of knowledge, in particular, is ambiguous
if not ambivalent. As its name indicates, this venerable
school of thought—whose ancestry may be traced beyond
Karl Mannheim and Max Scheler to Max Weber, Wilhelm
Dilthey, and Karl Marx[11]—has been primarily occupied
in demonstrating the "social construction of reality":[12]
i.e., the internalization or introjection of cultural norms

and values. It has exposed the ideological component of ideas, the nonrational dimension in reasoning itself. Therefore, on one side, the sociologists of knowledge have appeared to support the positivist impulse to diminish and disparage the autonomy of mind and the independence of man, reducing the status of ideas to reflexive and compulsive reverberations of the grimly determining forces in the social environment.

But the critical thrust of the sociology of knowledge has also cut the other way. While it has been uncovering the social construction of ideas and ideals, it has also been revealing the reciprocal influence of ideas and ideals upon social constructions; that is to say, it has shown knowledge to be *personal* as well as social.[13] *Wissensociologie* has focused attention upon "the human nature of science"[14]—the underlying personal reference point (to use Bridgman's term) in all human enterprise, however abstract or aloof or antiseptic. More specifically, these investigations of the nonempirical, nonrational ingredients of thought and theory have demonstrated that, contrary to the positivist pretension, such thought can never be "disinterested" but must always embody a powerful element of *interest*: which is to say that the investigator, the thinker, the doer, has a stake in what he is doing— a motivation or impulsion under and beneath the logic of pure Reason and the pursuit of disembodied Truth.

But it was not the intention of Mannheim and his disciples to translate "interest" simply as "bias" and then to excoriate it. Interest meant to them not only prejudice or passion but commitment and concern; it was the basis of insight and the source of understanding. "It is the participation in an activity," according to Louis Wirth, "that generates interest, purpose, point of view, value, meaning and intelligibility, as well as bias."[15] Not only was there no escaping this element of interest and involvement; there *should* be none, for it was precisely what made the work of science and scholarship a human, rather than a mechanical, enterprise.

To speak of interest and commitment as essential to the process of inquiry is, of course, to repudiate the established canon of ethical neutrality and to replace it with what Richard L. Means has called "the ethical imperative."[16] It is to reassert for the study of man, if not also that of nature, the name given to it by John Stuart Mill of the *moral science* (as distinct from positive or behavioral science); and it is to reinstate the fundamental distinction made by Dilthey and others in the last century between *Naturwissenschaften* and *Geisteswissenschaften* —between the sciences of nature, concerned with the discovery of cause and effect, and the sciences of the "human spirit," concerned with the explanation of meaningful relations and purposive actions. In this tradition of German scholarship the physical sciences were conceded the realm of objectivity while the human sciences occupied the realm of *intersubjectivity*. Even that prudent distinction, as we have seen, has come under challenge from the new generation of physical theorists who perceive in the creative work of natural scientists the unmistakable ingredients of what Michael Polanyi defines as "heuristic passion" and Arthur Koestler bluntly labels "sleepwalking."[17] Polanyi in particular has meticulously documented the thesis that (as Abraham Maslow summarizes it) "a scientist is at all times a gambler, a connoisseur, a man of good taste or bad taste, a man who makes acts of faith and leaps of commitment, a man of will, a responsible person, an active agent, a chooser and therefore a rejector."[18]

If the "myth of objective consciousness" (in Theodore Roszak's phrase) may be said to have come under challenge in the natural sciences, it is under something like total siege in the sciences of man. And although it would be reckless to say that the myth has yet been dispelled

or dethroned, the assault upon it has become so widespread and thoroughgoing as to signal the advent of a
crisis and to foreshadow the coming of a revolution. Thus,
so reputable a sociologist as Alvin W. Gouldner has enu-
merated "the varied signs of an impending transformation in the social sciences," and has entitled his survey
The Coming Crisis of Western Sociology.[19] The late
Abraham Maslow, founding father of contemporary humanistic psychology, wrote shortly before his death of the
new trend in his field as "a revolution in the truest, oldest
sense of the word, the sense in which Galileo, Darwin,
Einstein, Freud, and Marx made revolutions, i.e., new
ways of perceiving and thinking, new images of man and
of society, new conceptions of ethics and of values, new
directions in which to move."[20] Even more sweepingly,
Willis Harman anticipates a "new Copernican Revolution" in human knowledge with its source in the infant
science of man's subjective experience;[21] and Robert W.
Friedrichs discerns a fundamental "paradigm shift" in
sociology away from the regnant "priestly" mode of chaste
detachment to the insurgent "prophetic" style of committed participant-observation.[22] Meanwhile, in the vanguard of the revolution of hope, the vision of apocalypse
and transfiguration looms in the writings of missionaries
of the academic counterculture such as Charles Reich,
Philip Slater, and Theodore Roszak.[23]

Whatever its outreaches and overreachings, this new
wave of social-scientific humanism (more accurately, of
personalism) is no ephemeral efflorescence of a neo-
Romantic revolt. It has persisted long enough and penetrated deeply enough already to be identifiable as a
coherent movement of thought grounded in a distinctive
idea of man: a new image of being and of minding. Its
central proposition is the personal and contingent character of all knowledge, and more specifically of social
or *self-observing* knowledge—that which bears upon the

nature and destiny of man. And the major significance of this new idea lies in its powerful reinforcement of the freedom and responsibility of the actor and thinker and observer, whatever his vocation or pretension. It maintains that underlying and overarching all research and observation are the "hidden images of man," as Maurice Friedman has called them:[24] the tacit assumptions about human nature—about himself and other selves—held by the observer. His interpretations, however rooted in observation and drenched in data, are inescapably projections from this personal base; and even the consensual validation of his report by scientific peers and colleagues, as Thomas Kuhn among others has made us aware,[25] is no proof of purity or timeless truth but an *agreement* founded on a common paradigm—a shared framework of interest, value, and belief embraced by the community of scholars. "Background assumptions," as Gouldner has designated this underlying framework, "are embedded in a theory's postulations. Operating within and alongside of them, they are, as it were, 'silent partners' in the theoretical enterprise. . . . Background assumptions also influence the *social* career of a theory, influencing the responses of those to whom it is communicated."[26]

To say that knowledge is personal and its validation interpersonal is not, of course, to say it is *only* that—thereby recommitting the nothing-but fallacy of the behavioral positivists with their myopic "single vision." The recognition of the intersubjective serves to correct that visual defect and to restore the unitary perception of knowledge as experience, of science as human, of thought as dialectical and complementary. "Coextensive to their Without," as Teilhard de Chardin observed, "there is a Within to things."[27] Most significantly of all, to take the view of the new humanism is to accentuate the crucial function of personal decision—of *choice* on the basis of commitment, value, ideology, and interest—undertaken by the student of man and society. The case he presents is not only a matter of (logical) demonstration, it is also one of (psychological) persuasion—which is to say that the social scientist, dealing with man, is never merely reciting facts but *conducting an argument*. The mode of discourse he employs, however cloaked in methodological asceticism, is not purely descriptive and denotative but also rhetorical and hortatory. In short, the language of social science is not one of abstract monologue but of human dialogue; and what holds for the sender of the communication holds equally for the receiver—the partner in dialogue. The receiver, in attending to the presentation, is never simply "convinced by the evidence" but persuaded by the argument. In accepting or rejecting it, the receiver makes his own act of choice—his judgment. And he does so, no less than his partner, on the basis of "background assumptions"—values, commitments, and interests—for the most part only dimly seen and rarely made explicit.

This act of choice, of personal decision and subjective judgment, on either side of the dialogue—being a moral act—carries a large burden of responsibility. To be sure, the choice may be made irresponsibly, out of ignorance or prejudice or indifference; but it may also be made responsibly, in self-awareness and "sympathetic introspection" (to use the phrase of Charles Horton Cooley).[28] Nor is this decision making a matter simply of personal integrity or private ethics; the act of choosing represents a commitment of undeniable social relevance and political concern. For if it is true, in general, that "ideas have consequences," then men's ideas about man have the most far-reaching consequences of all. Upon them may depend the structure of government, the patterns of cul-

ture, the purposes of education, the design of the future
—and the human or inhuman uses of human beings.

> The danger lies [as Richard L. Means has written]
> in what man thinks he is, for this may shape what
> he becomes. If the fascist and totalitarian revolu-
> tions have taught us nothing else, they should at
> least suggest that the views of the nature of man,
> the reigning metaphors of social interpretation, can-
> not be taken lightly. One must continually cross
> swords with the dominant views of man, for if these
> views in any way become rationalizations for the
> destruction and manipulation of men or for warfare,
> then they are of the deepest concern to all rational
> and humane men.[29]

Most of the present book (Parts i and ii) represents a
crossing of swords with two currently dominant views of
the nature of man—those that I have called the bestial
model and the mechanical model, both of which threaten
to "become rationalizations for the destruction and manipulation of men." It will be argued that the grip of
these ideas upon us is not the compelling hold of reality
or the force of truth but the persuasive grasp of ideology
and mythology—and therefore that the natural history of
these ideas of man is not a record of progressive enlightenment but a nightmare of intellectual darkness from
which we should be trying to awake. And it will be argued,
further, that the act of choosing among competitive
visions of human nature and social order is not primarily
a scientific exercise but an existential and moral task: a
challenge to each human being to forsake the passive
posture of acquiescence before immutable cosmic law, so
long imposed upon us by religion and science, and to
assume the active role of self-creator—the maker of cul-

tures and shaker of foundations—which is no longer forbidden by the reformed science of nature and is boldly encouraged by the revitalized science of man. *To become or not to become*: that is the question. Or, as Gouldner has put it:

> The question here is not simply which parts of an intellectual system are empirically true or false, but also which are liberative and which repressive in their consequences. In short, the problem is: What are the social and political consequences of the intellectual system under examination? Do they liberate or repress men? Do they bind men into the social world that now exists, or do they enable men to transcend it?[30]

This book, then, represents an exercise in the psychohistory of an idea: the idea of man. More specifically it is an account, avowedly partial and partisan, of three variations on the theme—only three, out of the immensity of collective self-representations that have beguiled and bemused humanity from the neolithic to the neotechnic millennium. Even within that restricted frame of reference, the discussion is far from exhaustive or conclusive; the purpose has not been to make the study comprehensive but to make the ideas comprehensible. Little is said, for example, of the premodern history of these contesting approaches to the heart of man. (The image of *la bête humaine* is older even than Original Sin; the model of the "mega-machine," as we know from Lewis Mumford, was in use among the early Egyptians; and the humanist alternative was thoroughly worked out, in terms not yet improved upon, by Socrates of Athens.) Nor have all the modern bases of human self-imaging and imagining (such as those of art and literature) been touched upon here; this is not a survey but a reconnaissance. What transpires in these pages is not a rounded sociology of knowledge, a la Mannheim, but a microsociology of self-knowledge, a la Goffman.[31]

And something more. If all of written history is an act of faith, as Beard supposed, contemporary history (reflection on what someone has called the "recent present") is egregiously so. But ours is not an age of faith, least of all in man himself; acts of devotion and celebrations of humanism are distinctly out of vogue. This book has been written in the backwash of Watergate and the ashes of Vietnam, during the prolonged winter of our discontent with the rhetorics of righteousness and the Tin Pan Alley lyrics of liberalism. It is an era of antifaiths, of fallen idols and broken images—when old revolutionaries of hope have become anatomists of human destructiveness, when the manipulative technology of behaviorism is "mod," when novelists have abandoned realism and embraced the "schlemiel" as hero, when even popular culture is composed of situation tragedies—and when it seems that everywhere "the best lack all conviction while the worst are full of passionate intensity."

The thesis of this book runs counter to that prevailing mood. It is plainly optimistic. Its essential point is that, just as art can never be merely the "holding of a mirror up to nature," so the arts of collective self-portraiture (the human studies) cannot be merely a reflecting and recording of objective data—the mirroring of a fixed and determinate human nature. The artist intervenes, as he must; he interprets, as he should; he creates an image that embodies his vision, and seeks to persuade us of its truth. But it is an image, no more than that, until we are so persuaded; only then does it take on the power of truth and the aspect of eternity. That is the crux of the matter: The image has no hold upon us until we assent to it; truths about man are prophecies self-fulfilled. The real power, therefore, is ours: the power to choose among competing images of ourselves, grounded in contending ideologies and conflicting values. And so, with Lewis Mumford, "We must now ask ourselves, for the first time, what sort of society and what kind of men are we seeking to produce?"[32]

I

MAN AS KILLER:
The Natural History
of a Myth

CHAPTER 1

DARWINISM:
The Biologizing of Social Thought

"Darwinism" is the name conventionally given to a body of scientific theory presenting the case for biological evolution in terms of certain key concepts such as natural selection and the struggle for existence. "Social Darwinism" is the title historically applied to an ideological doctrine of the nineteenth century seeking to extend Darwin's theory from the animal kingdom to human society in such a way as to furnish a cloak of scientific authority and respectability for the prevailing social practices of rugged individualism, unbridled competition, imperialism, war, and aggression. In the annals of cultural and intellectual history, Darwinism is customarily regarded as a magnificent example of natural science at its best—rigorous, objective, and value-free. Social Darwinism, on the other hand, is seen as a kind of illegitimate spin-off or by-product, scientifically spurious and philosophically obsolete. In short, the social theory of Darwinism has been repudiated at the same time as the scientific theory has been vindicated; in this manner Science and Ideology are happily distinguished from one another, and the Darwinian theory of evolution is neatly extricated from the context of cultural bias and political apologetics.

Extricated along with that theory, however, and retained within the aura of science, is the image of Nature—human as well as animal—which is implicit in Darwinism. The image of Nature, in a word, is that of the Jungle ("Nature red in fang and claw"); and the image of human nature is that of *la bête humaine*—the man-beast, predator and aggressor.

The conventional distinction between the biological and social theories of Darwinism has long been suspect as arbitrary and, at certain points at least, artificial. In its premises if not in its proofs, Darwin's theory of evolution through natural selection was first of all a sociological, rather than a biological, concept. Darwin, as J. Arthur Thomson was among the first to point out, "projected on organic life a sociological idea, and showed that it fitted." In his 1910 study, *Darwinism and Human Life*, Thomson found nothing strange or inappropriate in the process of anthropomorphic analogy which he perceived to underlie Darwin's thought:

> The formula "struggle for existence," familiar in human affairs, was used by Darwin in his interpretation of organic life, and he showed that we gain clearness in our outlook on animate nature if we recognize there, in continual process, a struggle for existence not merely analogous to, but fundamentally the same as, that which goes on in human life. . . .[1]

More recently, the anthropologist Marvin Harris has demonstrated at length that "Darwin's principles were an application of social-science concepts to biology";[2] and the biologist Garrett Hardin has spelled out the manner in which Darwin "introjected into the scientific world the cybernetic scheme that pervaded the economic thinking in which he grew to manhood."[3] It is well known that

Darwin came upon the principle of natural selection and the struggle for survival, not from his meticulous observations and collections, but from reading Malthus' *Essay on Population*—and that the phrase "survival of the fittest" (which first appeared in the second edition of the *Origin of Species*) was contributed by Herbert Spencer, the ranking philosophical champion of laissez-faire economics and the ethics of rugged individualism. (It is noteworthy that Darwin's competitor Alfred Wallace, working independently, also happened upon the insight of natural-selection-through-struggle in the same way—that is, through reading Malthus.[4])

These evidences of extrascientific influence and unconscious bias in the development of Darwin's thought are less important for themselves than for the clues they provide to a deeper biographical fact which is not so widely appreciated: namely, the extent to which Darwin was a product of his culture and a child of his time. "The principle of the survival of the fittest," as John Maynard Keynes remarked, "is just a vast generalization of Ricardian economics." Expressed another way, the image of *struggle* in nature was a projection of the principle of *competition* in human society; and that principle in turn was the dominant metaphor, the main supporting pillar, of the conventional wisdom of Darwin's century. The pervasive apprehension of struggle and conflict was not only "in the air" of social and political speculation; it was already imported into biology by Spencer himself, some years before the publication of the *Origin*. As Harris puts it:

> In Spencer's earliest as well as in his most mature works, the discussion of evolution, struggle, and perfectibility takes place within an avowedly political framework. His open defense of economic liberalism and his condemnation of cooperativism, social-

ism, and communism again illustrate the futility
of isolating the development of theories of culture
from their sociocultural context. . . . Taking all these
factors into consideration, it seems evident not only
that the word "Spencerism" suffices for naming the
biocultural theories that have come to be known as
Social Darwinism, but that the term "Biological
Spencerism" would be an appropriate label for that
period of the history of biological theory in which
Darwin's ideas gained their ascendancy.[5]

To a reader from another and different cultural epoch,
one of the striking features of Darwin's narrative is the
prominence and recurrence of its images of struggle and
conflict. Stanley Edgar Hyman, in his study of Darwin
as an imaginative writer, demonstrates in detail that "the
archetypal image of the *Origin* is the war of nature."[6]
"All through the book, [Darwin] refers to 'a constant
struggle going on,' 'the constantly-recurring Struggle for
Existence,' 'victory in the battle for life,' and so on."[7] On
the basis of his close textual analysis, Hyman is led to a
pertinent conclusion: "We realize that this dramatic and
tragic vision of life *comes from Darwin, rather than from
his subject-matter*, when we see how undramatic most
present-day formulations of natural selection are."[8] In
other words, the dark vision of nature red in fang and
claw, which Darwin shared with Tennyson, was not out
there in the world but in the eye of the beholder—a
poetic intuition rather than an empirical observation.
Hyman goes so far as to maintain that the *Origin of
Species* "caught the imagination of its time as a dramatic
poem, and a dramatic poem of a very special sort."[9] Much
the same point is made in less lyrical terms by Harris in
his contention that the acclaim received by the *Origin*
cannot be explained simply on the grounds of its scientific character:

[These features] do not by themselves account for the passion with which such prestigious leaders of the scientific community as Sir Joseph Hooker, Thomas Huxley, and Charles Lyell rallied to Darwin's defense, nor for the enthusiasm of whole cohorts of younger scientists and intellectuals. *Origin* was much more than a scientific treatise; it was a great book precisely because of the diverse cultural themes it consolidated and expressed. It dramatized and legitimatized what many people from scientists to politicians had obscurely felt to be true without themselves being able to put it into words.[10]

The doctrine of evolution—that is, of *progress*—through conflict may be said to reflect the Victorian climate of opinion not only on its pessimistic side but on its optimistic side as well. The optimism of the age was conveyed by the idea of progressive change, of steady improvement and ultimate perfection both of man and society; its pessimism was conveyed by the images of war and aggression, of suffering and poverty, as inherent and inevitable features of the natural history of man. In many of the thinkers of this period—Darwin and Spencer were only the most conspicuous—the two moods occurred in alternation, fluctuating between the utopian optimism of a Saint-Simon or Comte, on the one hand, and the apocalyptic broodings of a Malthus or Gumplowicz on the other. Thus, a philosophical historian, Henry D. Aiken, has written of Spencer and his peers:

Like most of his fellow Victorians, Spencer was not unaware that the evolutionary march of history has its seamier side. He well understood that change is a process of dissolution as well as evolution, of disintegration as well as integration. In this respect Spencer was not alone. Nearly all of the philosophers

of development, evolution, and progress, who view
human life and institutions under the form of history rather than of eternity, at some point sound the
same note of the transitoriness, mutability, and conflict inherent in all things human. Underneath the
superficial buoyancy and hopefulness and the complacent assurance which we tend to identify with
the Victorian mentality there is nearly always something very like fear. This is hardly to be wondered
at, for the majestic portrait of evolutionary development is also a portrait of the predatory struggle for
existence.[11]

It is this Victorian affinity for scenarios of predatory
struggle and aggression which is especially pertinent to
our inquiry; for it indicates that, in the case of Darwinism,
the source of the violent images of struggle for existence
and survival of the fittest—with all their implications for
the nature of human nature—lay not in biology but in
sociology and ideology. Once these intuitions had been
imposed upon nature, they could be reclaimed by social
theorists as objective scientific evidence of the necessity
of struggle and conflict in human affairs. In this vein,
the late Richard Hofstadter has described the movement
of Victorian thought as proceeding "along a path which,
it was believed, would finally lead to a completed system
of thought, in which society would be understood as a
segment of nature and social evolution would be understood simply as an extension of biological evolution."[12]
He added significantly: "It is easy to see, in the light of
such intentions, how central a place would be played by
one's assumptions about human nature and what a central role the conception of instinct might play."[13] Hofstadter's characterization of the (Social) Darwinian
theory of instinctual aggression in man constitutes a
succinct outline of its main ingredients:

If I were to summarize schematically the rather rigid and mechanical conception which the post-Darwinian thinkers had to overcome, I would put it under these headings: First, there was the assumption that there is a fixed quantum of aggression with which man is endowed constitutionally, and that this gives to the aggressive instincts a special, "natural" authority, as against other aspects of his constitution. Second, that the forms in which aggression is expressed are determined largely or wholly by man's biological and instinctual constitution rather than by his social and historical environment. Third, that there are no countervailing natural instincts or impulses of compassion, or mutual aid, or no countervailing natural mechanisms to blunt or inhibit lethal violence within a single species. *Or*, fourth, that even if there are such, their potential is wholly accounted for or limited by their biological content.[14]

During the heyday of the fang-and-claw school of Darwinism, the idea of conflict as a law of nature was carried to its extreme not only in terms of aggression between and within species but also in terms of individual organic growth. Loren Eiseley, in his chronicle of "Darwin's century," has emphasized the excesses committed in the name of this guiding principle.

So complete was the triumph of the new philosophy that the struggle for existence, the "war of nature," was projected into the growth of the organism itself. Darwin's shadow dominates, in this respect, the rest of the century. Moreover, it provides an apt illustration of the way in which a successful theory may be carried to excess. The co-operative aspects of bodily organization, the vast intricacy of hormonic interplay, of cellular chemistry, remained to a considerable degree uninvestigated. Instead, "struggle" was the leading motif of the day.[15]

A feature of Eiseley's historical narrative is his demonstration that neither Darwin nor those who followed him had much feeling for the characteristics of stability and harmony within the organism. "Their success with the concept of struggle in the exterior environment had led them to see everything through this set of spectacles. A whole generation of neo-Darwinians persisted in this point of view."[16] But that was not all there was to it; the emphasis of the Darwinians upon instinct and animality as the essence of mankind—their concentration upon the archaic past—blinded them to the recognition of "mankind evolving," of the emergent evolution of consciousness and self-consciousness which would make of man (in René Dubos' phrase) so human an animal. Summarizing the legacy of this classical Darwinism, Eiseley concludes:

> We have frightened ourselves with our own black nature and instead of thinking "We are men now, not beasts, and must live like men," we have eyed each other with wary suspicion and whispered in our hearts, "We will trust no one. Man is evil. Man is an animal. He has come from the dark wood and the caves."
>
> As Huxley said, it is easy to convince men that they are monkeys. We all know this in our hearts. The real effort lies in convincing us that we are men.[17]

The first significant revision of the conflict theory of Darwinism, however, lay along a different course—not in establishing the humane characteristics of man but in demonstrating the pacific and cooperative aspects of animal behavior. The case for nonaggression in nature was impressively argued by Kropotkin, whose *Mutual Aid* (1902) challenged the notion of aggressive struggle between members of the same species and presented the evidence for cooperative and sociable practices as primary tendencies of living forms. Kropotkin's conclusions, based on extensive observation of various animals in the rugged conditions of Siberia and Manchuria, was (as Hofstadter has summarized it)

> that the widespread presence of mutual aid in the animal world was evidence for a "pre-human origin of moral instincts" and "also as a law of Nature and a factor in evolution." A large and interesting part of his book consists of a recital of instances observed by him and many more professional naturalists of types of intra-species animal cooperation and compassion. . . . The sum total of his evidence for mutual aid in the animal world was imposing and immensely suggestive.[18]

The Russian Prince Kropotkin was, to be sure, a political and philosophical anarchist whose ideology intruded upon his empiricism no less (perhaps even more) than had that of Darwin half a century earlier. The very basis of philosophical anarchism is an a priori assumption of natural solidarity, of intrinsic sociability and tolerance, among animals as among men. On both sides of the issue the dimension of cultural bias and temperamental disposition was equally substantial, if not equally appreciated; the main difference between the two sides, then as now, appears to have been that one vision conjured up the children of darkness and the other the children of light.

That difference reflected a shift in the intellectual climate or temper of the times which soon found expression in the form of a second wave of Social Darwinists—

the founders of pragmatism—whose deliberate purpose
was to refute the ethical and political generalizations of
their predecessors. No less than the Spencerians, the
pragmatic revisionists claimed to draw their inspiration
from Darwin's text. As Hofstadter has put it:

> Working primarily with the basic Darwinian
> concepts—organism, environment, adaptation—and
> speaking the language of naturalism, the pragmatic
> tradition had a very different intellectual and prac-
> tical issue from Spencerianism. . . . As Spencer had
> stood for determinism and the control of man by
> the environment, the pragmatists stood for freedom
> and control of the environment by man.[19]

In short, times had changed; and with them the felt
needs and urgencies, the images and imperatives, of late
Victorian society. Darwinism became neo-Darwinism, and
Social Darwinism virtually reversed its direction—becoming the counsel of cooperative social action and progressive reform, a preachment of the active mind and the
open system. Among the casualties of this ideological
sea change—along with fatalism, rugged individualism,
and survival of the fittest—was the concept of instinctual
aggression.

As we know, however, that concept was not permanently laid to rest as a scientific proposition. It was to be
resurrected and given a new career under other auspices,
first those of Freudian psychology and later those of
popular zoology and ethology. In the field of evolutionary
biology, meanwhile, the concept of an innate aggression
drive or instinct came to enjoy a kind of twilight existence, along with the grimmer features of Social Darwinism, during the heyday of "scientific racism"—which
lasted approximately from the 1890s to the end of World

War I. There is no need to recapitulate the pseudoscientific polemics of the Houston Chamberlains, Lothrop Stoddards, and Madison Grants, which were soon enough rendered obsolete not so much by disproof (of which there was plenty) as by general disenchantment and disbelief. The radical instinctivism of their racist doctrines has flared up recurrently in other vocabularies and disciplines; but it has not again captured the imagination of evolutionary biologists following in the giant footsteps of Darwin.

The reasons for the decline of that instinctivist creed in human biology are numerous; but the most significant is surely the emergence of a new and broad-scale theoretical approach that has all but swept away the old assumptions of genetic-hereditary determinism with regard to the progress of human development and social affairs. That new understanding is usually conceptualized as the idea of *cultural evolution*—the "new method of evolving by the cumulative transmission of experience," as Julian Huxley has put it.[20] This cultural approach, so widely shared today among evolutionary biologists as to constitute a consensus, maintains that man "is undergoing a two-phase evolution, the older organic and the newer social evolution."[21] It asserts that both phases are equally observable and demonstrable empirically; and that, in biological terms, "the distinction between them is that the one is genetical and the other is not."[22] The one that is *not* genetical is, moreover, paramount and controlling in the biology of man; hence it is not by instinctual and involuntary processes of "natural selection," but by conscious and deliberate actions and choices, that the significant evolution of humanity takes place. In short, through his creation of culture and recording of history, "man makes himself." George Gaylord Simpson has summarized the full meaning of what may be called the new humanistic biology:

Through this very basic distinction between the old evolution and the new, the new evolution becomes subject to conscious control. Man, alone among all organisms, knows that he evolves and he alone is capable of directing his own evolution. For him evolution is no longer something that happens to the organism regardless but something in which the organism may and must take an active hand.[23]

It would be difficult to overstate the significance of this new theory of human development drawn from post-Darwinian biology. It repudiates all the determinisms of fate and blood and circumstance; it casts out the dark mythology of bestial drives and atavistic impulses commanding the careers of men and civilizations. For now we know, as Theodosius Dobzhansky declares, that "evolution need no longer be a destiny imposed from without; it may conceivably be controlled by man, in accordance with his wisdom and his values."[24] No longer must we accept, on the evidence of science, that conflict and aggression—or any other dooms—are locked into the natural order of things. The whole litany of scientific fatalism, once held to be beyond dispute, has been simply swept aside. Thus P. B. Medawar observes:

That competition between one man and another is a necessary part of the texture of society; that societies are organisms which grew and must inevitably die; that division of labour within a society is akin to what we can see in colonies of insects; that the laws of genetics have an overriding authority; that social evolution has a direction forcibly imposed upon it by agencies beyond man's control— all these are biological judgments; but, I do assure you, bad judgments based upon a bad biology.[25]

On the basis of these authoritative statements on the "evolution of human evolution"—and hence on the nature of human nature—there would seem to be, not one, but *two* distinctive ways in which cultural values and beliefs come to be smuggled into scientific research, no matter how meticulous or objective. The first is through the unconscious penetration of thought, manifested in the spontaneous emergence of metaphors and analogies which appear irresistibly plausible and compelling, not because of their descriptive accuracy, but because they embody and articulate the underlying world view of the age and the culture—as in the case of the metaphor of competition which came to be transliterated, in the course of its passage from social thought to biological theory, into the perception of a predatory struggle for existence. On this subliminal level, the role of ideology and interest is generally unacknowledged (and probably "repressed," in the literal sense of that Freudian term). As Margaret Mead has pointed out, in discussing the clash of competing ideas of human nature in anthropology:

These curious crossings and interweavings of ideas, characteristic of different positions, illustrate vividly the extent to which a climate of opinion, of which explicit political and religious ideologies are only components, provides the atmosphere in which the scientists of a period make the very choices which they regard as dictated rigorously by the contemporary state of their particular disciplines.[26]

Besides that surreptitious penetration of thought, there is another way in which the deepest commitments and convictions of a culture—the climate of opinion or spirit of the age—enter into the actions and reflections of men. This second way, unlike the first, is conscious and volitional: In short, it is the way of cultural evolution. Illustrations of this intentional infiltration of assumptions and beliefs are to be found wherever values are enacted into laws, taught in schools, pronounced from pulpits, put into print, or otherwise broadcast through the media of communication. "Its achievement," as C. H. Waddington has said of cultural evolution, "has been the bringing into being of societies in which contributions deriving from such sources as Magna Carta, Confucius, Newton and Shakespeare can be both perpetuated and utilized."[27]

In other words, the ideas and images men hold about themselves and their world—concerning what is good and what is true and what is beautiful—provide the essential key to their character and condition. "It might not be unreasonable," writes Waddington, "to define humanity by this fact"—the fact, that is, of its *choice* (both conscious and unconscious) of myths to live by. And E. A. Burtt, in presenting his classic study of the metaphysical foundations of modern science, came to much the same conclusion: "In the last analysis it is the ultimate picture which an age forms of the nature of its world that is its most fundamental possession. It is the final controlling factor in all thinking whatever."[28]

In support of that pronouncement—and as a kind of concluding nonscientific postscript to this chapter on the unacknowledged debts of Darwinism—it is appropriate to review the main conclusions reached by R. G. Collingwood in his deservedly famous inquiry of a generation ago into the "idea of nature." Collingwood took his departure from the premise that there have been no less than three great periods of "constructive cosmological thinking" in the history of Europe: "three periods, that is to say, when the idea of nature has come into the focus of thought, become the subject of intense and protracted reflection, and consequently acquired new characteristics which in their turn have given a new aspect to the detailed science of nature that has been based upon it."[29] In each one of these periods—those of classical Greece, of the sixteenth to seventeenth centuries, and of the nineteenth century —a coherent science of nature came to be formulated *on the basis of assumptions drawn from the general culture.* Thus, "Greek natural science was based on the principle that the world of nature is saturated or permeated by mind"; the sixteenth-to-seventeenth century science of nature was founded on a peculiar juxtaposition of divine and mechanical models; and the "modern view of nature" formulated in the nineteenth century has been based on the evolutionary concepts of social change, progress, and conflict.

The common denominator of all three historical episodes, according to Collingwood, was the process of *analogy:* specifically, the assumption of an intimate likeness between familiar operations in the human world and the (otherwise mysterious) operations of the natural world. What is especially in point is the way in which this process was made to work in Darwin's century:

> Modern cosmology, like its predecessors, is based on an analogy. What is new about it is that the analogy is a new one. As Greek natural science was based on the analogy between the macrocosm nature and the microcosm man, as man is revealed to himself in his own self-consciousness; as Renaissance natural science was based on the analogy between nature as God's handiwork and the machines that are the handiwork of man . . . so the modern view of nature, which first begins to find expression towards the end of the eighteenth century and ever since then has been gathering weight and establishing itself more securely down to the present day, is based on the analogy between the processes of the natural world as studied by natural scientists and

the vicissitudes of human affairs as studied by historians.[30]

In explanation of the modern "cosmological analogy" —the reasoning from history to nature—Collingwood argued that the new view of nature could have arisen only from widespread familiarity with historical studies, "and in particular with historical studies of a kind which placed the conception of process, change, development in the centre of their picture and recognized it as the fundamental category of historical thought."[31] He pointed out that this kind of history had begun to appear around the middle of the eighteenth century—in Turgot, in Voltaire, in the *Encyclopédie* (1751–65), and thereafter almost everywhere. "Transposed during the next half-century into terms of natural science, the idea of 'progress' became . . . the idea which in another half-century was to become famous as that of 'evolution.' "[32] Collingwood's summary pronouncement on this event is particularly to the point: *"Once more, the self-consciousness of man,* in this case the corporate self-consciousness of man, his historical consciousness of his own corporate doings, *provided a clue to his thoughts about nature.* The historical conception of scientifically knowable change or process was applied, under the name of evolution, to the natural world."[33]

The very similar judgments of the English philosopher Collingwood and the American philosopher Burtt—both of them seeking independently to illuminate the metaphysical underpinnings of modern natural science— serve to reinforce and corroborate the thesis we have seen to be advanced by leading evolutionary biologists. To Burtt, the pictures that men form of themselves and their world "are their most fundamental possession, . . . the final controlling factor in all thinking whatever"—and, one might add, in all doing and dreaming and aspiring whatever. To Collingwood, the "self-consciousness of man," his thoughts about himself, provide the clue to his thoughts about nature—and also, one might add, to his thoughts about history and possibility, fate and freedom, good and evil. The two philosophers of history, in their insistence upon the emergent trait of self-consciousness, echo the consensual opinion of the biologists that, in creating man, the evolutionary process transcended itself;[34] that man as man is no longer the creature of organic evolution but *the creator of human evolution.* It is this new scientific theory—more "Lamarckian" than Darwinian in its acceptance of the hereditary (if non-genetic) transmission of acquired characteristics—that furnishes the hard evidence for what Dobzhansky has called "the biological basis of human freedom."[35] Even if it should be held that the testimony of philosophers is inadmissible in the court of scientific opinion, the fact remains that it is not from their ivory tower but from the ground-floor laboratories of evolutionary biology that there has emerged the most sweeping refutation of the claims of biological determinism. It goes without saying that this refutation includes, as an incidental detail, the myth perpetrated by "anti-social Darwinism" of the instinctual basis of human aggression.

CHAPTER **2**

FREUD:
Thoughts for the Times on War and Death

The most enduring and influential of the various instinct theories of aggression—at least until the advent of Lorenz, Ardrey, and company—has been Sigmund Freud's concept of the death instinct, first formulated in 1920 (*Beyond the Pleasure Principle*) and given its most forceful expression a decade later (*Civilization and Its Discontents*):

> In all that follows I take up the standpoint that the tendency to aggression is an innate, independent, instinctual disposition in man, and I come back now to the statement that it constitutes the most powerful obstacle to culture. . . . The natural instinct of aggressiveness in man, the hostility of each one against all and of all against each one, opposes this programme of civilization. This instinct of aggression is the derivative and main representative of the death instinct we have found alongside of Eros, sharing his rule over the earth. And now, it seems to me, the meaning of the evolution of culture is no longer a riddle to us. It must present to us the struggle between Eros and Death, between the instincts

of life and the instincts of destruction, as it works itself out in the human species. This struggle is what all life essentially consists of and so the evolution of civilization may be simply described as the struggle of the human species for survival.[1]

In the pronouncement of his dramatistic vision of the forces of death and destruction within the human soul, Freud, like Darwin before him, was surely giving authentic expression to the spirit of his age: the age of the war-scarred Lost Generation, embittered and disenchanted by the scenes and acts of carnage at which they had been participant-observers. It is noteworthy that, before the coming of the war, the phenomenon of aggression had been very differently explained by Freud—mainly in terms of frustration of the sexual instinct. In this earlier and happier framework, aggression was not itself a primary instinct: It was the product of experience and nurture, literally of "thwarted love."

For Freud, as for most Europeans, the shock of the war exerted a traumatic effect upon traditional values and assumptions. The optimism of the preceding century of progress, and of the Enlightenment faith in the rationality and perfectibility of man, disintegrated in the trenches. None of the established categories of social or religious thought—including Freud's own previously developed theory of instinctual motivation and behavior—seemed adequate to account for the wartime upheaval of mass hatred and massive slaughter. Freud was far from alone in suspecting there must be something in man himself, beyond the dreams of Eros, beyond the pleasure principle, that would explain this apparent urge to destruction and death.

It was during the war that Freud began to move toward the new theory of instincts which marked a fundamental change in his outlook and conceptual framework. As early as 1915, in "Thoughts for the Times on War and Death," the revision was foreshadowed. During the next five years—a time of successive privations and deprivations for Freud himself, involving among other things a series of deaths in the family, his own deteriorating health, and the continuing disruption of the original Vienna circle of psychoanalytic colleagues, as well as the miseries of Austria and Europe—during this period of personal and social tragedy Freud conceived and developed his account of the human tragedy. In his own metaphorical terms, the tragedy consisted in the primordial urge of all life to seek its own death—the tendency of the organic to return to the inorganic. Turned inward, upon the self, this urge took the form of the death instinct; turned outward, toward external objects and persons, it became the instinct of aggression. "After long doubts and vacillations," wrote Freud many years later, "we have decided to assume the existence of only two basic instincts, *Eros* and *the destructive instinct.* . . . We may suppose that the final aim of the destructive instinct is to reduce living things to an inorganic state. For this reason we also call it the *death instinct.*"[2]

At first, in the provisional and exploratory formulation of *Beyond the Pleasure Principle*, Freud was uncertain of the validity of his dark vision of love against death, and even of his own belief in it. With the insight of a professional self-questioner, he mused about his motives: "Perhaps we have adopted the belief [the death instinct] because there is some comfort in it. If we are to die ourselves, and first to lose in death those who are dear to us, it is easier to submit to a remorseless law of nature, to the sublime necessity, than to a chance which might perhaps have been escaped. . . ."[3] Freud had indeed lost in death one who was dear to him, his daughter Sophie, in January of 1920; *Beyond the Pleasure Principle* was published in May of the same year. The coincidence of the two events was so striking that Freud took extraordinary pains to establish that the book in fact was completed before his daughter fell ill; but he did nothing to deny that the times themselves were conducive to the most despairing thoughts on war and death. Thus, a recent biographer, Marthe Robert, has remarked concerning Freud's elaborate explanations:

> However logical it might appear to the psycho-analysts, this strictly biographical explanation was inadequate if one accepts the fact that between 1919 and 1920 there were good reasons why the ideas of death and destruction would impose themselves on and even dominate people's minds. Surveying the terrible and still almost incalculable devastation, as well as the material, moral and intellectual collapse of mankind which, it was by then clear, neither victors nor vanquished had escaped, what thinker would not have wondered what was the reason for the chaos and what meaning lay behind the brutal fall of man and his civilization?[4]

For whatever reason, Freud came in the course of succeeding years to overcome his doubts and to embrace the idea of Thanatos (as the death instinct become known in contradistinction to Eros) with a fervor evidently beyond the dimensions of ordinary scientific conviction. "To begin with it was only tentatively that I put forward the views I have developed here [*Civilization and Its Discontents*], but in the course of time they have gained such a hold upon me that I can no longer think in any other way."[5] What Freud meant, of course, was that the hold these views had gained upon him was the grip of logical and empirical truth; but the tone of his writings in these later years—apocalyptic in its forebodings, grim and cheerless in analysis—makes clear how deeply personal

and metaphysical his commitment had become. The following passage, a fair sample of the argument of *Civilization and Its Discontents*, is more akin to a cry of despair
than to the disciplined generalizations of a scientific
observer:

> The bit of truth behind all this—one so eagerly
> denied—is that men are not gentle, friendly crea-
> tures wishing for love, who simply defend them-
> selves if they are attacked, but that a powerful
> measure of desire for aggression has to be reckoned
> as part of their instinctual endowment. The result
> is that their neighbour is to them not only a possible
> helper or sexual object, but also a temptation to
> them to gratify their aggressiveness on him, to ex-
> ploit his capacity for work without recompense, to
> use him sexually without his consent, to seize his
> possessions, to humiliate him, to cause him pain, to
> torture and to kill him. *Homo homini lupus*; who
> has the courage to dispute it in the face of all the
> evidence in his own life and in history? This aggres-
> sive cruelty usually lies in wait for some provocation,
> or else it steps into the service of some other pur-
> pose, the aim of which might as well have been
> achieved by milder measures. In circumstances that
> favour it, when those forces in the mind which
> ordinarily inhibit it cease to operate, it also mani-
> fests itself spontaneously and reveals men as savage
> beasts to whom the thought of sparing their own
> kind is alien. Anyone who calls to mind the atrocities
> of the early migrations, of the invasion by the Huns
> or by the so-called Mongols under Jenghiz Khan and
> Tamurlane, of the sack of Jerusalem by the pious
> Crusaders, even indeed the horrors of the last world
> war, will have to bow his head humbly before the
> truth of this view of man.[6]

Not all of Freud's colleagues and followers, by any
means, were prepared to bow their heads before the truth
of his view of man. Indeed, the record of discussions and
conferences during this period indicates that many—
perhaps most—of those who accepted it did so reluc-
tantly, in deference to Freud's authority; and there were
those even among the orthodox, like Otto Fenichel and
Wilhelm Reich (at that time), who repudiated the idea
altogether.[7] It is probably the case that, as Leonard Berkowitz maintains, "Very few psychoanalysts today accept
Freud's hypothesis of a death instinct."[8] The consensus
of the field appears rather to favor an explanation of
aggressiveness and hostility much like that of Freud's
original instinct theory, and even more like the frustration-
aggression hypothesis contributed by American social
psychologists in the 1930s.[9] Beyond psychology, on the
other hand, the death-instinct theory has not only been
kept alive but has recently enjoyed a remarkable revival
—carried on, for the most part, with dramatic flair and
great popular impact, by a number of literary scholars
(e.g., Norman O. Brown and Lionel Trilling) and political
theorists (Herbert Marcuse and Paul Roazen). But before
turning to an appraisal of this popular revival of the "dark
side" of Freud, it is pertinent to look more closely at the
alternative approach to the problem of human aggression
—what may be called the "humanist alternative"—which
has emerged over the past forty years in psychoanalysis
and psychotherapy.

The central tenet of the post-Freudian view is that, in
the words of Abraham H. Maslow, "destructiveness or
aggressiveness is secondary or derived behavior rather
than primary motivation." Maslow goes on to state: "By
this I mean that aggressive or destructive behavior in the
human being will practically always be found to result
from an assignable reason of some sort, to be a reaction
to another state of affairs, to be an end product rather

than an original source."[10] Much the same definition was provided in the 1940s by Erich Fromm (who has subsequently qualified his view through greater attention to the varieties of human destructiveness, but without apparent fundamental alteration): "Destructiveness is a secondary potentiality in man which becomes manifest only if he fails to realize his primary potentialities. . . . We have shown that man is not necessarily evil but becomes evil only if the proper conditions for his growth and development are lacking."[11] In his own idiosyncratic fashion, Harry Stack Sullivan expressed a similar view:

But under what circumstances does so remarkable and, may I say, so ubiquitous a thing as malevolence appear as a major pattern of interpersonal relations in childhood? A great many years of preoccupation with this problem has eventuated in a theory which is calculated to get around the idea that man is essentially evil. One of the great theories is, as you know, that society is the only thing that prevents everybody from tearing everybody to bits; or that man is possessed of something wonderful called sadism. I have not found much support for these theories—that man is essentially a devil, that he has an actual need for being cruel and hurtful to his fellows, and so on—in the study of some of the obscure schizophrenic phenomena. And so as the years passed, my interest in understanding why there is so much deviltry in human living culminated in the observation that if the child had certain kinds of very early experience, this malevolent attitude toward his fellows seemed to be conspicuous. And when the child did not have these particular types of experience, then this malevolent attitude was not a major component.[12]

Clara Thompson, a neo-Freudian historian of the psychoanalytic movement, has emphasized what might be termed the growth-potential premise of this cultural approach to aggressive behavior: "The tendency to grow, develop and reproduce seems to be a part of the human organism. When these drives are obstructed by neurotic parents or as a result of a destructive cultural pattern, then the individual develops resentment and hostility either consciously or unconsciously or both. In short, far from being a product of the death instinct, it is an expression of the organism's will to live."[13]

Where Freud had been insistently *biological* in his orientation, the post-Freudian generation of the thirties and forties was conspicuously *cultural* in its emphasis upon the determinants of character and conduct—and of "misconduct." In retrospect it seems apparent that the cultural revisionists of psychoanalysis were responding to the spirit of their own age no less faithfully than Freud had done in the shell-shocked period following the first great war. As I have written elsewhere:

> The [later] period, conditioned by the social conscience and reformist spirit of the thirties, was the heyday of revisionism in psychoanalysis—dominated by the hopeful figures of Fromm, Horney and Sullivan. In an age of reform the mind characteristically turns outward, away from somber introspection toward affirmative social action; evil then is likely to be perceived as a feature of lagging institutions, not as an irremediable flaw of the human heart. . . . In the generation of the New Deal, the custody and interpretation of the Freudian texts was by common consensus the prerogative of social scientists—whose ideas, in turn, were weapons.[14]

During this period, moreover, there was emerging what John Seeley has called "the Americanization of the

Unconscious,"[15] which produced a much more optimistic, gregarious, and pragmatic psyche than Freud could ever have envisioned, through the marriage of European psychoanalytic theory and American social psychology.

Today, after a full generation of revisionism in the professional provinces of psychoanalysis, psychiatry, and psychotherapy, the noninstinctual post-Freudian consensus seems to hold the field still. But elsewhere, in certain neighboring groves, owing to a dramatic and polemical revival of the doctrine of instincts, the issue is once again in doubt and the battle has been resumed. Much of the apparent reason for the revival of the death instinct, and of Freudian instinctivism in general, stems from another shift in intellectual and ideological fashion which has been characterized by a strong reaction against the neo-Freudian revisionists—the culturally oriented optimists of the thirties—and a return to the original teachings of the master (or, more precisely, to the darker and more pessimistic metapsychological musings of Freud's later years). It should be emphasized, however (and not just in passing), that the revivalist movement has been inspired and carried on predominantly by individuals and groups *outside* the professional fields of psychoanalysis and therapy—most notably by students of literature and political philosophy. Among the leading spokesmen for this "neoclassical" orientation have been Norman O. Brown, Herbert Marcuse, Lionel Trilling, Stanley Edgar Hyman, John H. Schaar, and Paul Roazen.[16] Although there are significant differences among these writers (as we shall see), they share a common distaste for the "liberal-rationalist" school of neo-Freudians and a common affection for those very tenets of Freud's psychology and metapsychology which have been least acceptable to professional psychologists and psychoanalysts.

In order to understand the revival of sympathetic attention to the shadow side of Freud, it is necessary to have recourse once more to the shopworn image of the *Zeitgeist*. It was the shock and disillusionment of war, with its evidence of mass destructiveness and fratricide, that put Freud in the frame of mind to write his tragic scenario of life against death, of the individual against society, and of man against himself. (And just as Darwin had had his alter ego Wallace, because the idea was "in the air," so Freud had his Spengler—for whom also man was a beast of prey, a destroyer by nature.) A generation later, it was through the shock and disillusionment of another great war—with its evidence not only of actual destruction but of the potential annihilation of all human life—that the stage was set for a revival of Freud's classical drama. After Hiroshima and Nagasaki, after the death camps, after the paranoia of Stalinism—above all, after the failure of the war to bring peace—the liberal ideas and ideals of the thirties, including their psychological counterparts, appeared anachronistic and irrelevant. In this mood of alienation and disenchantment, Lionel Trilling composed his famous essay on the relevance of Freud to "the crisis of our culture,"[17] and Norman O. Brown, perhaps the most impassioned and influential of the Young Freudians, published his manifesto, *Life Against Death*:

> In 1953 I turned to a deep study of Freud, feeling the need to reappraise the nature and destiny of man. . . . I, like so many of my generation, lived through the superannuation of the political categories which informed liberal thought and action in the 1930's. . . . This book is addressed to all who are ready to call into question old assumptions and to entertain new possibilities. . . .
>
> But why Freud? It is a shattering experience for anyone seriously committed to the Western traditions of morality and rationality to take a steadfast,

unflinching look at what Freud has to say. It is humiliating to be compelled to admit the grossly seamy side of so many grand ideals. It is criminal to violate the civilized taboos which have kept the seamy side concealed. To experience Freud is to partake a second time of the forbidden fruit. . . .

But to what end? When our eyes are opened, and the fig leaf no longer conceals our nakedness, our present situation is experienced in its full concrete actuality as a tragic crisis . . . Freud was right; our real desires are unconscious. It also begins to be apparent that mankind, unconscious of its real desires and therefore unable to obtain satisfaction, is hostile to life and ready to destroy itself. Freud was right in positing a death instinct, and the development of weapons of mass destruction makes our present dilemma plain: we either come to terms with our unconscious instincts and drives—with life and death—or else we surely die.[18]

For Brown and others drawn from the literary and humanistic studies, the case for Freudian instinctivism is not scientific but ethical and ontological. The pessimism of Freud meets the despair of those for whom "the Western tradition of morality and rationality" no longer carries conviction or credibility. The felt need is for a new belief system, a radical *Weltanschauung*, which will break fundamentally with the liberal-democratic tradition. Indeed, Brown makes his ambitious purpose quite explicit: "We . . . are concerned with reshaping psychoanalysis into a wider general theory of human nature, culture, and history, to be appropriated by the consciousness of mankind as a whole as a new stage in the historical process of man's coming to know himself."[19] A preliminary step on the way to this wider general theory is the clearing of the undergrowth of post-Freudian thought which obstructs the path—all that Brown bluntly describes as "the catastrophe of so-called neo-Freudianism." The very vocabulary in which Brown proclaims his villains and heroes betrays the nature of his enterprise: It is not at all a judicious assessment of truth and error, but an apocalyptic account of calamity and redemption. In plain fact it is a revolutionary manifesto calling for a genuinely radical break with the liberal tradition of the past and the liberal society of the present—in favor of a daring leap into a truly free (repressionless) society. The repudiation of the neo-Freudians is a repudiation of liberalism; the call for the "abolition of repression" is a call for the abolition of prevailing institutions of authority—and for the design of a radically new and different culture.

As the writings both of Brown and Herbert Marcuse[20] demonstrate, the wave of "new Freudianism" is closely linked to the radical romanticism which grew up in academic and intellectual circles during the riotous sixties. In the service of this commitment to sweeping change, the Freudian texts have undergone a revision at least as substantial as that carried out earlier by the neo-Freudians, and one which would have startled Freud himself. For what is envisaged by the New Freudians is nothing less than the abolition of all repression and the transcendence of the death instinct through emancipation of the natural energies of life and libido. Indeed, in the strifeless society prophesied by Marcuse, death itself becomes transfigured into something almost pleasant to contemplate: "Death can become a token of freedom. The necessity of death does not refute the possibility of final liberation. Like the other necessities, it can be made rational—painless. Men can die without anxiety if they know that what they love is protected from misery and oblivion."[21] It is difficult to see how this softening of the hard edges of Freud's pessimism and instinctivism is any less "heretical" or "utopian" than the neo-Freudian modifications which have been rejected so scornfully by Brown, Marcuse, and others. These spokesmen for a new psychological and social order may turn out to be right in their prophecies and jeremiads; but, right or wrong, they do not appear to be genuinely Freudian. A more faithful rendering of the texts, directly contrary to theirs, is that of Philip Rieff:

> Short of Nirvana, if sexuality could conceivably cease to trouble man, his destructive instincts would trouble him more. . . . But the instincts cannot be taught to abide each other; their fusion creates tension and the possibility of abrupt reversals. Besides, were aggression merely a response to the frustration of some sexual or social need, it could be resolved, or at least ameliorated, by a specifically social reform of the conditions of frustration. But an aggression that is built in, due to the presence of a "death instinct," cannot be entirely manipulated, let alone abolished. . . .
>
> Here is no Swinburnian romance of free sexuality versus the moral law. Rather, Freud takes the romance out of sexuality, . . . Love is not a final solution for Freud, but a therapeutic one. . . . As a psychologist of fulfillment, Freud predicts disappointment; he sees the social value of repression, the complex nature of satisfaction. It is only in the therapeutic context—which is, after all, not life— that he rejects repression.[22]

In their effort both to have the theory of the death instinct and consume it too—to accept Thanatos as real and innate but somehow ultimately conquerable or at least tamable—the advocates of "instinctivist radicalism" (as Fromm has characterized their position) have moved beyond Freud to an eschatological vision of distant harmony and reconciliation of polarities remarkably like that of Marx. At some point in the arguments of both Marcuse and Brown, the categories and concepts of Freud dissolve almost into their opposites; for there is no theory of instincts in Marx, only a theory of forces and relations which operate to defer the final realization of the non-repressive society of nonaggressive men. It is not necessary here to assess the viability of the neo-Marxist psychology; it is enough to recognize that the theory of aggression presented by these radical revisionists comes eventually to rest less upon a doctrine of instincts than upon one of *institutions*. As adumbrated by Marcuse in his essay "Aggressiveness in Advanced Industrial Society," the once-dreaded death instinct is no longer a force in opposition to all culture, and therefore renounced by it, but rather has become a source of energy (on the order of electricity) which a repressive society may freely tap and exploit for its own nefarious purposes. "Destructive energy becomes socially useful aggressive energy, and the aggressive behavior impels growth—growth of economic, political, and technical power."[23]

This campaign on the part of Marcuse and Brown to politicize and "radicalize" psychoanalysis, mainly through rehabilitation of the death instinct, represents, however, only one side of a broader contemporary tendency to repudiate the liberal neo-Freudian "heresy" and restore the Freudian orthodoxy. Counterbalancing the radical left, there is also what may be termed a conservative right wing—a school of interpretation that relies no less heavily upon the instinctual theory of aggression but that does so in the interest of demonstrating the necessity of authority, order, discipline—and repression. It is difficult to say which of these two politically polar views is closer to the master or which is more likely to prevail; both are equally ideological in their source and consequence, and both have gained whatever plausibility they possess from the shifting currents of academic thought in the late sixties and early seventies. Where the radical instinctivists bespeak the fading message of the strawberry statement, the conservative instinctivists are representative of the backlash of opinion and apprehension that followed not only on the prairies but in the ivory towers. In its theoretical form that reaction has been one of subtle denigration of the supposedly overindulgent and permissive liberalism of the thirties and forties, which found expression in the humanistic psychology of Fromm and others (as well as in the educational philosophy of John Dewey, the social theory of David Riesman, the personality theory of Gordon Allport, and so forth). In the academic context the retreat from liberalism has commonly taken the form of a turn toward *determinism* in one or another of its variations: that is, toward doctrines of finality and certitude which offer authoritative assurances and solutions, as opposed to the open-ended ambiguities of the liberal tradition. One such determinism, lately favored in various disciplines, is the doctrine of instincts—and more particularly of the instinct toward destructive aggression.

Whereas the radical instinctivists have focused upon the death instinct in order to support their view of Freud as the prophet of social and erotic revolution, the conservatives have used the same data to project a very different image; for them Freud is the apostle of law and order, the advocate of parental discipline and social controls. In that voice, Freud doubtless speaks persuasively to the condition of all who have felt threatened by the eruption of rebellious impulses and the general show of violence, whether on the well-tended campuses or down the mean streets of their once-secure society. It is not surprising that this interpretation of Freud, relying upon his own pessimism and dread as well as upon his conceptual framework, should have come into vogue in the service of the conservative reaction in social and political theory.

The most sustained elaboration of the posture of conservative instinctivism has been furnished by the political theorist Paul Roazen in his 1968 study of the educational (as well as sociopolitical) implications of Freudian thought. Chapter 4 of his book, which deals directly with the aggression-instinct theory, makes the point clear. Throughout the discussion, the emphasis is upon "the directive aspect of social controls," "the constructive uses of civilized restraints," and even "the advantages to the individual of restrictions and self-sacrifices." The operative words are *authority, discipline, restraint*, and *control*; the pejorative terms are *permissiveness, indulgence* (without corresponding deprivation), *spontaneity*, and *anarchism*. The last of these terms is applied specifically to the neo-Freudian school: e.g., ". . . the revisionist tendency to drop the innate character of aggression has led to plainly anarchistic conclusions."[24] (Roazen's strictures on this score are closely similar to those of another political scientist, John H. Schaar, whose book-length critique of Erich Fromm is entitled *Escape From Authority*.[25])

The consequences for education and child rearing which follow from this interpretation of aggression are immediately evident. If the child is, as Roazen puts it, "assailed by murderous inclinations which terrorize him"; and if "the boy, for example, wants to eliminate both father and siblings, and have his mother sexually all to himself"—then it follows that repression and discipline are not only necessary but salutary. Hence a Freudian psychoanalyst, Melanie Klein, is quoted as saying: "He [the child] himself actually wants to be restrained by the adults around him in his aggression and selfishness. . . ." "Without external controls," Roazen adds, "the child may be even harder on himself."[26] In this view—reminiscent of the Calvinist doctrine of infant depravity—the natural condition of the child is one of possession by murderous and incestuous wishes which can be exorcised only by stern measures on the part of influential adults, notably parents and teachers. Roazen makes a point of citing the note left at the scene of the crime by an adolescent murderer—"Catch me before I kill more; I cannot control myself."[27] Elsewhere, also, Roazen appears to regard the suppressive methods used in treatment of psychotics as appropriate evidence for the value of similar restraints and controls in the rearing of normal children.[28] Given the major premise of innate destructive inclinations, it could hardly be otherwise. ". . . it has not been noticed," according to Roazen, "that implicitly within Freud's work, and quite explicitly in psychoanalytic theory since his death, limitations are shown to have a positive, directive aspect. Freud is always more articulate about the usefulness of restrictions when he is talking of the aggressive drives."[29]

If Freud himself was firm in his conviction of the "usefulness of restrictions," along with a few hyper-Freudians such as Melanie Klein, the trend of the main body of psychoanalytic theory since Freud is not at all as clear-cut as Roazen suggests. On the contrary, the weight of the evidence points in the opposite direction—the direction taken not only by the neo-Freudians but by Adlerians, Jungians, Rankians, most ego psychologists, and a broad variety of non-Freudian psychotherapists and clinical psychologists—the direction, that is, of increasing reliance on the human potential for healthy growth and constructive self-direction, and correspondingly upon educational and social measures designed to release rather than repress the natural inclinations and talents of the human person.

The two alternative theories of aggression—the instinctual and the social—which have been produced in the field of psychoanalytic psychology over the last fifty years represent almost a pure case of the venerable nature-nurture controversy. As we shall see in subsequent chapters, that controversy endures with obdurate persistence throughout the study of man—in biology, anthropology, ethology, and all the corners of psychology—despite the recurrent disclaimers of scientists that the troublesome dispute has been laid to rest. As Morris Opler has observed, "The conception of a future for man dependent on and guided by the genetic and physical is actually enjoying a renewed popularity in our day."[30] We have reviewed a few of the sources of this popular revival in an age of violence and rumors of violence; for the fields of psychology and psychoanalysis, at least, they are sources which bear no clear relation to the state of the science—but a very intimate relation to the state of mind of those who are persuaded by them. It is paradoxical, but not surprising, that doctrines of the darkest pessimism regarding human nature and conduct should find a responsive audience in our time. "For if it is all in human nature, and if we are all guilty," writes the psychiatrist Frederic Wertham, "then nobody is guilty. And if we are all responsible, no man is responsible. We make it too easy for ourselves."[31] Wertham goes on to point out:

> The theory that violence is ingrained in man and is an intrinsic manifestation of human nature is very widely held. It has been qualified, mitigated, embellished, and camouflaged, but in one form or another, usually with the ambiguous use of the term "aggression," it dominates our intellectual life. . . .
>
> The instinct-of-aggression theory makes violence a biological, natural phenomenon. That really legitimizes and rationalizes it. It is not an explanation but the evasion of an explanation. Human violence is not a product of nature, though; it is a product of

society. It is socially conditioned and socially preventable. . . . The violent man is not the natural man with destructive aggressions but is the socially alienated man.[32]

Who shall decide, when doctors of the mind disagree? And how shall the decision be made? If the choice between competing theories of human aggression cannot be made strictly on scientific grounds—and if in fact that choice must be made and will be made, either openly or tacitly—it would seem important to make the grounds for decision as responsible, reasonable, and humanely relevant as possible. The criteria for choice surely include attending to the evidence assembled by the experts; but the experts are sorely divided and their evidence thoroughly mixed. Fortunately there are other resources at hand—among them those suggested by Richard L. Means: "Does man wish to be a 'destroyer' or a 'helper'? On what basis will man construct his social world? On the basis of an appreciation of the full potential worth of human beings or on the basis of extrinsic, mechanical evaluations of human life? The choice is simple, direct, but unequivocally stark."[33]

CHAPTER **3**

LORENZ, ARDREY, AND COMPANY:
The Ethics of Ethology

The study of aggression may well be among the most important undertakings of science, both natural and behavioral. Yet, despite decades of research and centuries of theorizing, there is an astonishing lack of agreement among those who have made a speciality of that study, not only in one field but virtually in all: biology, ethology, psychology, anthropology, and sociology. Specialists on aggression inhabit a house divided, and the division is along classical lines—namely, those of nature versus nurture or heredity versus environment. On one side are the several *biological* theories, centering upon the concept of aggression as instinctual or genetic in character; on the other side are the *social* or *cultural* theories, centering upon the concept of aggression as a learned response.

This division of the experts reflects a persistent difference of scientific opinion which is more than a century old—a controversy very much at odds with the popular conception of scientific knowledge as cumulative, consistent, and consensual. But while the dispute is persistent and shows no signs of abating, there have been significant shifts in the relative influence and standing of the opposed viewpoints. Half a century ago, in the wake of the

Darwinian revolution and the rise of modern biology, instinct theories were as prolific in the social studies as they were in the life sciences, and prominent among them was the concept of an aggression instinct—such as William McDougall's "instinct of pugnacity" and Wilfred Trotter's "warring instinct of the herd."[1] During the twenties, however, and for nearly three decades thereafter, "biologistic" explanations came to be widely discredited —owing in part to effective critical work by L. L. Bernard and Knight Dunlop, as well as to the prevalence of environmental psychologies such as behaviorism.[2] The extent of this anti-instinctual consensus in the human sciences was such that to some present-day writers with a renewed biological interest it seems to have been flagrantly biased; accordingly they claim to find in the annals of the earlier period the evidence of something like a plot against any scientist who dared to defy the environmentalist "dogma" by insisting upon instinctual or genetic theories in explanation of human behavior.[3]

However, if the alleged bias of the interwar years resulted "from fashion and Zeitgeist," as Lionel Tiger suggests, it would appear that the Zeitgeist has reversed itself in recent years. As early as the fifties, Freud's theory of the death instinct was undergoing a popular (as distinct from professional) revival. In 1961 there appeared Robert Ardrey's widely read African Genesis, which posited a "killer instinct" in man on the basis of australopithecine artifacts and gave new currency to the Social Darwinist theories of anthropologists like Sir Arthur Keith and Raymond Dart.[4] More than anywhere else, however, it has been in the comparatively new science of ethology (the study of animal behavior) that the most compelling evidence for the instinctual origin of aggression has apparently been found. But—to anticipate the summary to follow—not all ethologists are agreed on the interpretation of the evidence. Their science, in short, appears as deeply divided on the issue of aggression as are the other sciences of nature and man.

The principal data and interpretations in favor of instinctual aggression have been derived from the researches of two pioneer ethologists: Konrad Lorenz, of the Max Planck Institute for the Physiology of Behavior, in Germany, and Niko Tinbergen, of Oxford University's Department of Zoology. These investigators are not in accord on all the issues (e.g., Tinbergen is less convinced than Lorenz of the validity of analogies between men and other animals), but they are generally agreed on the instinctual character of aggressive behavior in animals and the probability of its similar occurrence in man. Lorenz has been the chief publicist of his own views—most famously in *On Aggression*, which appeared in English translation in 1966—with strong assists from Ardrey and Tiger.[5] Tinbergen's views have been summarized by him in a 1968 paper and presented in more lively fashion by his former student, the British sociologist Desmond Morris.[6]

The essential features of the Lorenz-Ardrey theory of instinctual aggression have been well summarized by John Hurrell Crook, a leading British ethologist, in the course of a critique of Ardrey's *The Territorial Imperative* and Lorenz's *On Aggression*:

> Certain assertions occur in both books. First, that man, in common with many other animals, has an innate territorial or aggressive drive seeking consummation in periodic performance. Second, a superficial comparison of animal societies reveals a variety of territorial and social dispersion patterns to which simple survival values are attributed in terms of optimum utilization of commodities, selective elimination of the least fit, security and stimulation for the survivors. Third, man is defective in his

control of his aggression by reason of his recent evolution without concomitant development of innate ritualized restraints. In both books the possibility that the leopard may change his spots through learning is dismissed. The instinct, rather, must be diverted into conventional substitutes for war. The case for social engineering rather than education is complete.[7]

Other aspects of the instinctivist hypothesis should be mentioned. Aggression is defined, by Lorenz and his followers, as "the fighting instinct in beast and man which is directed against members of the same species."[8] It is therefore to be distinguished from predation against *other* species (although Ardrey frequently juxtaposes references to man as a "killer" and as an "armed predator"). Underlying this specific instinct is the assumption that "human behavior, and particularly human social behavior, far from being determined by reason and cultural tradition alone, is still subject to all the laws prevailing in all phylogenetically adapted instinctive behavior."[9] Two conclusions follow from these premises: that animal behavior studies tell us most of what we need to know about human behavior, especially in matters of war, murder, and other "militant excitements"; and that the "phylogenetically programmed" drive toward war and destruction cannot be unlearned or outgrown but can only be sublimated, redirected, or repressed.

The instinct theorists differ somewhat in the degree of their pessimism concerning the prospects of survival of the human species under the compulsions of the aggressive or territorial imperative. The bleakest outlook is that of Desmond Morris, who rejects virtually all proposed solutions and sublimations as incompatible with biological laws. For example, he writes: "Another solution is to de-patriotize the members of the different social groups;

but this would be working against a fundamental biological feature of our species."[10] Again, he rejects the suggestion that aggression can ever be overcome by intelligence or intellectual control: "Unhappily, where matters as basic as territorial defence are concerned, our higher brain centres are all too susceptible to the urgings of our lower ones. Intellectual control can help us just so far, but no farther. In the last resort, it is unreliable, and a single, unreasoned, emotional act can undo all the good it has achieved."[11] The only sound biological solution to the human dilemma, according to Morris, is one not likely to be soon effectuated: ". . . massive de-population, or a rapid spread of the species on to other planets. . . ."

Ardrey's monocausal approach, which reduces aggression along with most of human behavior to the primordial instinct for territory, is not much more hopeful regarding the possibility of bringing the destructive urges under control. "The territorial nature of man is genetic and ineradicable," he maintains.[12] Again: "The territorial imperative is as blind as a cave fish, as consuming as a furnace, and it commands beyond logic, opposes all reason, suborns all moralities, strives for no goal more sublime than survival."[13] Ardrey's position on the issue is somewhat ambiguous since his thesis requires that the advantage in war must lie almost insuperably with the defender of territory rather than with the "aggressor"— which appears to make the territorial imperative "non-aggressive," and which also leads Ardrey to attribute an affirmative moral quality to the territorial instinct, despite his previous contention that it "suborns all moralities." Nevertheless, believing as he does that war represents man's most exhilarating experience and that it is the expression of instinctive drives beyond rational control, Ardrey is far from optimistic regarding the prospects of peace on earth or goodwill among men.

Lorenz's attitude on this question may be summed up

in the observation that the survival of mankind is a race between instinctual gratification and instinctual sublimation. Thus he has written: "An unprejudiced observer from another planet, looking upon man as he is today, in his hand the atom bomb, the product of his intelligence, in his heart the aggression drive inherited from his anthropoid ancestors, which this same intelligence cannot control, would not prophesy long life for the species."[14] Those characteristics which are unique to man, such as moral aspiration, are seen to be fundamentally at odds with the biological characteristics that he shares with the animals:

> That indeed is the Janus head of man: The only being capable of dedicating himself to the very highest moral and ethical values requires for this purpose a phylogenetically adapted mechanism of behavior whose animal properties bring with them the danger that he will kill his brother, convinced that he is doing so in the interests of these very same high values.[15]

However, in what he terms an "avowal of optimism," Lorenz outlines several varieties of sublimation which he considers might operate as safety valves for the aggression drive and cheat it of its natural object. Among them are the development of science and the arts, the cultivation of brotherly or neighborly love, and especially the expansion of international sporting contests such as football. (Ironically, the most forceful rebuttal to the last suggestion has been that of Morris, who observes that one proposed solution "is to provide and promote harmless, symbolic substitutes for war; but if these are really harmless they will inevitably go a very small way towards resolving the real problem. It is worth remembering here that this problem, at a biological level, is one of group

territorial defence and, in view of the gross overcrowding
of our species, also one of group territorial expansion.
No amount of boisterous international football is going
to solve this."[16])

THE OTHER ETHOLOGY

The impression conveyed by advocates of the aggression-
instinct theory is that their views are representative of
the modern science of ethology and that nearly all studies
of animal behavior, especially in recent years, support
their theoretical position. Moreover, there is a marked
tendency among them to suppose that what little evidence
may exist to the contrary arises from an unreasonable
public resistance to the truth and from a "radical misunderstanding of certain democratic principles" such as
equality and freedom.[17] Ardrey and Tiger both hint at the
presence of a prejudice among scientists and scholars in
favor of fashionably "liberal" views and against the less
palatable findings of ethologists.[18] It is noteworthy that
scientific criticism of their own theory and data is, for the
most part, either disregarded or discredited on ideological
grounds rather than directly confronted.

Contrary to this impression of near-unanimity on the
part of serious researchers, however, the field of ethology
and related animal studies is deeply divided on the issues
involved. Moreover, both the interpretations and the general approach of Lorenz, Ardrey, Morris, and company
are widely regarded by their fellow scientists as unrepre-
sentative, outdated, oversimplified, and injudicious. Specifically, the two main charges brought against them are
that their writings are unfaithful to the observed facts of
animal behavior and that their extrapolations from that
behavior to the conduct of human life are unwarranted.
The first charge has been documented by such scientists

as T. C. Schneirla, Sir Solly Zuckerman, and J. P. Scott, among others; in brief, the contention is, as Schneirla puts it, that Lorenz bases his interpretations on work carried out as much as fifty years earlier and ignores or is unaware of "current scientific theory and methodology which is at odds with Lorenz's outdated negative view."[19] Scott adds that Lorenz's "ideas of instinct are thus pre-Mendelian and pre-physiological, and in this day and age such a classical theory of instinct forms a very incomplete and inadequate explanation of behavior."[20]

The second major criticism of Lorenz and his followers —that their projections from the animal kingdom to human society are unjustified—is shared by an even larger body of scientific reviewers of their work. The conclusion of Sir Solly Zuckerman may be taken as typical: "Speculations such as these—and Lorenz indulges in many—may be fascinating, but they are not science. The complexities of human social and political behavior cannot be explained on the basis of oversimplified homologies and analogies with highly selective aspects of animal behavior."[21]

Contrary to the impression given by proponents of the instinctivist theory of aggression, it is not only *social* scientists who, as might be expected, resist their thesis and argue the case for nurture as against nature in the etiology of violent behavior. A large number, perhaps a majority, of life scientists who have written on this question emphasize the primacy of social learning and cultural experience, of external stimuli producing internal frustration, and generally of variable conditions in the environment. The conclusion reached by Crook, after a lengthy review of the evidence, is representative of "the other ethology":

> Instead of resulting from an innate and ineradicable force demanding repetitive expression, aggressive

behavior occurs normally as a response to particular aversive stimuli and ceases upon their removal. . . . In many, also, aggression is commonly associated with frustrations born of the delay in responding imposed largely by his learning to play social roles in a community. There is every reason to suppose that individual sensibility likely to evoke aggression is determined during socialization. The manifestation of aggression in human society is thus largely a cultural attribute.[22]

Among some of those who criticize the instinctivist theory of aggression, there is also recognition of another and more specific implication—i.e., its significance for education and child rearing. Given his conviction of the spontaneous urge toward aggression in the human animal, it is not surprising that Lorenz should express outright disapproval of "permissive" American methods of education which allegedly "supposed that children would grow up less neurotic, better adapted to their social environment, and less aggressive if they were spared all disappointments and indulged in every way" but which in fact produced "countless unbearably rude children who were anything but nonaggressive."[23] The clear inference from his theory, even apart from such remarks, is that education and child rearing require for good results an atmosphere of strict discipline, moral and even physical restraints upon aggressive "spontaneity," and the Freudian therapy of contact sports. It is this connotation which has led Ashley Montagu to refer to the Lorenzian doctrine as a "new litany of innate depravity," reviving an ancient belief, one of whose expressions was the schoolmen's assumption of infant depravity. The potential consequences of reestablishing this doctrine as social and educational policy have been pointed out by Schneirla in a passage which might well stand as a coda to the present chapter: "It is as heavy a responsibility to inform mankind about aggressive tendencies assumed to be present on an inborn basis as about 'original sin'—and this Lorenz admits in effect. A corollary risk is advising societies to base their programs of social training on attempts to inhibit hypothetical innate aggression, instead of continuing positive measures for socially constructive behavior."[24]

What stands out from this competition of viewpoints in contemporary ethology, as in the earlier disputes of Darwinian biology and Freudian psychology, is the extent to which the dichotomy of opinion appears to be governed by factors other than those supposedly involved in empirical observation and scientific theory building. The presence of strong feelings on both sides, of underlying commitments of value and belief which cut beneath the level of fact and measurement, is apparent in the crosscurrents of the literature. Where, on one hand, Lorenz, Ardrey, and Tiger raise the cry of prejudice against their opponents, on the other hand the charge is made against them of ideological and political bias. Thus Ralph Holloway writes of Ardrey that his "book is an apology and rationalization for Imperialism, Pax Americana, Laissez Faire, Social Darwinism, and that greatest of all evolutionary developments, Capitalism."[25] Kenneth Boulding warns similarly:

> We have seen in the Nazi movement how appallingly dangerous a pseudo-science can be in the legitimation of an absurd and evil system. I am not suggesting that either Lorenz or Ardrey is a racist theorist like Gobineau or Houston Chamberlain. However, one could imagine their superficially attractive neo-Social-Darwinism applied to very ill uses indeed, and the fact that it is scientific humbug does not unfortunately detract from its attractiveness.[26]

The basis for these accusations is to be found in the evident readiness of aggression-instinct theorists to derive definite ethical, political, and ideological inferences from the prehominid records of the wilderness and the aviary. Ardrey's territorial urge, in particular, serves as the foundation for a wide-ranging "philosophy of real estate" (as one reviewer has called it) which is reminiscent of Machiavelli's famous dictum that avarice for property exceeds all other loves and aspirations in man. Among other things, this theory leads Ardrey to make a curious distinction between so-called true "biological nations" (e.g., Britain, France, Greece) and pseudo-nations or "noyeaux" (such as Italy, modern France, and all the new countries of black Africa). Indeed, Ardrey goes so far as to endorse the remarkable prediction that "were South Africa physically invaded by white forces, 80 percent of South African blacks would join in the country's defense; were the invasion to be mounted by black forces, the defense would be total."[27]

In view of all this, it does not seem excessive to suggest that the scientific literature on the roots of aggression is a graphic illustration of the extent to which personal beliefs and cultural values come to be woven into the fabric of any research that bears upon the springs of human action—or upon its ends. Even where that bearing is remote and indirect, as in the case of nonprimate animal studies, it may be sufficient to activate those human capacities of commitment, conviction, and concern which are not so much *un*scientific as *trans*scientific; they would seem to be the source of all interest and incentive, no less in the work of science than in the works of art. One kind of testimony to their existence and their relevance is provided by the aggression-instinct theorists, who do not hesitate to make the leap from fact to value (although they deny that they have first plunged from value to fact). Another kind of testimony to the presence of the "ethical imperative" is furnished by the opponents of the instinct theory. Nearly all these critics, in the course of their refutations, make the same point: that the work of Lorenz, Ardrey, and company is not only bad science, it is bad *counsel*. As Sally Carrighar has put it, ". . . a widespread belief that human wars are instinctive, by which biologists mean inevitable, would of course tend to make them inevitable. . . . If aggression, as these authors insist, is a doom carried in human genes, we are predestined to wage wars and hopes for peace would seem to be slim."[28]

This emphasis upon the prophetic self-fulfillment of such beliefs about human nature and conduct conveys the awareness that these ideas have consequences beyond their descriptive character and objective verifiability. They carry, in fact, an inescapably normative dimension; insofar as they are believed and acted upon, they become confirmed and "validated." Accordingly it would seem to be appropriate, even within a scientific context, to inquire which images and models of behavior—what ideas of man—lend support to the common values of humanity (such as liberty, dignity, and fraternity) and which ideas place them in jeopardy. At the conclusion of his critique of the Lorenz-Ardrey thesis, Crook states the issue in trenchant terms:

> The image of man, already demoted from his place near the angels through the popularization of Darwinian and Freudian ideas, is all too vulnerable to further erosion. The *Zeitgeist* extols the mechanism, and we may perhaps see ourselves as no more than that; but the mechanism is wonderfully complex, its properties poorly understood, and as subjects we remain uniquely self-aware. Although the phenomenon of man cannot be explained by simplistic argument pandering only to the pessimism of an age, the image that most of the people acquire

is apt to shape the values of a community. Indeed, a parallel is apparent in the recent past when ideas derived from a misunderstanding of "Social Darwinism" played their part in the history of European fascist politics. Who knows whence a New Right may gather a cloak of respectability to condone, perhaps in some new "Report from Iron Mountain," the defense of racial garrisons in the noyeaux of the near future? The new genre of popular biological exposition neglects the humanity of man. We would do well to meditate upon the reasons.[29]

II

MAN AS MACHINE:
The Inhuman Uses of
Human Beings

CHAPTER 4

TECHNOLOGICAL REVOLUTION:
The Paradox of Power

It is a truism that the technological revolution of our time has enormously enhanced the power of man to control natural forces which once were assumed to be forever beyond his capacity to alter or affect. "Technology," as Robert L. Heilbroner has put it, "is altering life to its existential roots before our very eyes." It might be said that the Age of Invention, coterminous with the First Industrial Revolution, has given way to the Age of *Intervention*, synonymous with the Second Industrial Revolution. Those impenetrable mysteries of nature and the universe, of which poets and contemplatives once spoke with awe and wonderment, have been reduced to the status of technical problems routinely "solved" in operational terms, printed out on IBM cards, and stored as software in the data bank.

The sheer magnitude of the power which this revolution is putting into the hands of men—power to change their outer world and inner selves—is without precedent in human history and probably without equal in the fantasies of human imagination. "Humanity today," writes Victor Ferkiss in *Technological Man*, "is on the threshold of self-transfiguration, of attaining new powers over itself and its environment that can alter its nature as fundamentally as walking upright or the use of tools."[1] More specifically, according to Emanuel G. Mesthene, "We have now, or know how to acquire, the technical capability to do very nearly anything we want. Can we transplant human hearts, control personality, order the weather that suits us, travel to Mars or Venus? Of course we can, if not now or in five or ten years, then certainly in 25 or 30 or 100."[2]

That word *control* may well be, as Norbert Wiener anticipated a score of years ago, the key term in the vocabulary of the new technology. But it is, of course, a double-edged sword: The very techniques which are granting us such extraordinary control over the natural and human world also create new dilemmas of control with regard to those techniques themselves. The problem is at once obvious and subtle. It is obvious at the level of most physical and technical bottlenecks such as atmospheric pollution, traffic congestion, resource depletion, and the like; there the answer to technological breakdown is, simply enough, technological breakthrough. It is more subtle at the point of intersecting values and contradictory frames of reference—where, in Anatol Rapoport's phrase, strategy and conscience meet. On both levels, illustrations of what might be termed the *paradox of power*—that is, expanding technological control matched by diminishing social control and disappearing self-control —are abundant throughout our society. Nor are they perceived solely by rebels and romanticists. Everyone remembers the prophetic admonition of President Dwight Eisenhower, in his Farewell Address to the nation in January, 1961, that "in the councils of government, we must guard against the acquisition of unwarranted influence, whether sought or unsought, by the military-industrial complex." Less well remembered is the corollary warning in the same speech: "Akin to, and largely responsible for, the sweeping changes in our industrial-military posture, has been the technological revolution during recent decades. . . . [I]n holding scientific research and discovery in respect, as we should, we must also be alert to the equal and opposite danger that public policy could itself become the captive of a scientific-technological elite."[3]

The clear presumption underlying Eisenhower's warning is that the interests and imperatives of the "scientific-technological elite" are not those which should guide a free society—indeed, that they imperil its fundamental values. In this apprehension, the late President has been joined by a great many critics of unchecked technology—conservative, liberal, and radical alike. The point of agreement among them all is the intuition that the natural course of technology rampant leads directly through technolatry to technocracy: that is, to a sociopolitical order in which the instrumental values of efficiency, impersonality, and a purely technical rationality predominate over the human values of liberty, dignity, privacy, and responsibility. "Must the miracle of the person," asks Lynn White, Jr., "succumb to the order of the computer?"[4]

That eventuality, which once seemed only the fantasy of fevered poets and writers of science fiction, has gained plausibility in the wake of recent developments on a variety of fronts: among them the biological revolution, with its impulse toward the "manufacture of man"; the psychological revolution, with its tendency to engineer behavior through "psychotechnological intervention"; the political counterrevolution of the Nixon years, which produced an Orwellian technocracy of anonymous managers equipped with a sophisticated armory of espionage and surveillance devices directed against the citizenry; and, underlying everything, the cultural evolution of a "postmodern," "postindustrial" style of thought and performance which we may call the technological ethos. That ethos—the cluster of norms and values implicit in the operations of technology—has long been viewed with suspicion by humanists (an early and eloquent statement of the case was Friedrich Juenger's *The Failure of Technology*[5]); but their criticisms have been generally ignored or derided by the mainstream of professional and scientific authority. The two camps are today as far apart as ever; but the balance of forces has become markedly less unequal, and the odds on tomorrow have shifted accordingly. A succession of unanticipated consequences of industrial and technological "progress"—concerning which the new science of ecology in particular has made us aware—has raised the public consciousness and brought about something like a shock of recognition. No longer does the voice of Lewis Mumford cry alone in the wilderness; the prophet at last is honored in his own country. His premonitions and admonitions of the past half-century, directed to the irrepressible conflict of technics and civilization, have come finally to sound like the home truths which, for all their erudition and originality, they always were. Meanwhile we have had the far more pessimistic projections of Roderick Seidenberg regarding the fate of "posthistoric man," and the all but overwhelming vision of technological Armageddon presented by Jacques Ellul.[6] By the end of the sixties the climate of opinion concerning the relationship of technology and human values had so altered that Herbert J. Muller, a distinguished cultural historian of unshakable calm and prudential wisdom, was prepared to entitle his own examination of the issue *The Children of Frankenstein*.[7]

A representative critique of the technological ethos and its dehumanizing potentialities, building upon the strictures of Ellul and Mumford as well as upon his own earlier design for a "sane society," is Erich Fromm's *The Revolution of Hope: Toward a Humanized Technology*. The argument of the book is that technology and human individuality are on a collision course: the requirement of "maximal efficiency and output," which underlies the technological process, "leads to the requirement of minimal individuality."[8] Foremost among the losses suffered by the person under this relentless order is that of self-direction or self-control: "The passiveness of man in industrial society today is one of his most characteristic and pathological features. . . . Man's passiveness is only one symptom among a total syndrome, which one may call the 'syndrome of alienation' . . . he feels powerless, lonely, and anxious. He has little sense of integrity or self-identity."[9] Fromm's diagnosis of the condition of technological man, bleak and forbidding as it is, pales before the portrait given us by the sociologist Lewis Yablonsky in his grimly titled study, *Robopaths: People as Machines.* The condition of "robopathology," according to Yablonsky, is the product of "the growing dehumanization of people to the point where they have become the walking dead. . . . Robopaths are the reverse of Čapek's technological robots, they are people who simulate machines. Their existential state is ahuman."[10]

This theme of individual alienation and collective anomie is, to be sure, a dominant motif in the expressive art and literature of Europe and America over the past generation; and it is no less central in the psychological and sociological literature, where it dates back at least to Marx. There is tragedy as well as irony in the observation that, at the same time as man collectively is gaining control over his physical world and his evolutionary fate, man individually feels himself to be losing control over his personal world and his private life. Both phenomena, moreover, are traceable to the same source: both are products of the technological ethos.

Among professional observers of technological society,

there are at least two distinguishable schools of thought regarding the probable future outcome. The larger group, whom we may call the *technological determinists*, perceive the issue (of identity versus technology, of liberty versus order) as already closed and the struggle as lost. This school, moreover, is in turn divided into celebrants and mourners—between those who embrace the future "technetronic society," if occasionally with minor reservations (e.g., Zbigniew Brzezinski, Herman Kahn, Marshall McLuhan, Alvin Toffler),[11] and those who deplore its coming but can see no possibility of averting it (e.g., Ellul and Seidenberg). Opposed to the technological determinism of both these groups is a school of thought— let us call it *humanistic indeterminism*—which holds that the issue is far from closed, that mankind possesses a viable choice between alternative futures, and that this power of choice imposes a responsibility to comprehend the crucial differences between the competing paradigms or myths which undergird the issue. The most influential spokesman for the indeterministic view is still Mumford, whose magisterial two-volume work *The Myth of the Machine* (the second volume is entitled *The Pentagon of Power*) directly challenges the master metaphor of conventional anthropology: that is, the image of *Homo faber*, of man as toolmaker or technician.

To consider man, then, as primarily a tool-using animal, is to overlook the main chapters of human history. Opposed to this petrified notion, I shall develop the view that man is preeminently a mind-making, self-mastering, and self-designing animal; and the primary locus of all his activities lies first in his own organism, and in the social organization through which it finds fuller expression. *Until man had made something of himself he could make little of the world around him.*[12]

The contest between this humanistic image of man and his world, with its skeptical irreverence toward the technological imperative, and the contrasting vision of those who embrace the future technocratic order (whether with resignation or rejoicing) is manifested in a variety of forms and acted out upon numerous stages. A pertinent example, which illuminates not only the paradox of power but the ambiguity of ethics in the post-machine age, is the surveillance scheme known as the "national data bank."

THE DATA BANK DICK

The revelations and scandals of the Watergate Era—which resulted in the decline and fall, card by card, of the imperial House of Nixon—have heightened the nation's awareness of the vulnerability of those personal and private rights which, enshrined within the isolation of the first ten Amendments, stand against the mighty demands for public order and national security that pervade the body of the Constitution. For a time at least, illegal buggings and surreptitious entries are unlikely to be tolerated, and the more dramatic and notorious forms of assault upon the dignity and privacy of the citizen may decline in frequency. But the underlying conflict of interest—the tension between the requirements of order, efficiency, and regulation on the one hand and those of simple human liberty on the other—will not go away. For the issue is not one of legality versus illegality, or morality versus corruption; rather it is one of competing social claims, each of which carries legitimacy and plausibility. On one side are the imperatives of technology, governmental or otherwise; on the other side are the needs of the person.

A graphic illustration of the persisting conflict between

technological and humane perspectives may be seen in the repeated proposals for a "national data bank" (i.e., a centralized computer system pooling information on individuals from a score or more of public agencies). Recommendations to this effect have been voiced with increasing frequency at least since 1959, when the American Economic Association and the Social Science Research Council established a study committee, under Professor Richard Ruggles of Yale University, to explore the problem of preserving and disseminating economic research data.[13] The Ruggles Committee, after three years of study, recommended the creation of a federal data center to store and make available basic statistical materials originating in some twenty agencies of the federal government. Then, as now, the arguments for such a bank were entirely cogent and reasonable. It would preserve in one convenient file the diverse information scattered among numerous agencies; it would reduce the length of questionnaires; it would act as a servicing facility, somewhat like the Library of Congress, and therefore would be of aid to scholars and researchers, and so on. The initial proposal of the Ruggles Committee was later reinforced by other authoritative reports, all of which emphasized the obvious advantages of a national data bank in terms of coordinated planning and decision-making as well as of all-around efficiency. The primary justification was succinctly stated by the then chairman of the Civil Service Commission, John Macy, in the late sixties: "In forecasting manpower needs and important decisions of career planning for proper decisions in these areas, we must have integrated information systems. This will require the use of information across departmental boundaries."[14] What is noteworthy about Macy's argument is that, in extolling the virtues of the computer generally and of the computerized data bank in particular, he could envision no possibility of misuse or manipulation of the data. To all those "who fear that computers will de-emphasize humanity," Macy had a positive reply: "Far from it! . . . It has liberated the manager to give his mind to greater scope of creativity. Rather than degrading the worth of the human being, the computer has placed a premium on man at his best."[15]

But the man who is at his best in this tableau is, as Macy indicates, the *manager*—the individual on top of the data bank. There is little doubt that administrators and executives would be rendered more efficient and resourceful by such means; what is in question is the well-being of the man at the bottom of the data pool, the person whose vital statistics are being reported, recorded, indexed, researched, and distributed across departmental boundaries. In short, the issue is one of *privacy*—or, more narrowly, of confidentiality—as against the plausible and persuasive demands for access to personal information by various interested groups. Fortunately this client-centered outlook—the view from below, as it were —has been gaining more adherents as the data bank proposal has come under closer scrutiny. Arthur R. Miller has described the negative potential of the scheme in specific terms:

> First, if all the information gathered about an individual is in one place, the payoff for snooping is sharply enhanced. Thus, although the cost or difficulty of gaining access may be great, the amount of dirt available once access is gained is also great. Second, there is every reason to believe that the art of electronic surveillance will continue to become more efficient and economical. Third, governmental snooping is rarely deterred by cost.[16]

More than that, even if the contents of a federal data bank are primarily "statistical" rather than of an "intelligence" character, it would seem that the material could easily be foraged and manipulated for intelligence purposes. The notorious episode of the White House "enemies list," involving among other underhanded things the commandeering and exploitation of income-tax records from the Bureau of Internal Revenue, should be enough to demonstrate the potential abuses of such information sources by devious men of high office. But even apart from sinister or ulterior motives, the danger of misuse of the massive data files arises from the best of intentions and the most constructive of purposes—such as those of sound administration, informed decision-making, and scientific research. "For one thing," observes the sociologist Edward W. Shils, the administrators of a national data center "would acquire a professional vested interest in the satisfaction of their cognitive appetite. As long as computers could cope or could be designed to cope with such quantities of material, there would be what would sound like good and reasonable arguments for making the informational archives of the government complete."[17]

Even before the disclosures and disasters of Watergate, there was growing apprehension among those sensitized to personal rights as the signs of increasing electronic surveillance in both the public and private sectors began to multiply—most ominously, perhaps, in the exposure of widespread gathering and storage of information by the Army on millions of civilian Americans whose activities and advocacies were clearly legitimate but conveyed, to certain trained eyes, all the earmarks of eccentricity. Both houses of Congress have held hearings on the issue of "computer privacy" (or, as someone has termed it, "the pollution of privacy") in an effort to assemble defenses against the oppressive presence of automated and cybernated information dossiers. Nor has there been any dearth of critical literature; numbers of articles and books

—notably among them Jerry M. Rosenberg's *The Death of Privacy*[18]—have documented the increasing resort to data banks and other computerized information systems not only by public agencies but also by industrial corporations and private institutions. An example of the versatility of potential exploitations of the new information technology is the centralized data system called LOGIC (Local Government Information Control) set up for one million residents of Santa Clara, California, in 1968. "Included in this alphabetic index record are data such as name, alias, address, record of birth, driver's license, Social Security number, position if employed by county, property holdings, voter and jury status."[19] One of the many hazards of such a system is illustrated by the action of New York State a few years ago in selling the names and addresses of the state's 6.4 million vehicle owners to a marketing service, in order to net the treasury some $86,000. That the officials involved could see no harm in such a transaction speaks volumes for the discrepancy between bureaucratic-technological interests and the merely "private" concerns of individual citizens. Episodes like these led Rosenberg to declare—on the eve of Watergate—that "the Big Brother of 1984 may not be a greedy power-seeker, but rather a relentless bureaucrat or opportunist obsessed with efficiency, who may use information for purposes other than those for which it was collected."[20]

The value which is chiefly at stake in this issue—that of privacy, or perhaps more accurately of *personal security*—is more than just another of those functional and sociometric variables (like status, power, wealth, affection, and so on) that behavioral scientists are inclined to treat in the sterile quantitative terms of allocation and distribution. Privacy is a fundamental right of the person clearly guaranteed by the Constitution (directly by the Fourth Amendment, implicitly by the First and Fifth); and, what is more in point, it is a right perhaps more critically endangered than any other by the conditions and consequences of our high-speed, high-density, high-rise mass society. More than a few observers believe it is already later than we think; thus W. H. Ferry, lately of the Center for the Study of Democratic Institutions, asserts that privacy is "today a goner, killed by technology."[21] The rapid proliferation of electronic eavesdropping, pointed up by the Watergate disclosures and by successive congressional hearings, dramatizes only one aspect of the threat to privacy; another danger grows out of the progressive weakening of legal controls against police interventions and intrusions. But the most fundamental and far-reaching of all is the simple pressure for information and knowledge, necessary to the maintenance of adequate records, on the part of innumerable agencies, bureaus, and institutions dealing with the public as clients or petitioners. The federal agencies of public assistance and welfare, of vocational rehabilitation and public health, of educational assistance and special employment, all require data on the tens of millions of Americans who make use of their services. Increasingly, in an age of psychology and behavioral science, the information which is thought to be necessary includes highly personal (and typically negative) material, of a kind easily misunderstood and misused—not to say malignly used.

The challenge to privacy is, of course, a challenge to personal liberty; more basically still, it signals an erosion of that capacity of *respect for the person* which has its deepest roots in the Judeo-Christian heritage, and which over the centuries since the Renaissance has become a central element in what Walter Lippmann termed the "traditions of civility."[22] Where privacy is challenged, it is the human person that is under attack. The idea of the person rests upon the moral perception of the human being as subject rather than object, as an end rather than a means—as unique, incommensurable, and *inviol-*

able. It is a conception of man altogether alien to that postmodern spirit of classification, analysis, and organization which finds its characteristic expression in the technical mind and the technological order. The spreading incursions upon privacy by computerized intelligence —like the imminent intrusions upon personality by the biological revolution—are merely items in a general trend toward the ever more efficient and total organization of society which more than one prophetic observer has perceived as an already inexorable and irreversible tide. The chilling prediction of Roderick Seidenberg, in *Posthistoric Man*, may stand as a suitable epigraph to this case study of the pressures of technological society upon the person:

> Under the momentum of this universal trend, the individual will indeed find himself churned into an ever smaller particle, into a minute and at length irreducible atom of the social system. As the significance of the individual is thus steadily diminished, his status and identity must necessarily approach that of a statistical average, while at the same time the mass will become correspondingly enlarged and dominating in its new and terrifying totality. Under the pressure of this transformation we will have crossed the threshold of a collectivist age.[23]

CHAPTER 5

BIOLOGICAL REVOLUTION:
The Nurture of Nature

The startling succession of discoveries in microbiology and related life sciences over recent years—well described by one observer as the "evolution revolution"—have become generally familiar through a number of revelatory popularizations (such as Alvin Toffler's *Future Shock* and Gordon Rattray Taylor's *The Biological Time Bomb*),[1] through James D. Watson's true detective story of *The Double Helix*,[2] through press reports of sensational transplants and other medical breakthroughs, and through countless commentaries estimating the awesome consequences of what can only be termed our rampant biological technology.

The potential reach of these discoveries is such that many observers regard our ventures into biological "inner space" as more far-reaching in their significance for human existence than our "Star Trek" adventures into outer space. The most important of these implications bears upon the age-old controversy of determinism versus freedom (or blind determinism versus *self*-determinism). As R. Michael Davidson puts it: "This is the new era of Participatory Evolution. No longer is man the offspring of Nature, the creature of natural selection. Science has provided him with the technology to become his own maker."[3]

Among the more spectacular developments which the life scientists, and their counterparts the "genetic engineers," regard not only as possible but imminent are: the control of aging, with extension of the life span; the creation of life, through synthesis of (increasingly complex) living organisms; vast enhancement of intelligence in man and animals, through "brain biology" and genetic intervention; reproduction (by cloning) of exact living duplicates of animals and thereafter of men; perfection of an artificial placenta and subsequent establishment of true "baby factories" (i.e., the production of infants a la Huxley's fable); organ regeneration; creation of mixed man-machine chimeras or "cyborgs" (cybernetic organisms); extensive mind modification and personality reconstruction via drugs . . . and much more.[4]

The problem of *control*—the paradox of technological power—is so great in this one vital sector of technology as to boggle the imagination. That paradox, to restate it once more, is the coexistence of immense physical power with immense psychical powerlessness. On one side, man has, or is about to have, seemingly limitless power to change his nature—to reconstruct his past (by manipulating heredity), to control his future (by cloning, genetic surgery, postponement of death), to manufacture humanoids or androids virtually to measure. On the other side, this very power of control is at present uncontrolled and potentially out of control. It is uncontrolled because, as yet, the virtue of unlimited scientific and technological development has not seriously been called into question, either by scientists themselves or by the rest of us (except in a few extreme circumstances such as those of enforced psychosurgery). And the situation is potentially out of control because the powers, forces, and futures being provoked by biological technology may soon exceed our ability to restrain or recall them.

A single example, not more ominous or extraordinary than many others, may serve to make the point. It arises from the galloping advances in molecular biology; and the warning comes from Sir Macfarlane Burnet, a Nobel Award winner for his work on tissue transplants. The common practice in his field of culturing viruses and developing new mutants carries the risk that a dangerous mutant might escape the laboratory and bring about an epidemic against which the world would be helpless, lacking natural defense systems to protect against it. "The human implication," writes Burnet, "of what is going on in this sophisticated universe of tissue-cultured cells, bacteria and viruses which can be grown at the expense of one or other are at best dubious and at worst frankly terrifying." If a seriologically unique virus of great virulence should appear, which is not at all unlikely, and should then get into general circulation without being immediately controlled, the result could be an "almost unimaginable catastrophe . . . involving all the populous regions of the world." Sir Macfarlane goes on to speculate that we may already be unwittingly introducing episomes (or genetic messages) into human genetic material in the course of molecular experiments—messages that may lie dormant for years before emerging in the form of radical alterations of the human genotype, such as "monsters," defective individuals, cancerous outbreaks, new diseases, and the like. On the basis of these distinct possibilities, he has been moved to make an extraordinary declaration: "It seems almost indecent to hint that, as far as the advance of medicine is concerned, molecular biology may be an evil thing." And Burnet concludes: "It is a hard thing for an experimental scientist to accept, but it is becoming all too evident that there are dangers in knowing what should not be known. But no one has ever heeded the words of a Cassandra."[5]

Not a few other life scientists, contemplating the possibilities of calamity opened up by their powerful research, share Burnet's nightmare premonition and echo his call for a moratorium in certain crucial corners of the laboratory. Some years earlier, in *Can Man Be Modified?*, Jean Rostand dared to ask the question: "Has science reached a frontier beyond which its program might be more harmful than advantageous?"[6] And Sir George Pickering, considering the prospect of the indefinite extension of human life, has declared:

> I find this a terrifying prospect, and I am glad I shall be dead and will have ceased to make my own contributions to this catastrophe before it happens. However, we may ask ourselves whether it is not time to halt the programme of research and development which will make such a thing possible. The hint of such an idea by a man who has spent most of his adult life in research of this kind savours of intellectual treason. It is inhumane. It is at variance with the age-old ideas and ideals of the medical profession. Nevertheless, we should face up to the probable consequences of our ideas and ideals and be prepared to revise them.[7]

It should be said, however, that if such expressions of concern are no longer rare among biologists, they are also far from common. In a striking commentary of a few years ago, Donald Fleming drew attention to the peculiar constellation of beliefs, values, and purposes which he ascribed to the "new revolutionaries" in biology—primarily biochemists and molecular biologists. Observing that "one of the stigmata of revolutionaries in any field is their resolute determination to break with traditional culture,"

Fleming maintained that the new biologists have broken not only with professional procedures in their own field but also with traditional moral and religious values in the wider culture. "The parallel is very marked," he wrote, "between the original Christian Revolution against the values of the classical world and the Biological Revolution against religious values." On this view, the current revolution is not only biological but cultural and ethical in its meaning; it contains a discernible ideology which embraces "despair at our present condition, but infinite hope for the future if the biologists' prescription is taken." Indeed, according to Fleming, it is more than hope that is held out: "If the world will only listen, they *know* how to put us on the high road to salvation."[8]

It is especially noteworthy that, in this interpretation, the gospel of the biological revolutionaries is a *technological* creed, and that in describing it Fleming finds the jargon of technology ironically appropriate:

> What exactly does their brand of salvation entail? Perhaps the most illuminating way to put the matter is that their ideal is the manufacture of man. In a manufacturing process, the number of units to be produced is a matter of rational calculation beforehand and of tight control thereafter. Within certain tolerances, specifications are laid down for a satisfactory product. Quality-control is maintained by checking the output and replacing the defective parts. After the product has been put to use, spare parts can normally be supplied to replace those that have worn out.
>
> This is the program of the new biologists—control of numbers by foolproof contraception; gene manipulation and substitution; surgical and biochemical intervention in the embryonic and neonatal phases; organ transplants or replacements at will.[9]

It is not necessary to embrace all the particulars of this argument in order to recognize Fleming's central point concerning the conflict "between traditional values, however moderately indulged, and the values appropriate to the Biological Revolution." The latter complex of values, as set forth in the writings of such of the "revolutionaries" as Joshua Lederberg and Herman G. Muller,[10] is plainly a new form of naturalistic ethics which equates the good of man with the progress of science in general and with the research interests of microsurgeons and genetic engineers in particular. It is, in fact, simply our old friend the technological ethos, as interpreted by specialists in biology; and it illustrates, as vividly as any example drawn from industrial or governmental technology, the peculiar ambiguity of the problem of *control* with respect to this ungoverned phenomenon. Surprisingly, that ambiguity has not generally been confronted in the voluminous literature dealing with the very problem under discussion here—the problem, that is, of controlling, planning, and directing technological change.

The ambiguity arises from the fact that, in addition to the two familiar options with respect to the future course of technology, there is also a third. Everyone is aware of the first two options—those of "drift" and of "mastery"— the first implying a general lack of social regulation or planning, and the second implying conscious and concerted effort to bring the process under control. The large and fashionable body of literature known as futurology or futuristics represents, almost uniformly, the second of these two options. The futurists, impatient with the confusion and chaos resulting from unchecked technological growth, seek to apply the principles of rationality, systems analysis, strategic priority allocation, technical forecasting, long-term multiform trend projection, and the like. These are, of course, the very principles of the technological ethos, as we have been reviewing it. Contrary to some appearances, therefore, the perspectives of futurology are not genuinely critical toward the miracles and mystiques of technology but only toward its irrational or uncoordinated development. The futurists are, more or less undisguisedly, themselves *technologists*; and the future order they envisage is that of a planned technological society.[11]

The third option—an alternative to technofuturism as well as to old-fashioned technological drift—is encountered rarely in the works of future thinkers and strategic planners but has begun to appear elsewhere in the social and physical sciences with such frequency as to foreshadow the advent of a coherent new movement of thought—virtually (to adapt the phrase of Charles Reich) a "new consciousness."[12] Its common denominator is conveyed in a slogan contributed by W. H. Ferry: "People First, Machines Second."[13] Still more pertinently, it is illuminated in the distinction drawn by Anatol Rapoport between the values of "strategy and conscience."[14] In short, the third alternative is nothing more nor less than the application of *humanism* to the problems of technological society; it amounts to a reordering of social priorities and a transvaluation of social values, centering upon a new (or resuscitated) image of man radically different from the conceptual models and metaphors which have dominated the modern world. "Not the Power Man," as Mumford has put the case, "not the Profit Man, not the Mechanical Man, but the Whole Man, Man in Person, so to say, must be the central actor in the new drama of civilization."[15]

THE NURTURE OF NATURE

The "nature-nurture" controversy—otherwise known as heredity versus environment or, in its broader philosophical form, determinism versus freedom—is an ancient quarrel which has often been pronounced dead, obsolete, or irrelevant. But the old issue has a habit of reviving— or, more accurately, of persisting. And it has seldom been more lively or more warmly contested than it is today. Much of the reason for its current vitality arises from the series of fundamental scientific discoveries known collectively as the "biological revolution." (Another reason, discussed in Chapters 1 to 3 above, has to do with the recrudescence of instinct theories of aggression, territoriality, the "male bond," and so on, advanced in explanation of human behavior.)

The salient facts of the biological revolution, centering upon the discovery of the double-helix structure of DNA, have been spelled out in preceding pages. What is in point here is the powerful impetus which these breakthroughs have given to the nature-nurture debate. In the long run, one of the most portentous aspects of the biological revolution may well be the *conceptual* revolution which it is bringing in its wake. That great shift of ideas—which implies nothing less than the turning around of all our concepts regarding the interrelationship of human nature and social nurture—is already under way. There can be little doubt about the reality and profundity of this modification of perspectives; but, like other revolutions, its precise direction and final outcome are not foreseeable with certainty. In effect, its course may lead along either of two divergent paths, toward either of two opposite conclusions: It may turn out to support the argument from *nature* (genetic or instinctual determinism) or the argument from *nurture* (cultural indeterminism and conscious self-determination). This is not to say that these incompatible alternatives are equally probable or plausible on the record; the second of the two, as we shall see, would seem to be more positively indicated. But the point is that neither option is quite certain to prevail; nor is it a matter simply of waiting until the scientific returns are in from the laboratory. It is becoming clearer that, in this field as in others relating to life and man, the scientific returns are never finally or incontestably in. The resolution of the issue, the outcome of the conceptual revolution instigated by the new biology, is fundamentally a matter of *choice* or decision to be made on grounds independent of the scientific facts and figures themselves.

THE NEW CASE FOR "NATURE"

The most formidable statement in recent years of the case for genetic determinism with respect to such matters as intelligence, learning, scholastic attainment, and (inferentially) social and cultural achievement was the comprehensive 1969 paper by Arthur R. Jensen, an educational psychologist whose primary concern has been with individual differences in human learning.[16] Although virtually all of Jensen's findings and conclusions had been published by him before,[17] the 1969 paper stirred wide attention and controversy owing to the vigor of Jensen's insistence upon two central claims:

1. "That genetic factors are strongly implicated in the average Negro-white intelligence difference. The preponderance of evidence is, in my [Jensen's] opinion, less consistent with a strictly environmental hypothesis than with a genetic hypothesis, which, of course, does not exclude the influence of environment or its interrelation with genetic factors."

2. "[That] compensatory education has been tried and it apparently has failed."[18]

Thus, Jensen's principal conclusion—on the basis of a wide-ranging review of research studies in genetics, psychology, anthropology, intelligence testing, and much else—was not only that there are genetic differences between individuals but that there are genetic differences in intelligence between *races*, and in particular between whites and blacks. This led him to the further conclusion that educational policies and school curricula should be designed (in most cases thoroughly overhauled) to meet these racially specific aptitudes and limitations.

It is worth noting that this approach places Jensen squarely within a tradition of research and argument reaching back at least three hundred years—a tradition characterized by one unsympathetic anthropologist (Juan Comas) as "scientific racism,"[19] and by another (Manning Nash) as "the ideology of race."[20] The central characteristic of this literature is the imputation of mental (and usually of physical) inferiority to some races, and of mental superiority to others—a difference which is taken to be innate and ineradicable. The role played by extra-scientific assumptions and values in the periodic recrudescence of this school of thought will be discussed later; here it is enough to take note of the continuity and consistency of its main propositions. The essential preliminary claim is that intelligence is, to a controlling degree, a heritable characteristic rather than a product of experience and learning; in other words, intelligence is genetically fixed and predetermined. When that crucial premise has been accepted, the next step in the argument involves a link between races and Mendelian or "breeding" populations (aggregates or groups statistically distinguishable from others by virtue of some genetic frequencies). If races constitute such breeding populations, then the genetic theory of intelligence comes into operation to explain (or rationalize) differences of performance and behavior, as between such groups as blacks and whites.

Such biologistic explanations have appeared with considerable frequency in recent years, following a long period of dormancy during which it was supposed that

concepts of racial inferiority had been extinguished with
the Nazi regime. In 1961, the distinguished anthropologist
Juan Comas called attention to a revival of the school
in a widely discussed article, " 'Scientific' Racism Again?"
His concern centered upon the appearance of *The Mankind Quarterly*, "a supposedly scientific journal whose
comments are the cause of profound concern to those
interested in racial questions in the biological and anthropological fields as well as in the social field."[21] At
about the same time, two books were published which
gave clear support to the racial-inferiority thesis: Audrey
M. Shuey's *The Testing of Negro Intelligence* and Carleton Putnam's *Race and Reason*.[22] In 1967 (and repeatedly
in subsequent years), the Nobel prizewinning physicist
William Shockley sought to persuade the National Academy of Sciences to undertake studies of heredity and race
in relation to "our national human quality." Shockley's
appeal, which in its later form leaned heavily on the
work of Jensen, maintained that the United States may
be undergoing serious "downbreeding" by the comparatively high birth rates among Negroes, said to be born
on the average mentally inferior to whites.[23]

What is "new" in the case for nature presently advanced
by Jensen, Shockley, and others is not so much the theory
(which has remained fairly constant over at least half
a century), nor even the data (drawn mainly from IQ
testing and performance scales), but rather the *climate
of opinion* in scientific and academic circles resulting
from the successive shocks of the biological revolution.
Although that revolution has actually been carried out
only in specialized corners of the field (molecular biology
and genetics), biology as a whole has gained immense
prestige and has already replaced physics as the queen
of sciences in academic and popular esteem. A rash of
theories claiming biological origin and sanction have
begun to appear in psychology, sociology, anthropology,

and political science—often promoted with the vigor of insurgency and an air of shaking the foundations. Thus, Lionel Tiger, a social anthropologist, writes: "Have we now the greater and more accurate findings of biology on which can be based a biological or zoological view of man? We have." He then adds: "So far, in relatively few places have the new data and theories of zoologists, geneticists, palaeoanthropologists, etc., penetrated the methodological array and graduate school catechisms of the dominant traditions of sociology and anthropology."[24] Of more immediate interest is the effort of Bruce Eckland to advance a genetic theory of intelligence applicable to the subject matter of sociology, notably to differences of social class.[25] It seems likely that biological models and metaphors may soon acquire the prominence in social science once accorded those of physics—with equally significant consequences for the image of man and the perspectives of society.

However, the advent of biologism in social science presupposes the theoretical victory of "nature over nurture"—that is, the thesis of the fixed genetic determination of intelligence and other significant factors in behavior. The accumulation of claims to this effect from various scientific quarters—not only from "Jensenists" but from zoologists like Desmond Morris, ethologists like Konrad Lorenz and Niko Tinbergen, psychologists like H. J. Eysenck and Anthony Storr, and so on—lends substance to the possibility that the case for "nature" may yet prevail over the case for "nurture" in the behavioral sciences. Some early interpretations of the DNA–RNA discoveries—the "breaking of the genetic code"—have strongly conveyed this deterministic message. The psychologist Gardner Murphy, estimating the future impact of such discoveries in biology, has observed that "[t]hese genetic terms, of course, will be held by some to be fatalistic, as indicating the genetically given limitations upon all human endeavors."[26] But Murphy goes on to identify other features of the biological revolution which point in the opposite direction: "Through respect for the genetics of human individuality, how to become better *environmentalists* will be understood." Paradoxically, a possible result of the revolutionary breakthrough in genetics may be not to strengthen the cast for genetic "predestination" but to give new and powerful support to the other side of the controversy based upon the capacity of man to intervene in his own destiny.

THE NEW CASE FOR "NURTURE"

In addition to the traditional argument, there are actually two distinct "new" cases for the thesis of environmental modifiability with respect to intelligence and other factors in behavior. The first and more familiar is contained in the general trend of recent (post–World War II) research and theory surrounding heredity-environment *interactions*. Summarizing these developments, Thomas F. Pettigrew has written: "This newer view of the nature-nurture controversy and a mounting accumulation of new developmental evidence has resulted in a revised conception of the nature of intelligence."[27] Such researches, as presented especially by J. M. Hunt in his important volume, *Intelligence and Experience*, affirm the crucial role of early childhood environment as well as of life experience generally. "Intelligence, then, is not merely an inherited capacity, genetically fixed and destined to unfold in a biologically predetermined manner. It is a dynamic, on-going set of processes that within wide hereditary limits is subject to innumerable experiential factors."[28] That this new perspective on intelligence as "a relatively plastic quality" is a considerable departure from earlier orthodoxy is stressed by Pettigrew:

"Hunt's view upsets two long-unquestioned dogmas about intelligence, dogmas critical in the area of race difference. He terms them the assumptions of 'fixed intelligence' and 'predetermined development.' . . . Indeed, the assumption of fixed intelligence became so established before World War II that many psychologists regarded all evidence of substantial shifts in I.Q. as merely the product of poor testing procedures."[29] Hunt himself has reemphasized the major conclusions which have gained wide endorsement among psychologists and other scientists during the past score or so years:

> I had thought, though, that at least in the years since World War II we had learned something about most of these matters. I had thought we had learned that it was no longer tenable to conceive of intelligence tests as indicators of fixed capacity of innate potential in children. I had thought we had learned that it was quite wrong to think we could predict an adult's intellectual competence from his score on a test taken as a child without specifying the circumstances he would encounter in the interim.[30]

This line of thought is, to be sure, not strictly a defense of nurture as against nature but rather represents a new emphasis upon the *interaction* of inherited and environmental factors as a corrective to the preponderantly genetic orientation of the preceding generation. However, it is plain that to accept the principle of interaction is to sacrifice the dogma of fixed biological predetermination and to admit the relevance of experience, learning, and culture in the assessment of intelligence. For most environmentalists, this recognition of the relative plasticity of intelligence is victory enough.

But not for all environmentalists. There is a newer case for nurture which goes a great deal farther—some would say it goes all the way. This argument derives directly from the biological revolution of very recent years, which has been appropriately labeled the "Evolution Revolution" and "the new era of Participatory Evolution." R. Michael Davidson states the main point boldly: "No longer is man the offspring of Nature, the creature of natural selection. Science has provided him with the technology to become his own maker."[31] Something of the mind-boggling potentiality of this new power of human self-generation is suggested by the prediction of the biologist Jean Rostand that, in the coming era of germinal choice and ectogenesis (test-tube pregnancy), "it will be little more than a game to change the subject's sex, the color of its eyes, the general proportions of body and limbs, and perhaps the facial features."[32] Moreover, as the burgeoning science of fetology gains access through fetal surgery to what some one has coyly called "the littlest astronaut"—making possible the removal, treatment, and reimplantation of the fetus for whatever reason—"the possibility of programming personality and increasing intelligence will be considerably enhanced."[33] The control of the chemical messengers known as hormones is meanwhile giving medical science a vastly increased "power to intervene," as Gordon Rattray Taylor puts it, in the operations of the human body. "The day when growth and development can be controlled, as an orchestra is controlled by a conductor, is in prospect."[34]

There is more even than this to the new science of biological intervention. Another medical technique— genetic surgery—promises still greater control over the nature of human nature. Now that man has broken the chemical code of life by discovery of the structure of DNA, writes Davidson, "he can undertake to manipulate the DNA molecule and the genes that make it up, thus becoming master of his own heredity."[35] Some geneticists, such as Edward L. Tatum and Joshua Lederberg, foresee

a time within the next decade or two when genetic sur-
geons "will be able to delete undesirable genes, insert
others, and mechanically or chemically transform still
others—foreordaining, at the molecular level, the physical, mental, even racial characteristics of the incipient
individual."[36]

The new case for "nurture over nature" has still more
strings to its bow. Brain biology, wrote James Bonner a
few years ago, "is the next great challenge—the challenge
to break the brain code." Predicting a succession of advances in augmenting and preserving brain power and
mental vigor, Bonner was led to prophesy an era not too
far distant when "man will have the opportunity to
literally remake himself in whatever image he chooses."[37]
More and more experimental evidence is accumulating,
at all levels of development from fetus to mature adult,
in support of the thesis of the modifiability of intelligence
(if not of its unlimited potential). Most remarkable of all,
perhaps, in its implications for education is the long-
sustained work of David Krech, E. L. Bennett, and other
Berkeley psychologists with young rats segregated and
raised in two very different environments—one "intellec-
tually enriched" and the other "deprived." The enriched
setting provides ample opportunities for learning and
stimulating; the deprived environment is limited to the
minimum essentials for survival. When, after about
eighty days of this, the animals are killed and their brains
subjected to various chemical analyses, "[the] results are
convincing. The brain from a rat from the enriched
environment—and presumably, therefore, with many
more stored memories—has a heavier and thicker cortex,
a better blood supply, larger brain cells, more glia cells,
and increased activity of two brain enzymes, acetylcholinesterase and cholinesterase, than does the brain
from an animal whose life has been less memorable."[38]

Krech himself draws several inferences of far-reaching

significance from his twenty years of laboratory experimentation. "First, the growing animal's psychological environment is of crucial importance for the development of its brain. By manipulating the environment of the young, one can truly create a 'lame brain'—with lighter cortex, shrunken brain cells, fewer glia cells, smaller blood vessels, and lower enzymatic activity levels —or one can create a more robust, a healthier, a more metabolically active brain." Second, these environmental and educational actions are more influential even than the powerful brain-changing chemical agents which are becoming available: "Indeed, a review of all the data indicates that manipulating the educational and psychological environment is a more effective way of inducing long-lasting brain changes than direct administration of drugs." Finally, Krech contends that for every species, including man, there must be a set of "species-specific" experiences which are particularly enriching and effective in developing its brain; his guess is that these ideal learning experiences for man will prove to be related to the defining human characteristics of language and symbolic interaction. (In passing, it is pertinent to note the strictures of this hard-boiled rat psychologist concerning the behavioristic dogma of stimulus-response or conditioning as the basis of all learning: "Whatever value so-called reinforcement or stimulus-response theories of learning may have for describing acquisition of motor skills by people, maze-learning by rats, and bar-pressing by pigeons, these theories are assessed as completely trivial and utterly irrelevant when it comes to understanding that 'stunning intellectual achievement,' the acquisition of language by the child.")[39]

If these various new lines of biological and psychobiological discovery do not demolish the doctrine of fixed genetic predetermination of intelligence, they must surely leave it profoundly qualified and seriously compromised.

No doubt there are outer limits to the plasticity and modifiability of human "nature" and in particular of mental development; but it seems clear from the laboratory evidence—even from that of the science of heredity itself—that those limits have not yet been envisioned, let alone attained.

In view of this authoritative array of scientific evidence, it should not be necessary to undertake another detailed evaluation of the arguments advanced by Jensen in his controversial monograph linking race and IQ. There are, however, a few problematic features of the Jensen paper which seem to have escaped the attention of most commentators. These aspects involve speculations of a philosophical nature, bearing upon the assumptive frameworks of value and belief which underlie the investigations of scientists—not just "bad" scientists but *all* scientists— into the sensitive regions of intelligence, race, aggression, human nature, and social nurture.

THE IDEOLOGY OF IQ

Jensen to the contrary, it is far from the prevailing view among psychologists that intelligence is some sort of fixed entity or substance which persists more or less unchanged over time and can be measured "once and for all" by IQ tests. More representative is the viewpoint expressed by Alexander G. Wesman in terms of two propositions: "1. Intelligence is an attribute, not an entity. 2. Intelligence is the summation of the learning experiences of the individual." This alternative approach insists upon the variability of learning and acquired knowledge, not only across cultures, but across *time* in the life of any individual; and it asserts that the search for "culture-free" or "culture-fair" tests of intelligence is both futile and undesirable. Such a search, according to Wesman, is futile because there is no escaping the role of environment: "A culture-free test would presumably probe learnings which had not been affected by environment; this is sheer nonsense." And the search for such a pure measuring instrument is undesirable because it would neglect the principal value that instrument serves: "A culturefair test attempts to select those learnings which are common to many cultures. In the search for experiences which are common to several different cultures or subcultures, the vital matter of relevance of the learning for our purpose is subordinated or ignored."[40]

This thesis of the cultural bias of IQ tests is by now, commonly accepted among psychologists; but what is uncommon is Wesman's conviction that the bias is not only inevitable but *constructive*—once the limitations and special purposes of such tests are recognized. In this view, society defines intelligence in terms of its dominant values; if these values have to do with, say, the manipulation of verbal symbols and the solution of technical problems (perhaps in competitive frameworks involving rewards and reinforcements), then intelligence will be taken to consist in the relative prevalence of these learnings. It is interesting that one of the clearest statements of this point of view, that of O. D. Duncan, has been quoted by Jensen himself without reservation or demurrer: "[I]ntelligence is a socially defined quality and this social definition is not essentially different from that of achievement or status in the occupational sphere. . . . When psychologists came to propose operational counterparts to the notion of intelligence, or to devise measures thereof, they wittingly or unwittingly looked for indicators of capability to function in the system of key roles in the society."[41] Jensen also quotes Duncan's elaboration of this point, which deserves to be reproduced in full:

> Our argument tends to imply that a correlation between IQ and occupational achievement was more

or less built into IQ tests, by virtue of the psychologists' implicit acceptance of the social standards of the general populace. Had the first IQ tests been devised in a hunting culture, "general intelligence" might well have turned out to involve visual acuity and running speed, rather than vocabulary and symbol manipulation. As it was, the concept of intelligence arose in a society where high status accrued to occupations involving the latter in large measure, so that what we now *mean* by intelligence is something like the probability of acceptable performance (given the opportunity) in occupations varying in social status.[42]

The proper inference from this would seem to be that *intelligence is whatever is valued*, in terms of performance and behavior, within a given society. In the prestigious scientific form of IQ—Intelligence Quotient—it is a cultural ranking system for the repertory of social roles and skills, a "mirror for man" in its reflection and reinforcement of his favored preferences and purposes. More than that: It is also, if this much be granted, a reflection and reinforcement of his *prejudices*. It should not be surprising, then, to find that intelligence ratings and quotients become the instruments of ideology—consensually validating the established hierarchies of status and achievement in much the same way as the *Social Register*. It might be argued further that the very concept of "IQ"—the doctrine of intelligence as a fixed objective entity—is not merely sociological but ideological in character (like such other murky concepts as "leadership," "development," "primitive," and so on). The ideology which the concept of IQ serves is that of the permanent inequality of men and races—what David Spitz referred to as the pattern of antidemocratic thought. On the other hand, there is a countervailing "democratic dogma": an alternative ideology grounded in the liberal tradition and recognizable through its commitment to the ideas and ideals of equality, indefinite perfectibility, and unrestricted opportunity. At the level of ideological dispute, scientific evidence is used selectively and expediently rather than impartially; there is an irresistible tendency to leap from descriptive data to normative conclusions and programmatic proposals, amid an atmosphere of mutual suspicion and the imputation of ulterior motives. Because the ideology of IQ is analogous to the ideology of race, the comments of Manning Nash are pertinent here:

> Along with the study of race there may exist the "ideology of race." The ideology of race is a system of ideas which interprets and defines the meanings of racial differences, real or imagined, in terms of some system of cultural values. The ideology of race is always normative; it ranks differences as better or worse, superior or inferior, desirable or undesirable, and as modifiable or unmodifiable. Like all ideologies, the ideology of race implies a call to action; it embodies a political and social program; it is a demand that something be done. The ideology of race competes in a political arena, and it is embraced or rejected by a polity, not a scientific community.[43]

It is noteworthy that the opening sentence of Jensen's 1969 study of intelligence and race declared: "Compensatory education has been tried and it apparently has failed." Thus, even before the presentation of his data— virtually none of which was new and all of which was strictly related to the comparative influence of genetic and nongenetic factors upon intelligence—Jensen leaped dramatically to conclusions and recommendations regarding social policy which went far beyond the scientifically tenable deductions from the evidence presented. Jensen's readiness to move directly from the laboratory to the political forum is remarkable on its face, and leaves him open to the charge of ideological bias. Nash makes the point in terms which might have restrained Jensen's dubious extrapolations:

> Scientists will go on trying to describe and explain differences in all sorts of performances between and among all sorts of categories of persons, but it is not likely that they will ever take the differences they find to be fixed, immutable, or unmanipulable; it is much less likely that they will ever evaluate the meaning of these differences apart from specific environments; and it is impossible that they will recommend courses of social action on the basis of their findings.[44]

With regard to the selective use of research data, some critics of Jensen have called attention to the curious gaps in a paper which gives the appearance of being a comprehensive overview of the literature. For example, Nicholas Anastasiow remarks: "What is troubling about Jensen's hypothesis of racial differences in IQ is that he appears to seek truth and make known his findings, yet seems to close off alternative hypotheses to explain the data. At the same time, he asks us to consider the tenability of an older hypothesis of racial differences which his data, to this reviewer, fail to support."[45] Apart from specific examples of uncongenial research findings which are omitted by Jensen despite their relevance and prominence, there is a general neglect of the literature of cognitive and learning psychology (notably the classic work of Piaget) in its relation to intellectual development. Moreover, Jensen's selective inattention to some important data is supplemented by highly debatable interpretations of other data which he *does* include.[46]

In a brief article published a year earlier, Jensen expressed an attitude toward the prevailing climate of research on intelligence which implied that ideological influences, dictating an "official" line, were at work to discourage honest researchers from pursuing unfashionable hypotheses. Arguing the need for investigation of the hypothesis of innate racial (black-white) differences in IQ, he wrote: "But the question arises whether there has been an official decision to create the impression that such hypotheses have already been scientifically tested with conclusive results." Again: "My attempts to find comprehensive, scientifically based discussions of these issues lead me to the conclusion that the matter is not being studied or explored in any or all of its socially important ramifications. The policy of ignoring this problem might well be viewed by future generations as our society's greatest injustice to Negro Americans."[47]

What is singular about this demand for new avenues of inquiry into intelligence is Jensen's confidence that the significant differences will be found to fall along racial lines. That confidence is remarkable, among other reasons, because it is out of accord with the thinking of most geneticists on the subject. Far from subsuming the individual within some larger category such as race or class or other group membership, the preponderant emphasis of geneticists today is rather upon the *uniqueness* of individual character, personality, and potentiality. Interestingly enough, this point has been made by two scientific commentators in connection with Jensen's earlier article—one (Ernest Caspari) writing in the same journal issue as Jensen, the other (Gordon M. Harrington) writing in a subsequent issue. Harrington concluded his commentary with these two sentences: "Perhaps the essential concept of the geneticist for education is that the pupil is a unique individual. Any curriculum or any method which rests on the identification of the child by group membership or by measurement on some limited set of variables may have a limited range of effective application."[48] Caspari concludes his own article with a similar affirmation of the "dignity of the individual" as expressed in the recognition of his unique and distinctive identity:

> Genetically, every human being is unique, i.e., different from every other human being that is in existence today, that ever existed, and that will ever exist—excepting of course monozygotic twins. . . . The challenge to education appears to me to reside in the problem how to create educational methods and environments which will be optimally adjusted to the needs of unique individuals. The main contribution which a geneticist can make to educational research is to stress the fundamental biological fact that every human being is a unique individual and that his genetic individuality will be expressed in the way in which he reacts to environmental and educational experiences.[49]

These critical commentaries on the genetic-racial theory of intelligence, as proposed by Jensen and others, call to mind the pronouncement of Stanley Garn that "the study of human genetics is thoroughly complicated by the existence of culture." In a classic paper on "Cultural Factors Affecting the Study of Human Biology," Garn demonstrated in a number of vital areas "the extent to which cultural practices intrude into the study of human biology, making it quite different from the study of any other species."[50] The burden of his argument was that "man cannot be treated just as a large primate, amenable to the methods and techniques of mammalian biology."[51]

To his assertion that man, as creature *and creator* of culture, is unique among the animals may be added the proposition of the geneticists that each man is unique among men. For it is not only true that culture intrudes upon the biology of man; it is also true that biological man, in his "genetic individuality," *intrudes upon his culture.* It might be said that the difference of man is that he can make a difference. If his intelligence and abilities are not essentially fixed at birth, then his destiny is not foreordained and his options are not closed. It is interesting, in this connection, to observe how the geneticist Harrington deals with the psychologist Jensen's use of the idea of "genetic potential" in relation to intelligence and development. That concept "implies that, for a given individual, there is a ceiling of possible achievement"— but such a notion runs counter to the thinking of the geneticist whose predictions are in terms of probabilities rather than absolutes.

> Quantitative genetic theory suggests there is no ceiling for a given child but only that the probability of reaching a specified level in a specified environment decreases as the specified level increases. The concept of potential is reminiscent of the now fortunately demodé term, "over-achiever." At one time it was fashionable to talk of a child as an over-achiever as though he had committed an unpardonable sin in doing better than the school psychologist thought he should do.[52]

The present chapter has been occupied with the venerable question of the interaction between heredity and environment in the life of man—between human nature and social nurture. It may be, however, that there is a hidden bias in the very terminology of the discussion which distorts the reality and neglects the heart of the matter. To talk as if the only active forces in the equation are those of *nature* on the one hand and *culture* on the other is to treat man as a merely reactive organism—the "victim-spectator," in Gordon Allport's term, of blind forces working through him. In this sense, it matters little which of the two, nature or nurture, holds the upper hand; whichever side wins, man loses. But the traditional bias of mechanistic and deterministic thinking, which once pervaded all the sciences of man, is no longer convincing. The biological revolution, among other things, has radically altered the terms of the dispute. Man has been shown to hold the power, not only to act upon his environment, but to act upon his *heredity*—not only to change his world (to blow it up or redeem it), but to change his own being (to diminish or transfigure it).

Man has always possessed the capacity of saying No to his destiny, even as it closed in on him. He might dare to defy his fate; he could not think of daring to *change* it. Now, in a miraculous way confirmed by science as well as psychology, man has come into possession of the capacity to say *Yes*: to affirm his existence and to choose his destiny. Today, for the first time in history, to paraphrase Lewis Mumford, we must ask ourselves in all urgency and candor: What sort of society and what kind of man do we wish to have and to become? That, which was once an academic question, has suddenly become an existential choice. Ours is the power, quite literally, to make or break—to "murder and create." It is an awesome responsibility, perhaps more than mind and love and will can accommodate. But our successive technological, biological, and psychological revolutions have left us little time or room for leisured contemplation. At the close of the most terrifying chapter of his prophetic study of cybernetics and society, *The Human Use of Human Beings*, Norbert Wiener summed up the situation in one terse sentence: "The hour is very late, and the choice of good and evil knocks at our door."[53]

CHAPTER 6

PSYCHOLOGICAL REVOLUTION:
The Rise of Psychotechnocracy

It was Senator J. William Fulbright who gave currency, some years ago, to the phrase "the arrogance of power." The senator was referring to its political expression, but the phrase clearly has a wider and deeper reference. The power which technological science has conferred upon us is quite literally the power of life and death—specifically, of creating life and of cheating death. We have taken note of its arrogance in the form of the would-be "manufacturers of man"—the new revolutionaries in microbiology. There is another and perhaps more ominous form of this hubris which deserves equal consideration: one so far-reaching in its potential consequences as to warrant the observation that, in technology no less than in politics, power tends to corrupt—and absolute (or unchallenged) power, to corrupt absolutely.

Given the proximity of the two fields and their laboratories, it is not surprising that the biological manufacturers have their counterparts within psychology—in a school of thought and experiment variously self-styled "psychotechnology," the "technology of behavior," and "behavior modification." The founding father of the school, or movement, of applied behaviorism was John B.

Watson, an experimental psychologist turned advertising executive, who is best known for what might be called the Americanization of the conditioned reflex; and the contemporary dean of the school is B. F. Skinner, whose assorted writings—notably *Walden Two*, a utopian novel, and *Beyond Freedom and Dignity*, a philosophical speculation—have attracted a broad popular audience to the cause.

What we are advised by these engineers of behavior, to put it plainly, is not that we must cultivate science in the cause of man but that we must cultivate man in the cause of science. And the way to do that, as Skinner in particular insists, is to move as swiftly as possible beyond the obsolete ethics of freedom and dignity to the utilitarian ethics of the technocratic society—one which emphasizes the group over the individual, order over liberty, control over autonomy, and survival (of the culture, not the person) over all else. Skinner, in his wholesale repudiation of virtually the entire moral tradition of Western civilization, completes a work of philosophical ground clearing and demolition begun in the early years of the century by Watson and his followers. In order to comprehend the present and future potentialities of this ambitious program of behavior control and cultural design, it is useful to review its past history and performance.

"Behaviorism" is the title self-consciously embraced by a school of psychology which, in both its classical and contemporary forms, confines the attention of the scientist to observable behavior: "to what an organism is doing [in Watson's words]—or more accurately what it is observed by another organism to be doing."[1] The reason for this limitation is that, more explicitly and aggressively than any other approach to the study of man, behaviorism has viewed its enterprise as that of a natural science in the tradition of physics. "Psychology, as the behaviorist views it," wrote Watson, "is a purely objective, experimental branch of natural science which needs introspection as little as do the sciences of chemistry and physics."[2]

As that quotation suggests, behaviorism arose originally as a deliberate reaction against the emphasis of much nineteenth-century psychology upon introspection and consciousness—that is, upon the realm of mind considered as distinct from the realm of matter and accordingly governed by different rules and approached by distinctive procedures. In dramatic contrast, behaviorism presented itself to the world as a "psychology without a soul,"[3] the foe of superstition and the nemesis of mysticism. In its scorn of conventional scholarship, in its appeal for a return to scientific "first principles," above all in its self-confident rhetoric, behaviorism through its insurgent years bore the characteristics of a revolutionary movement of thought. The behaviorist must begin, exclaimed Watson, "by sweeping aside all medieval conceptions. He [has] dropped from his scientific vocabulary all subjective terms such as sensation, perception, image, desire, purpose, and even thinking and emotion as they were subjectively defined."[4] (In closely similar terms, Skinner wrote nearly sixty years later: "Physics did not advance by looking more closely at the jubilance of a falling body, or biology by looking at the nature of vital spirits, and we do not need to try to discover what personalities, states of mind, feelings, traits of character, plans, purposes, intentions, or the other perquisites of autonomous man really are in order to get on with a scientific analysis of behavior."[5])

The "revolutionary" ideology of behaviorism was manifested in a radical materialism which contained a definite moral and ethical component in addition to its explicit preference for "body" over "mind" in terms of scientific methodology. As Paul G. Creelan has noted:

Watson's radical rejection of the traditional psychological phenomena such as those of "consciousness" resides in the context of a vehement antipathy toward traditional religion and the closely related doctrine of the "soul." Moreover, his revolt was coupled with a thoroughly naturalistic interest in, indeed fascination for the study of animals precisely at the time when revolts against ascetic, puritanical spiritualism were commonplace, when the Scopes trial became a momentous national event.[6]

David Bakan, taking note of the "adamant emphasis on the body by the behaviorists" and the association of "mind-body with spirit-flesh" as comparable antinomies, concludes that "the implicit message of the behavioristic orientation was an assertion of the significance of the flesh over spirit," with the consequence that "in some sense the neutrality of the 'scientific' orientation lent moral neutrality to sexuality."[7]

Of course there was more to the appeal of behaviorism than its participation in the revolt against traditional religion and morality; it was also consistent with a broader-based naturalism and materialism which was already firmly anchored in what E. A. Burtt has termed the "metaphysical foundations of modern science."[8] For all its novelty, behaviorism was only the latest version of a centuries-old tradition in psychology—that of associationism or sensationalism dating back to Hobbes and Locke, which sought to translate the principles of Newtonian mechanics into psychological categories. The classic formulation was that of Locke, which presented a portrait of original human nature as a passive agent, a tabula rasa, that could (as Gordon W. Allport has put it) acquire mental "content and structure only through the impact of sensation and the criss-cross of associations, much as a pan of sweet dough acquires tracings through the impress of a cookie cutter."[9] During the eighteenth century David Hartley, the founder of associationism if not of psychology itself, systematized the approach in the form of a natural science of mind no less exact (in pretension at least) than the procedures of classical mechanics. Following Hartley, such mechanistic psychologists as Holbach, La Mettrie, and Cabanis openly proclaimed man to be a machine and nothing but a machine; and James Mill, in his *Analysis of the Phenomena of the Human Mind*, carried the mechanical model of man to its psychological culmination by setting out to "destroy the illusion of psychical activity," as Elie Halévy has put it, and "to reduce everything to constant and in some sort mechanical relations between elements which should be as simple as possible."[10]

The immediate precursor of behaviorism was the reflexology of Pavlov and Bechterev, founded on the discovery of the conditioned reflex. The concept of "conditioning"—the control and reinforcement of responses through manipulating stimuli—was recognized almost at once as a tool of immense power in the hands of psychologists. It is noteworthy that Pavlov's reflexology subsequently became the official psychology of the Soviet Union, where interest in the good behavior of citizens was more than clinical; while in America, in the form of behaviorism, reflexology gained an equivalent if less formal standing as the dominant school of psychological theory and of that practical form of behavior modification known as advertising and public relations. For to Watson and his followers, the conditioned reflex provided something more than an explanation of the full range of human behavior; it also held the key to the scientific management and control, not to say the transformation, of human life. Throughout the literature of behaviorism, from Watson to Skinner, there runs the vision of changing or manipulating behavior—of doing something with the malleable clay —not just of knowing about it. "The interest of the behaviorist," said Watson, "is more than the interest of a spectator; he wants to control man's reactions as physical scientists want to control and manipulate other phenomena."[11] As man was simply "an assembled organic machine ready to run," so the behaviorist visualized himself as the engineer or programmer ready to run it. Observing the enviable success of chemistry and biology in controlling and altering their subject matter, Watson asked plaintively: "Can psychology ever get control? Can I make someone who is not afraid of snakes, afraid of them and how?"[12] And he boasted elsewhere: "In short, the cry of the behaviorist is, 'Give me the baby and my world to bring it up in and I'll make it crawl and walk; I'll make it climb and use its hands in constructing buildings of stone or wood; I'll make it a thief, a gunman, or a dope fiend. The possibility of shaping in any direction is almost endless.' "[13] (That this immodest brag of the sculptor in human clay was not merely an idiosyncracy of John B. Watson may be seen from the nearly identical announcement of another reputable psychologist, James McConnell, in 1966: "The time has come when if you give me any normal human being and a couple of weeks . . . I can change his behavior from what it is now to whatever you want it to be, if it's physically possible."[14])

The idea of man projected by this classical behaviorism was that of an empty organism without inherent or prepotent directiveness, infinitely manageable and manipulable—in short, a stimulus-response machine. If this image held out no prospect of self-control for man, it opened up limitless vistas of external control—in the service of whatever norms or goals might command the allegiance of the controllers. For Pavlov, they were to become the norms of totalitarian society; for Watson, they were the norms of the prevailing social order in America

—the business society of the first third of the century. In a series of illuminating *obiter dicta*, the founder of behaviorism made clear his preference for conformity and conditioned good behavior over the unscientific claims of free speech and personal liberty. The behaviorist, he maintained, "would like to develop his world of people from birth on, so that their speech and their bodily behavior would equally well be exhibited freely everywhere without running afoul of group standards."[15] His moral and cultural vision was of a future "universe unshackled by legendary folklore of happenings thousands of years ago; unhampered by disgraceful political history; free of foolish customs and conventions which have no significance in themslves, yet which hem the individual in like taut steel bands."[16] The tragedy of past history was that "social experimentation" had always been carried out in the interest of nations or sects or persons "rather than under the guidance of social scientists."[17] Now, at last, all that could be changed; the scientist of behavior was mercifully at hand: "not asking here for revolution . . . not asking for 'free love' . . . [but] trying to dangle a stimulus in front of you, a verbal stimulus which, if acted upon, will gradually change this universe. For the universe *will* change if you bring up your children, not in the freedom of the libertine, but in behavioristic freedom."[18]

One of the many paradoxes of behaviorism is that, defining itself as an objective science free from commitment or value, it should move with what seems an inexorable impulse toward not only the shaping of men but the designing of cultures. Partly this would appear to be because, as Edna Heidbreder put it in the thirties, behaviorism "does not pretend to be a disinterested psychology. It is frankly an applied science, seeking to bring the efficiency of the engineer to bear upon the problem of reform."[19] However, with rare exceptions, it is not *social* reform that is pursued by the behaviorist but the reform of *persons*; not the changing of institutions to meet the needs of men but the processing of men to meet the needs of institutions—specifically, the institutions of technological society. It could hardly be otherwise; for it is only *society* which, in this perspective, has a "given" character —an intrinsic program of purposes, values, aspirations, and needs to be served. Where man himself is empty, passive, only awaiting the sculptor's hand, his society palpitates with ongoing motivations and manifest destiny. It is as if, unable to bring themselves to abolish mind and purpose from the universe altogether, the behaviorists have simply shifted its location from man to his environment. An early statement of the case was that of the Austrian sociologist Ludwig Gumplowicz in the nineteenth century:

> The great error of individualistic psychology is the supposition that man *thinks*. . . . A chain of errors; for it is not man himself who thinks but his social community; the source of his thoughts is in the social medium in which he lives, the social atmosphere which he breathes, and he cannot think ought else than what the influences of his social environment concentrating upon his brain necessitate. . . .
> The individual simply plays the part of the prism which receives the rays, dissolves them according to fixed laws and lets them pass out again in a predetermined direction and with a predetermined color.[20]

From Gumplowicz to Skinner may be a great stride for behaviorist psychology, but it is a small step for man. "A scientific analysis of behavior," according to Skinner, "dispossesses autonomous man and turns the control he has been said to exert over to the environment."[21] The way it works is this:

In the traditional picture a person perceives the world around him, selects features to be perceived, discriminates among them, judges them good or bad, changes them to make them better (or, if he is careless, worse), and may be held responsible for his action and justly rewarded or punished for its consequences. In the scientific picture a person is a member of a species shaped by evolutionary contingencies of survival, displaying behavioral processes which bring him under the control of the environment in which he lives, and largely under the control of a social environment which he and millions of others like him have constructed and maintained during the evolution of a culture. The direction of the controlling relation is reversed: *a person does not act upon the world, the world acts upon him.*[22]

Another of the paradoxes of behaviorism is that, despite its willful abolition of "autonomous man," its conspicuous aversion to the democratic dogma of individual freedom and responsibility, and its insistent shrinkage of human capacity to the level of the laboratory animal if not of the machine, it should have been greeted in its heyday of the twenties as a truly "democratic" psychology and a harbinger of the good society to come. "For a while in the 1920's," as E. G. Boring was to write, "it seemed as if all America had gone behaviorist."[23] A typical commentary of the period exclaimed that behaviorism was peculiarly "adapted to the American temperament because it is fundamentally hopeful and democratic";[24] and a reviewer of one of Watson's numerous volumes felt secure in declaring: "Perhaps this is the most important book ever written. One stands for an instant blinded with a great hope."[25] Why not? The power of behaviorism (as its spokesmen maintained and its audience was prepared to believe) was the power of science itself, caught up in the myth of progress through invention and of prosperity through manufacture. In the age of Edison and Ford, of scientific management and the Veblenian dream of technocracy (government as engineering),[26] who could withstand the blinding hope of a reconditioned and recycled race of men made happy and harmonious (not to say productive and efficient) through the miraculous intervention of the highest authority in the modern world: the scientific priesthood?

There is so much that was wrong with this behaviorist panacea—so much that is patently silly and morally irresponsible—that the episode would scarcely be worth rehearsing, other than as a footnote to the history of popular crazes, were it not for the remarkable recrudescence of the same "blinding hope"—the same visionary future of "behavioristic freedom"—in the later generation of the sixties and seventies when it has again come to seem that all America has gone (operant) behaviorist. In fact, during the half-century between the twin peaks symbolized by Watson and Skinner, behaviorism was continuously nourished and periodically revitalized in the laboratories of experimental psychology. According to Sigmund Koch, compiler of the most comprehensive history of twentieth-century psychology, behaviorism has gone through three distinct stages to date: first, the period of "classical behaviorism" under Watson's leadership, lasting from 1913 to 1930; second, the tenure of "neo-behaviorism" from 1930 to 1945, marked by a shift away from empirical concerns toward theoretical abstraction, as in Clark Hull's attempts to construct a "hypothetico-deductive" science; and, finally, "neo-neo-behaviorism," the present era dominated by Skinner.[27]

Skinner's influence, which began with his first published volume (*The Behavior of Organisms*) in 1938 but has been felt most strongly in the last twenty years, has extended far beyond the boundaries of the laboratory and professional journal; his work of behavioral-science fiction, *Walden Two,* has enjoyed a succession of popular vogues since its publication in 1948, and his bestselling treatise of 1971, *Beyond Freedom and Dignity,* has attracted a still broader audience responsive to the promise of operant conditioning and behavioral technology, both as personal therapy and as the basis for the scientific design of cultures.

While there are important differences between the behaviorism of Watson and that of Skinner—notably the latter's emphasis upon the consequences of behavior as well as upon its initial stimulus—the similarities are more fundamental and significant. Both spokesmen have been insistent upon the rigorous natural-science character of their experimental enterprise; both have been scornful of the "mentalistic" psychologies which give weight to concepts such as "mind" or "purpose"; both have considered the white rat and other animal subjects as adequate surrogates for man in the laboratory (with allowance only for differences of complexity and verbal behavior); and both have been messianically convinced of the power of their behavioral science to move beyond mere description to prescription—beyond prediction to control—in the laboratory of human society.

The potential power of a truly scientific psychology to shape behavior and remake the society of man was recognized by Skinner in his earliest book, which contained the declaration that "It is largely because of its tremendous consequences that a rigorous treatment of behavior is still regarded in many quarters as impossible."[28] Those consequences were philosophical as well as practical; for, as Skinner made clear later on, "If we are to enjoy the advantages of science in the field of human affairs, we must be prepared to adopt the working model of behavior to which [such] a science will inevitably lead."[29] What that model assumed as an axiom was the thoroughly determinate character of all behavior: "If we are to use the methods of science in the field of human affairs, we must assume that behavior is lawful and determined . . . that what a man does is the result of specifiable conditions and that once these conditions have been discovered, we can anticipate and to some extent determine his actions."[30]

To his credit, Skinner has never sought to evade or soften the implications of his thoroughgoing determinism; perhaps his most notorious pronouncement—repeated over the years like a litany and finally given titular status (*Beyond Freedom and Dignity*)—is that there is no place for the idea of freedom, in any of its forms or variations, within the system of scientific behaviorism. The essential point was tersely stated in *Science and Human Behavior*: "We cannot apply the methods of science to a subject matter which is assumed to move about capriciously."[31] (A few years earlier, the central character of *Walden Two* said the same thing more bluntly: "I deny that freedom exists at all. I must deny it—or my program would be absurd. You can't have a science about a subject matter which hops capriciously about."[32]) Skinner's insistence upon the irreconcilability of freedom and applied behaviorism tells much about his commitments and ambitions; like Watson before him, he attributes the absence of harmony and happiness in the world largely to man's unwillingness to apply scientific solutions—and the chief reason for that unreasonable attitude is the refusal to abandon an outworn tradition of beliefs surrounding "freedom, justice, and so on."[33] "A scientific conception of human behavior dictates one practice, a philosophy of personal freedom another. . . . The present unhappy condition of the world may in large measure be traced to our vacillation."[34]

In forthright language, Skinner presents us with a

choice between two contrasting—indeed, mutually exclusive—*ideas of man*: On one hand, "the conception of
a free, responsible individual [which] is embedded in our
language and pervades our practices, codes and beliefs";[35]
on the other hand, the conception of an organism in the
clutch of environmental circumstance (somehow allied
with hereditary or genetic factors left unspecified)—in
short, unfree and irresponsible. To linger on the traditional path, we are warned, is to court disaster; only by
abandoning the error of democratic ideology and pursuing
the rigorous course of behavioral science can we hope to
bring order to society and control into our lives. But to
accept the authority of science (i.e., of Skinner's peculiar
version of science) is necessarily to submit to its terms,
which involve giving up not only the old ethical codes
and human values but the very notion of *mind* itself—
the prescientific habit of interpreting behavior "in terms
of an inner agent which lacks physical dimensions and is
called 'mental' or 'psychic.' "[36] The full difference between
the old folkways and the new dispensation has been
spelled out by Skinner in an illuminating passage which
deserves to be quoted in its entirety:

> The use of such concepts as individual freedom,
> initiative and responsibility has, therefore, been well
> reinforced. When we turn to what science has to
> offer, however, we do not find very comforting sup-
> port for the traditional Western point of view. The
> hypothesis that man is not free is essential to the
> application of scientific method to the study of
> human behavior. The free inner man who is held
> responsible for the behavior of the external biological
> organism is only a prescientific substitute for the
> kinds of causes which are discovered in the course
> of a scientific analysis. All these alternative causes
> lie *outside* the individual. . . . These are the things

which make the individual behave as he does. For them he is not responsible, and for them it is useless to praise or blame him.[37]

As various critics have pointed out, there is a curious contradiction in this line of argument. For if Skinner is correct in his deterministic assumptions, then his argument is superfluous and futile, since (as Paul Kurtz has put it) "if everything we do is strictly determined, then we cannot choose to master or control the environment, nor can we choose to follow Skinner's recommendations, unless we are determined [by external forces] to do so."[38] On the other hand, if there is any point at all to the discussion—if we *can* act upon the environment, design our cultures and initiate behavioral technologies—Skinner is thoroughly refuted in his basic premises. For then there are contingencies in human existence which are not merely the "contingencies of reinforcement." There is an element of choice, for better or worse, over which we have some control; there is a need to reflect and a demand for decision which implies a large degree of responsibility and an irreducible element of freedom.

The dilemma here is not only logical but psychological as well; it bespeaks a deep aversion to the idea of freedom, in the sense of spontaneity, chance, unpredictability, and hence "autonomy." For an appreciation of the force of Skinner's rage for order, it is instructive to turn to the personality and career of the man himself. There is a pertinent passage in *Walden Two*, spoken by the character named Frazier (the author's middle name), who admittedly represents at least a part of Skinner's personality:

"I have only one important characteristic, Burris: I'm stubborn. I've had only one idea in my life—a true *idée fixe* . . . to put it as bluntly as possible, the idea of having my own way. Control expresses it, I think. The control of human behavior, Burris. In my early experimental days it was a frenzied, selfish desire to dominate. I remember the rage I used to feel when a prediction went awry. I could have shouted at the subjects of my experiments: 'Behave, damn you, *behave* as you ought.' "[39]

Even before he attempted to control experimental subjects, Skinner apparently showed the aptitudes of a mechanic and engineer. In childhood he reportedly built steerable wagons, scooters, rafts, bamboo water pistols, an ingenious toy steam cannon, even "a flotation system to separate green from ripe elderberries."[40] He was later inspired by the dramatic successes of Watson in shaping behavior through conditioning, and chose experimental psychology as his life work. Like Watson also, Skinner was not content with theoretical speculation or pure research but was soon caught up in behavioral engineering. His technological bent was manifested in such celebrated inventions as the Skinner Box, a specialized enclosure designed for the operant conditioning of rats and pigeons; the Air Crib, an isolation booth for babies; and a programmed-instruction machine. His most famous feat of engineering design, however, has been the hypothetical construction of an entire community, "Walden Two," governed by the principles of Skinner's applied science of behavior. In this model society, based upon the "new conception of man compatible with our scientific society,"[41] behavioral engineering has succeeded in extinguishing all inconvenient emotions and antisocial impulses in favor of the positive reinforcement of political indifference and a complacent life-style which bears a striking resemblance to a middle-class retirement community. There are no moral questions to be struggled with in Walden Two, nor any serious issues of choice; the residents (some would call them patients) are instead conditioned from birth to make the "right choices" automatically, without the anxiety of reflection. The government of the place, insofar as we are told about it, is ostensibly in the hands of a board of planners who in turn are actually controlled by a junta of "Managers"— among them a Manager of Personal Behavior and a Manager of Cultural Behavior—a self-selecting and (in principle) self-perpetuating elite. There is little or no political participation by the rank-and-file members of the community; control is willingly left to the custodial cadre. "In Walden Two no one worries about the government except the few to whom that worry has been assigned. . . . Even the constitutional rights of the members are seldom thought about, I'm sure. The only thing that matters is one's day-to-day happiness and a secure future."[42]

Skinner's alter ego in the novel, Frazier, outlines the key motifs of the fable in reflecting upon the question, "What is the original nature of man?"

> "That's certainly an experimental question—for a science of behavior to answer. And what are the techniques, the engineering practices, which will shape the behavior of the members of a group so that they will function smoothly for the benefit of all? That's also an experimental question, Mr. Castle —to be answered by a behavioral technology. . . . Experimentation with life—could anything be more fascinating?"[43]

This quotation makes clear both the assumption and the ambition of its author: the assumption as to human nature is that it is malleable clay awaiting the hand of the behavioral artisan, and the ambition as to the future is to design a technology that will—not enhance the freedom and dignity of individuals—but "shape the behavior of members of a group so that they will function smoothly for the benefit of all." Much of Skinner's subsequent research and writing may be viewed as a gloss upon that ambition. His increasing attention to the engineering and technology of behavior—particularly of collective behavior—is documented in various articles and books of the fifties and sixties, climaxed by the publication of *Beyond Freedom and Dignity*.[44] In an interview conducted by the Center for the Study of Democratic Institutions in 1972, Skinner restated his enduring interest as an engineer to mankind in these words:

> The things that impress me are not so much the laboratory experiments with human subjects but the success of the technological applications to humans. This is most easily done under controlled environments, such as institutions for the care of psychotics or the retarded, or with juvenile delinquents, or small children. There you have more control than in the world at large. . . . I have an interest as a citizen in applying operant conditioning principles to government and to international affairs, but I doubt that I will make any great contribution in those fields.[45]

Although the idea of man projected in Skinner's writings has remained unchanged over more than a generation, his concern with its broad cultural and social import has become intensified as his impulse to practice new technological applications of control-through-conditioning has become more prominent. The two sides of his thought, his psychology and sociology, are clearly complementary —as he himself has recognized in the oft-repeated assertion that his science and technology of behavior rest upon the "hypothesis that man is not free." The very possibility of the control he seeks over the conduct of men depends upon the negation or "abolition" of their freedom: that is, of their responsibility for the direction of their lives, their capacity to choose, their relative independence from the forces of external circumstance, of history and environment. The birth of psychotechnology means nothing less than the death of the *person*, as we had always thought we knew him:

> What is being abolished [writes Skinner] is autonomous man—the inner man, the homunculus, the possessing demon, the man defended by the literatures of freedom and dignity.
>
> His abolition has long been overdue. Autonomous man is a device used to explain what we cannot explain in any other way. . . . To man *qua* man we readily say good riddance. Only by dispossessing him can we turn to the real causes of human behavior. Only then can we turn from the inferred to the observed, from the miraculous to the natural, from the inaccessible to the manipulable.[46]

Reading this abolitionist brief, this gleeful epitaph pronounced over the ashes of "autonomous man," of "man *qua* man," it is not difficult to sympathize with the judgment rendered by Sigmund Koch after having devoted "half a career as a psychologist to the detailed registration of behaviorism." Why, he asks, has so implausible and ignoble a mode of thought as this persisted for so long? "What does behaviorism mean? I mean in a human way." Koch answers his own question thus: "Really very simple: behaviorism is the strongest possible wish that the organism and, entre nous, the *person* may not exist—a vast, many-voiced, poignant lament that anything so refractory to the assumptions and methods of eighteenth-century science should clutter up the world-scape."[47]

That may seem a harsh judgment upon a venerable and reputable theory of human nature; but in the light of so

many insistent depreciations of the very idea of man—
man as man, man as a whole, man for himself—it is
surely not without foundation. Throughout its "many-
voiced" career, behaviorism has in a real sense analyzed
"man" out of existence. It has done so, in fact, in more
than one way. First, it has reduced man analytically to a
set of physical dimensions and a repertoire of neuro-
muscular responses indistinguishable from those of other
animals except in degree of complexity; hence, man is
stripped of a distinctive identity in the world of natural
objects. Second, behaviorism has reduced the individual
person to the group or culture which forms and overarches
him; as Skinner says, "We may therefore find it necessary
to change from a philosophy which emphasizes the
individual to one which emphasizes the *culture* or the
group."[48]

There is also a third, possibly more fundamental,
reduction of man implicit in the behaviorist scheme. Not
only is individual man depersonalized, but mankind in
general is *dehumanized* to the level of a complex but
manageable mechanism ("an organic machine ready to
run"). If it is true that man "does not act upon the world,
the world acts upon him"; if there is nothing inside a
man's skin different (except in degree of accessibility)
from what is outside it; if there is no potential for
responsibility, resourcefulness, and reflection—in short,
if there is no *freedom* for man—then it is not too much to
say that man himself has been explained away and in his
place there grins the image of the cheerful robot.

If the psychology of behaviorism has conceived this
automaton through its program of psychotechnology, the
political sociology of behaviorism is prepared to enforce
it through its program of psychotechnocracy. We have
already reviewed the degradation of the democratic dogma
in the static society of Walden Two; that bland product
of the behaviorist imagination seems almost innocent a

quarter-century later, in the wake of successive developments in the biology and technology of behavior modification. A striking report on the possibilities in the political arena—in particular the prospects of controlling the conduct of statesmen and public decision makers—has been furnished by Kenneth B. Clark in his 1971 presidential address before the American Psychological Association. What is singular about this report, moreover, is not so much its recognition of the new battery of mind-controlling and behavior-changing devices as its enthusiastic endorsement of their application by the specialists of psychotechnocracy. Here are a few salient passages from Clark's address:

> The present generation of human beings is required to develop psychological and social sciences with that degree of precision, predictability, and moral control essential to survival. The awesome advances in the physical and biological sciences have made psychotechnology imperative. . . . The behavioral sciences are now the critical sciences; they will determine the answer to the ultimate moral question of human survival.
>
> The psychological and social sciences must enable us to control the animalistic, barbaric, and primitive propensities in man and subordinate these negatives to the uniquely human moral and ethical characteristics of love, kindness, and empathy. The redirecting of power away from the absurd, the pathetic, and the self-defeating can be and now must be seen as a responsibility and goal of science and psychotechnology. . . .
>
> The era of psychotechnology coincides with the abrupt recognition of the limits of the time within which the human brain can discover and use that knowledge which is requisite to control, protect, and

affirm humanity with precision and predictability. Already neurophysiological, biochemical, and psychopharmacological and psychological research has put forward provocative and suggestive findings. The work on the effects of direct stimulation of certain areas of the brain; the role of specific areas of the bid-brain in controlling certain affects; the impact of certain drugs on exciting, tranquilizing, or depressing the emotional and motivational levels of the individual; and the effects of externally induced behavioral changes on internal biochemistry of the organism—these and other findings suggest that we might be on the threshold of a scientific biochemical intervention which could stabilize and make dominant the moral and ethical propensities of man and subordinate, if not eliminate, his negative behavioral tendencies. . . .

It is a fact that a few men in the leadership positions in the industrialized nations of the world now have the power to determine among themselves, through collaboration or competition, the survival or extinction of human civilization. . . . We cannot predict the personal and emotional stability of these leaders with the life and death power over mankind. . . .

It would seem logical then that a requirement should be imposed on all power-controlling leaders and those who aspire to such leadership that they accept and use the earliest perfected form of psychotechnological, biochemical intervention which would assure their use of power affirmatively, and reduce or block the possibility of their using power destructively. Such psychotechnological medication would be an internally imposed disarmament. It would assure that there would be no absurd or barbaric use of power. It would provide the masses of human beings with the security that their leaders would not or could not sacrifice them on the altars of their personal ego pathos, their vulnerability and instability.[49]

There, in the strained rhetoric of psychotechnology, is an authoritative prescription for peace in our time—a total solution to any crisis of conscience, failure of nerve, or dilemma of democratic decision making—promising an end forever to all chance and choice, inspiration or intuition, on the part of statesmen at whose lonely desks the buck has traditionally stopped. The solution, breathtaking in its simplicity, is to *take the decision away from them*—indeed, to remove it altogether from the sordid forum of representative government and to hand it over to the psychotechnocrat. The operative terms in Clark's brief are "psychotechnological medication" and "psychotechnological, biochemical intervention." There is no mistaking who it is that alone can apply this type of "internally imposed disarmament," which will automatically "assure that there will be no absurd or barbaric use of power." It is the technologist of behavior, armed with his artillery of drugs and electrodes, conditioners and reinforcers, medications and interventions: all the sophisticated hardware and software of human engineering. There is no one else available; the old ways have been tried and found wanting; the need is urgent, we are told, and the time is short. The hour of the behavioral scientist is at hand; it is up to him to "determine the answer to the ultimate moral question of human survival."

What is implicit in this putative transfer of power and displacement of authority is nothing less than the destruction of the democratic process of government—the death of politics as a vocation, as a competition of viewpoints and a consensus of decision, and its replacement by the benevolent despotism of those whom Dwight Eisenhower referred to as the "scientific-technological elite." For these autocrats of the dissecting table, in their own eyes and dreams of glory at least, are the New Mandarins (as Noam Chomsky called them): the harbingers of a brave new world in which everyone will make the right choices automatically and from which all anxiety and ambiguity, not to say intelligence itself, will be banished.

Is it excessive, then, in view of the cosmic claims and pretensions of the mechanical modelers of man—the psychotechnicians—to speak of the arrogance of power and to caution against their potential betrayal of the political and moral tradition of Western civilization? Perhaps they are not very likely, after all, to gain access to the corridors of power or to the confidence of an informed citizenry. But it is well to recall the apprehension expressed a few years ago by a congressman (Cornelius J. Gallagher) that public opinion might not long be able to withstand the expert testimony and authoritative appeals of the New Mandarins: "The people seem dangerously prepared to surrender their age-old respect for the vast capabilities of the human mind and personality to the impressive and sometimes overwhelming knowledge which the scientific elite alone have mastered."[50]

The last word on this subject may have been spoken by Aldous Huxley, in a prophetic utterance some thirty years after the publication of his *Brave New World*:

> We have had religious revolutions, we have had political, industrial, economic, and nationalistic revolutions. All of them, as our descendants will discover, were but ripples in an ocean of conservatism—trivial by comparison with the psychological revolution toward which we are so rapidly moving. *That* will really be a revolution. When it is over, the human race will give no further trouble.[51]

Now the psychological revolution is upon us, together with the technological revolution and the biological revolution. This triple revolution—these three faces of the technocratic future—illustrates not only the paradox of power but the pathology of power. The signs indeed accumulate that the human race may soon give no further trouble, and that mechanization may take command over us all without a struggle.

But there are other straws in the wind: hints of a genuinely alternative future, a future worthy of man. They are portents of a fourth revolution in the making— what may be termed the *human counterrevolution*— grounded in the outrageous idea of man, at once radical and reactionary, which dares to view him as neither a tool user nor a tool, in his essential being and becoming, but rather as a *creator*: an artist, actor, lover, brother, maker, and shaker. In the prevailing climate of opinion, this dissonant conception—the very idea of Man—appears momentarily outweighed by the evidence from the laboratory and the computer center. But that evidence, as we have seen, is vulnerable and precarious; its authority has been deeply undermined both scientifically and morally. "For those of us," as Lewis Mumford has concluded in *The Pentagon of Power*, "who have thrown off the myth of the machine, the next move is ours: for the gates of the technocratic prison will open automatically, despite their rusty ancient hinges, as soon as we choose to walk out."[52]

III

MAN AS MAN:
The Revival of
Humanism

CHAPTER 7

DEMOCRATIC MAN:
The Human Image in the American Creed

In his classic study of black-and-white relations in the United States, *An American Dilemma*, first published in 1945, the Swedish social scientist Gunnar Myrdal was particularly impressed by the national consensus surrounding a body of beliefs and values which he termed "the American Creed." It seemed to Myrdal "that America, compared to every other country in Western civilization, large or small, has *the most explicitly expressed* system of general ideals in reference to human interrelations. This body of ideals is more widely understood and appreciated than similar ideals are anywhere else."[1] The basic character and sweep of the American Creed, which so fascinated Myrdal, were spelled out in a summary statement:

> These ideals of the essential dignity of the individual human being, of the fundamental equality of all men, and of certain inalienable rights to freedom, justice, and a fair opportunity represent to the American people the essential meaning of the nation's early struggle for independence. In the clarity and intellectual boldness of the Enlightenment pe-

riod these tenets were written into the Declaration
of Independence, the Preamble of the Constitution,
the Bill of Rights and into the constitutions of several
states. The ideals of the American Creed have thus
become the highest law of the land. The Supreme
Court pays its reverence to these general principles
when it declares what is constitutional and what is
not. They have been elaborated upon by all national
leaders, thinkers and statesmen. America has had,
throughout its history, a continuous discussion of
the principles and implications of democracy, a discussion which, in every epoch, measured by any
standard, remained high, not only quantitatively but
qualitatively. The flow of learned treatises and popular tracts on the subject has not ebbed, nor is it
likely to do so. In all wars, including the present one,
the American Creed has been the ideological foundation of national morale.[2]

In tracing the various ideological roots of the American
Creed, Myrdal devoted particular attention to the
eighteenth-century "philosophy of Enlightenment," summarizing its impact in these sentences: "The American
Creed is a humanistic liberalism developing out of the
epoch of Enlightenment when America received its national consciousness and its political structure. The Revolution did not stop short of anything less than the heroic
desire for the *emancipation of human nature*.' "[3] This
idea of total emancipation—not just the emancipation
of *men* from the bondage of tyranny and poverty but the
emancipation of *man* from the bondage of history and
heredity—represented the psychological equivalent of the
revolutionary political philosophy which found expression in the Declaration, the Preamble, and the Bill of
Rights. Known more familiarly as the concept of "indefi-

nite perfectibility," this article of the democratic faith conveyed for the revolutionary generation, as it still conveys today, the idea of man in the American Creed.

Among the various historical and ideological sources of the image of "democratic man"—for example, the English common-law tradition, the Christian emphasis on the dignity of personality, and, more particularly, the Protestant tradition of spiritual independence and dissent—two factors stand out as dominant influences. The first of these was the social and intellectual revolution which swept England and then France during the century of Enlightenment. Carl Becker, surveying the rapid advance of secular reason and the retreat of Divine mystery, has summarized the new faith in human nature which these developments entailed:

> The eighteenth century was the moment in history when men experienced the first flush and freshness of the idea that man is master of his own fate; the moment in history, also, when this emancipating idea, not yet brought to the harsh test of experience, could be accepted with unclouded optimism. Never had the universe seemed less mysterious, more simply constructed, more open and visible and eager to yield its secrets to common-sense questions. Never had the nature of man seemed less perverse, or the intelligence and will of men more pliable to rational persuasion. Never had social and political evils seemed so wholly the result of ignorance and superstition, or so easily corrected by the spread of knowledge and the construction of social institutions on a rational plan. The first task of political science was to discover the natural rights of man, the second to devise the form of government best suited to secure them. And for accomplishing this high task,

for creating and maintaining a society founded on justice and equality, the essential freedom was freedom of the mind.[4]

The European Enlightenment came to America, as Bernard Bailyn has demonstrated, through two parallel streams of thought and writing: straight from the great liberal spirits of the age—Locke most of all, along with Voltaire, Rousseau, Beccaria, Montesquieu, Grotius, and Pufendorf—and, still more immediately and powerfully, from the "coffeehouse radicals and opposition politicians" of England, whose innumerable pamphlets and speeches, more than any other factor, "shaped the mind of the American Revolutionary generation."[5] The first of these two streams of thought provided the philosophical foundations of the revolutionary ideology of natural rights and civil liberties; the second stream provided the spur and the whiplash, the rhetorical model and historical precedent, and the practical arguments against tyranny (stemming from the radical Levellers and Diggers of the English Civil War, among others) which were to be turned by the colonists to their own advantage as early as the middle of the century. The specific thrust of these arguments was toward political reforms—simply put, the defense of liberty against power—but more fundamentally they were expressions of that broad social movement compounded of humanism, populism, individualism, and equalitarianism which Myrdal later saw to be aimed at nothing less than the "emancipation of human nature."

The first of the two dominant influences in the shaping of the image of "democratic man" was, then, the importation of the European Enlightenment on its most polemical and radical side. The second factor, which served to reinforce and redouble the effect of the first, was the utopian vision of the American landscape as a New

Jerusalem—a fresh start and a clean beginning, where the taint of tradition and the burden of history might be swept aside and all men could be *re*created equal. If this was at first only a gloss on the old Puritan dream conceived in England and fed on millennial pieties before there was an America, it was soon vindicated by the testimony of the New England Puritans and their descendants. "What then is the American, this new man?" asked the "American farmer," Michel Guillaume St. Jean de Crèvecoeur, in the eighteenth century:

> He is an American, who leaving behind him all his ancient prejudices and manners, receives new ones from the new mode of life he has embraced, the new government he obeys, and the new rank he holds. He becomes an American by being received in the broad lap of our great *Alma Mater*.
>
> Here individuals of all nations are melted into a new race of men, whose labours and posterity will one day cause great change in the world. . . . The American is a new man, who acts upon new principles; he must therefore entertain new ideas, and form new opinions. From involuntary idleness, servile dependence, penury, and useless labour, he has passed to toils of a very different nature, rewarded by ample subsistence. This is an American.[6]

"It was inevitable," according to Don M. Wolfe, "that the New World should produce images of man in keeping with the revolutionary changes it made in the lives of the colonists."[7] Free from the structures of class and the strictures of feudalism, in the society of the wilderness and the culture of the frontier—as historians from Turner to Hartz have maintained—ordinary men were generally and roughly free, as never before, to choose their lives and to "make themselves." "In such a situation," wrote Tom

Paine in *The Rights of Man*, "man becomes what he ought. He sees his species, not with the inhuman idea of a natural enemy, but as kindred."[8] The image of man which was implicit (and often explicit) in the American Revolutionary ideology held in balance the distinctive values of equality and liberty, joined with a conviction of the simple reality of fraternity and community, and grounded in the no less evident fact of opportunity. Given these conditions, and indeed they seemed God-given, the nature of man was indefinitely perfectible—almost, as it seemed to some, *immediately* perfectible. The Americans in the generation of Paine and Jefferson, according to Wolfe,

> saw in themselves an embodiment of human nature expanded to powers unattainable in the restraints of the Old World. . . . In America, then, the concept of plasticity, the infinite malleability and teachability of the human organism, was to be tested as never before. . . . The New World was in essence a prodigious gamble on the unmeasured powers of the common man, a gamble scornful of nature's unique boundaries, and uninformed, then as now, by any body of measurable certainties about genetic inheritance.[9]

The liberation of man which the American adventure promised was a many-sided freedom. As we have seen, it included liberation from history (from the restrictive past of feudalism and ancient hierarchies), liberation from the fixed status and poverty of rigid class systems, and liberation from the ancestral subjugation to lords and masters. To these dimensions of freedom Hans Morgenthau has discerned another: liberation from a permanent enemy without, in terms of the "absence of serious competition from abroad." The combination of these factors has led Morgenthau to define the early American experience of freedom as having both "vertical" and "horizontal" dimensions:

> Out of this unique and exhilarating experience of being free, as it were, vertically and horizontally, without a permanent master from within and without a permanent enemy from abroad, the specifically American state of mind arises. To Rousseau's statement that "Man is born free, but everywhere he is in chains," that mind might well have replied: man may or may not be born free, but in America he is without chains. Man in America is free to rise within the nation as high as merit and opportunity will carry him, and the American nation is free to expand as far as its power will carry it. These two kinds of mobility—the vertical and the horizontal—were experienced as being interconnected, the latter serving as a supplement to the former.[10]

The human emancipation which the American experience appeared to presage was philosophically grounded in the venerable doctrine of natural rights—already old and well established in political theory and common-law practice, as well as the covenants and commitments of the Puritan tradition. The two preceding centuries had elaborated the preliminary concept of natural law—the higher law inhering in the nature of man which transcended the positive power of rulers—but it was the century of Reason and Revolution which drew out of that mixed body of dogma the fundamental message that came to characterize the American Creed. The idea of certain natural and inalienable rights pertaining to man *qua* man both depended upon a prior recognition of the dignity of the individual and constituted a reinforcement and demonstration of that value; and particularly was this so in the growing insistence of the colonists (and other

Englishmen) that those rights which were "beyond the law" should for that reason be written into the law. In fact, it was generally thought that they *were*—i.e., that the natural rights of life, liberty, property, mobility, freedom from intrusion and from arbitrary arrest or trial, were all guaranteed by English constitutional law;[11] and it is possible to maintain that the force of the natural rights doctrine in the eighteenth century owed less to the abstractions of moral and political philosophy than to the steady accretion of positive prescriptions and proscriptions delineating the sphere of personal autonomy, liberty, and privacy.

Whichever came first, it was the idea of natural rights which underlay the revolutionary consciousness of the latter part of the century; and that consciousness was not only political but psychological and ontological. In order for rights to be natural to man, there had to be a conception of human nature and an image of man supportive of those claims—a sense of man as sufficiently rational, equitable, and responsible to make the enterprise of freedom practical. Such an image was not to be derived from the famous Machiavelli, for whom the run of humanity were irresponsible creatures dominated by greed and impulse, fit subjects for the deceiving prince. Nor was it to be drawn from Hobbes, a very familiar name in the colonies, whose state of (human) nature was a permanent war of all against all, characterized by fear and hostility, in which the life of man was "solitary, poor, nasty, brutish, and short"—until he should surrender his dreadful freedom unequivocally to the sovereign of a total Leviathan-state.

The image of man which was most clearly supportive of the eighteenth-century premise of natural rights, and the corollary drive for constitutional rights, was derived primarily from Locke, whose conception of the natural state of mankind was the opposite of Hobbes's, and whose theory of government and society was antithetical. For Locke the presocial condition of man was not one of mutual hostility but of mutual tolerance and peace—virtually a state of grace. Nor was his social contract a surrender pact drawn up *between* the people and a sovereign; rather it was a limited agreement *among* the people to allow the regulation of some natural rights in order to gain protection for the remaining ones. As Saul K. Padover has summarized the doctrine: "If the rulers violate the natural laws, men, having freely made their compact with their governors, have a right to resist and, where necessary, to abrogate the agreement. In brief, Locke asserted the right to revolution."[12] Locke's psychology, with its denial of innate ideas (or instincts) and its emphasis upon experience as the source of knowledge and character, supplemented his political philosophy and gave encouragement to the colonists' growing conviction of themselves as new men, unfettered by inner or outer bonds, free to "become as they ought." Padover stresses the effect:

The implications of Locke's empirical position were far-reaching, particularly in a new country that was engaged in the pioneer effort of creating a new civilization. If men were the product of their experience, then it was logical to assume that the creation of a good (socially desirable) environment would result in virtuous people. . . . Here, then, we find the seeds of democracy, a political philosophy that is based on the fundamental assumption of human flexibility and, in consequence, of potential improvability.[13]

If this was the philosophy and psychology that furnished the "seeds of democracy" and the conceptual framework for the American Revolutionary ideology, it never held the field alone but was in active and persistent conflict with the opposing school of thought derived from Hobbes. That competition of viewpoints was, of course, already an old and familiar affair; in the great debate between Socrates and the sophists of Athens (notably Callicles and Thrasymachus), and again in the issue between mainstream Renaissance thought and that which Hiram Haydn has called the "counter-Renaissance," the same fundamental dispute about human nature was in evidence. On one side was a thoroughly mechanistic and deterministic psychology, portraying man as essentially irrational and irresponsible, the creature of blind forces working through him (whether instinctual or environmental), culminating in a pessimistic philosophy and an authoritarian political theory. Thrasymachus, Machiavelli, Hobbes—and Alexander Hamilton—were representative spokesmen for this viewpoint in their respective ages. On the other side was the view of man which underlay the adventure of democracy—stressing the faculties of reason and purpose, the moral attributes of dignity and responsibility, and the possession of individual rights flowing from those qualities. From these psychological and metaphysical foundations have developed the political ideas of limited government, constitutionalism, representation, divided or separated powers, natural and legal rights, consent of the governed, and the right of resistance to tyranny—in a word, democracy. Socrates, Cicero, Thomas More, Erasmus, Locke, Rousseau—and Thomas Jefferson —have been among the representative spokesmen for the latter viewpoint.

It is probable that, as Arthur O. Lovejoy and others have maintained, the pessimistic view of human nature and government was in fact more widely held in the eighteenth century than its opposite number, for all the power and excitement of the radical new philosophy of reason. At any rate, the generation that witnessed the American Revolution and the framing of the Constitution was one of "protracted conflict between the Hamiltonians, who were at bottom Hobbesian pessimists, and the Jeffersonians, who in the last analysis had a Lockean optimism regarding the creative role of reason and sense."[14] If it was the Jeffersonians who dominated the Revolutionary ideology, and the Hamiltonians who dominated the Constitutional Convention, there was also a third force at work whose moderating influence was perhaps chiefly responsible for the constitutional compromise that evolved between the two philosophical poles. That mediating element was symbolized in the commanding figures of Madison—"father of the Constitution," whose own philosophy was closer to Hamilton than to Jefferson—and of Franklin, doyen of the framers, whose viewpoint was closer to Jefferson than to Hamilton. The rationale for the constitutional solution that emerged was to be found in the work of Montesquieu, whose comprehensive and comparative study of political history, *Spirit of the Laws*, provided a typology of governmental institutions exactly suited to the attitudes of the constitution makers. Montesquieu, himself basically a conservative thinker, found the safeguard for human liberty in a tripartite division of governmental powers—which the Americans took over in the form of the executive, legislative, and judicial branches. In words that anticipated the arguments of Madison in the Federalist Papers, Montesquieu wrote: "There would be an end of everything, were the same man, or the same body, whether of the nobles or of the people, to exercise those powers, that of enacting laws, that of executing the public resolutions, and of trying the causes of individuals."[15]

It was in this notion of checks and balances, of countervailing and balancing forces in government and society, that the influence of Montesquieu was especially felt. There was also something more, as Padover has pointed out:

> The pragmatists among the Founding Fathers found Montesquieu's rational explanation of social phenomena highly plausible. They had a particularly keen appreciation of the Frenchman's emphasis on environmental factors as being of decisive importance in the molding of society. When Montesquieu pointed out the overriding influence of climate and soil, which he called "the first of all empires," as well as of "religion, laws, maxims of government, customs, manners," in the formation of human character and institutions, he spoke a language well understood by his American readers.[16]

The theory of balance among contending interests and powers was most fully developed by Madison, in his role as the *primum inter pares* of the Constitution makers, and still more famously in his contributions to the Federalist Papers. Particularly in the Federalist No. 10, Madison made plain his belief that it was not generosity or fellow feeling that ruled the conduct of most men but rather the spirit of "faction"—that is, of special and selfish interest. In this he was close to Hobbes and at one with Hamilton; but he was very far from Hobbes, and at odds with Hamilton (at least in the latter's private views), in the political solution which he propounded. That solution represented perhaps the first American declaration of the case for political pluralism—for the toleration and encouragement of diversity of opinion and interest, rather than the stifling of it. More than that, Madison's proposal foresaw the peculiar line of development to be taken by the American party system—for which no provision whatsoever had been made in the Constitution. Nowhere in our modern literature is there a more trenchant description than in the tenth Federalist paper of the unique function which the parties were to assume of moderating and controlling faction: of the prohibition of any one interest from obtaining a majority and dominating all the rest; of the virtues of diversity and multiplicity for purposes of mutual check and balance.[17] Madison clearly shared the prevailing view of party as synonymous with faction—a view as meaningful as ever today with respect to the minor parties of our own system or the extreme parties in such a system as the French. But Madison differed emphatically with those "theoretic politicians" from the time of Plato onward who held it to be axiomatic that a good society depends upon the possession of the greatest possible homogeneity and consensus, and therefore was unlikely in territories less insular than the British or less cohesive than the Athenian or less provincial than a Swiss canton (the ideal setting for Rousseau). The latent causes of faction, according to Madison, lie rather in the very nature of man; they arise from the diversity of human faculties, and it is the protection of this diversity which is the first object of government. The causes of faction, then, cannot be destroyed without either destroying liberty or imposing a uniform ideology upon all citizens—which comes to the same thing. If the causes cannot be removed, then it is the effects of faction which must be dealt with; and the way to do this is not by suppression but by liberation. Faction must be allowed to flourish, in all of its diversity and rivalry; what needs to be done is to devise means of composing and adjusting the rivalries. "The regulation of these various and interfering interests forms the principal task of modern legislation, and involves the spirit of party and faction in the necessary and ordinary operations of the government."[18]

The genius of Madison—which some later historians, like Daniel J. Boorstin, have equated with the "genius of

American politics"—was to defy the great tradition which had assumed that the regulation of these conflicting interests, the capacity of interpreting the general will, must lie either with an enlightened despot or with an enlightened elite. "It is vain," he wrote, "to say that enlightened statesmen will be able to adjust these clashing interests, and render them all subservient to the public good. Enlightened statesmen will not always be at the helm." The solution that Madison proposed was as simple as it was revolutionary: Enlarge the scope of the Republic. Encourage—not compression, reduction, homogeneity—but a broad extent of territory, a large increase of population, and a wide diversity of interests. "Extend the sphere, and you take in a greater variety of parties and interests; you make it less probable that a majority of the whole will have a common motive to invade the rights of other citizens." Among other things, for all his opposition to the concept of party as faction, Madison was in effect anticipating and adumbrating the institution of the two-party system and the modern conception of the political party as a loose confederation of diverse interests, regions, and classes. He was the foremost exemplar of that liberal theory of balance and accommodation, bargaining and compromise, which was the political equivalent of the doctrine of economic liberalism. (And also of the later doctrine of judicial liberalism, at least on its constitutional side; there is a direct line from the tenth Federalist paper to the belief of Mr. Justice Holmes that the test of truth for an idea should be its ability to get itself accepted in the marketplace.)

Between the affirmative faith in human nature of Paine, Samuel Adams, and Jefferson on the one hand, and the dark premonitions of men like Hamilton and John Adams on the other, the moderating pluralism of Madison was that of an enlightened conservative—an American Burke—who provided a balanced perspective embracing at the same time a substantive commitment to liberty and a procedural counsel of prudence. Neither he nor John Adams, nor even the Hamilton of the Federalist Papers, was quite exempt from the pervasive optimism of the Revolutionary generation concerning the educability and improvability of man under the influence of the American landscape. What together they contrived in the form of the Constitution was a document in the great tradition of Magna Carta, the common law, and English constitutionalism. With the Bill of Rights added, it became a document in a greater tradition—if one that was only beginning to find a voice and to gain a hearing in the councils of the powerful.

What was beginning to happen to American thought, in the gathering storm of pre-Revolutionary events and arguments, was no less than a transformation in the assumptions and premises that had ruled political speculation without effective challenge for upwards of two centuries. Of these premises the most fundamental was the belief that no government could be either equitable or orderly in which the major power was not held by a privileged class, whose superior fitness to rule clearly lay in the solid evidence of wealth, breeding, education, and the like. Equality as a political idea was not then seriously entertained; common people were unfit not only to rule but even to participate in the workings of government in any but carefully delimited and circumscribed ways. But in the crisis of the colonies, under the pressure to devise new styles of republican government, and with growing readiness to challenge any and all forms of traditional authority and superiority, the old formalities and abstractions simply did not work and began to break down. During the decade or so preceding the Revolution, a basic "paradigm shift" occurred in America; the idea of equality emerged, the concept of democracy was transformed, and a new image of man was born. Something of what that new paradigm was to be like has been described by Bailyn in terms of the doubts and apprehensions felt by Tories and other defenders of the status quo in the face of the developing intellectual unrest:

> What reasonable social and political order could conceivably be built and maintained where authority was questioned before it was obeyed, where social differences were considered to be incidental rather than essential to community order, and where superiority, suspect in principle, was not allowed to concentrate in the hands of a few but was scattered broadly through the populace? No one could clearly say. But some, caught up in a vision of the future in which the peculiarities of American life became the marks of a chosen people, found in the defiance of traditional order the firmest of all grounds for their hope for a freer life. The details of this new world were not as yet clearly depicted; but faith ran high that a better world than any that had ever been could be built where authority was disturbed and held in constant scrutiny; where the status of men flowed from their achievements and from their personal qualities, not from distinctions ascribed to them at birth; and where the use of power over the lives of men was jealously guarded and severely restricted. It was only where there was this defiance, this refusal to truckle, this distrust of all authority, political or social, that institutions would express human aspirations, not crush them.[19]

The fundamental shift in the categories of thought which this suggests embraced, among other things, the gradual abandonment of the "Hobbesian" view of man and its replacement by the "Lockean." Even as late as the Constitutional Convention of 1787, the issue was still being contested; but its outcome was no longer in doubt.

The idea of man in the American Creed was to be, not the constricted one of the Federalists, but the liberal and liberating one of the Jeffersonians. Myrdal has summarized the essential and enduring thrust of that creed in clear terms:

> . . . taking the broad historical view, the American Creed has triumphed. It has given the main direction to change in this country. America has had gifted conservative statesmen and national leaders, and they have often determined the course of public affairs. But with few exceptions, only the liberals have gone down in history as national heroes. America is . . . conservative in fundamental principles, and in much more than that. . . . But *the principles conserved are liberal and some, indeed, are radical.*[20]

At the outset of the American experiment, in the generation of Revolution and the trauma of national birth, it was not only an ideology of government that was forged in the legislatures and coffeehouses and tested in the crucible of a war of liberation; it was also an idea of man. The image of Democratic Man was no logical product, then, of science or history, or political experience, or even of conventional philosophy. Its adoption by the Americans —like the adoption of the Bill of Rights—was an act of faith. On that faith the nation was founded and its creed was grounded. Two hundred years later, that idea of man —tested again and again, abused, betrayed, and derided —appears as one of history's supreme illustrations of the self-fulfilling prophecy. It is hard proof of the visionary notion, once reserved for poets and romantics, that men at some time are masters of their fate—that they may choose themselves, make their history, and define their future.

CHAPTER 8

THE ACADEMIC
COUNTERCULTURE:
Toward a Radical Humanism

The central thesis of this book, as documented in the previous chapters, is that underlying the competition of ideas in the marketplaces of science, politics, and culture is a deeper and deadlier conflict of ideas about man himself—his essential nature, his salient features, and his alternative futures. During the decade of the sixties, both the overt competition and the covert conflict were carried on most dramatically in the colleges of America—not on their playing fields but in their classrooms, corridors, and campus commons. Everyone who was there recalls, whether with regret or relief, the swift waxing and waning of that impassioned confrontation between the Academic Establishment—standing in for the mainstream adult culture—and the young disestablishmentarians of what came to be known as the counterculture.[1] And everyone remembers also the abrupt end of ideology on the campuses at the end of the decade: the winding down of demonstration, agitation, protest, activism of all forms, and even (as it now seems) of the rebellious heart and the committed spirit.

But while one stage of the conflict, that between students and administrators, was drawing to a close in the colleges and universities, another was just beginning. It is remarkable that in most accounts of the campus revolt of the late sixties there is little mention of its most durable and perhaps its most significant aspect: the deep schism and altercation within the ranks of the faculties themselves, and specifically within the departments and disciplines concerned with the study of man. Some years after the wave of student activism has receded and the voices of protest have lapsed into a studied or stunned (or stoned) silence, the war of ideas and ideals continues to be waged across the campuses, less physically but no less fervently than before—although hidden from public view behind the protective walls of scholarly discourse and the academic traditions of decorum. The fault line which divides the community of scholars today has its epicenter in the social and behavioral sciences but also reaches throughout the curriculum—all the way from the humanities at one end to the hard sciences at the other. In the next chapters an attempt is made to chart the course of this division on three of its main battlegrounds —those of history, sociology, and psychology—with passing reference to neighboring groves of Academe. In each field the elements of conflict and the lines of opposition are essentially the same; the "conventional wisdom" of the field, articulated in a body of postulates and premises governing the scope and method of the discipline and resting upon an implicit paradigm of the nature of man and society, has come to be challenged by a competitive system of commitments, assumptions, and values: in effect, an academic counterculture. But before examining the particular expressions of this intramural "struggle of the dons," it may be well to summarize the general features and wider ramifications of the contemporary crisis of values which, if it does not yet seem to many a burning issue, cannot any longer be dismissed as merely an academic question.

Although the youth-based counterculture of the sixties
has passed into history, the sense of a genuine transformation of contemporary culture and society, one which
is already shaking the foundations and pointing us to
where the wasteland ends, is more widely felt and shared
today than ever. In their details the premonitions and
prescriptions vary; but there is a common thread of
prophecy regarding both the crisis of technological society
and the "transvaluation of values"—the obsolescence of
the modern technoscientific world view and the return of
the repressed ideas of humanism—which is seen to be ger-
minating beneath the asphalt and plastic of the "mega-
technic wasteland."[2] Thus George B. Leonard, declaring
that "the time is overdue for the emergence of a new
vision of human and social destiny and being," goes so
far as to maintain that "the current period is indeed
unique in history and that it represents the beginning of
the most thoroughgoing change in the quality of human
existence since the creation of an agricultural surplus
brought about the birth of civilized states some five thou-
sand years ago."[3] William Irwin Thompson, looking down
upon the American scene from a precarious vantage
point at the edge of history, subtitles his volume "Speculations on the Transformation of Culture."[4] Theodore
Roszak, who first drew our attention to the youth counterculture, now heralds the rise of a counterculture of the
spirit: "There is a strange, new radicalism abroad which
refuses to respect the conventions of secular thought and
value, which insists on making the visionary powers a
central point of political reference."[5] Eugene S. Schwartz,
in his sweeping and forbidding assessment of the rise and
denouement of technology in modern civilization, *Overskill*, finds hope of survival and revival in a humanistic
vision of posttechnological man: "Here is at once the
power that can hasten the decline of the technological
society and can transform it into a society based upon

man in nature, with human values and with faith in a sensate, erotic, and creative individual."[6] Lewis Yablonsky, observing the advent on a mass scale of *Robopaths: People as Machines*, concludes that "a reversal of the machine system's social death-dealing consequences" can come about only through "an effort at all levels, by all people in a social machine society," toward "humanistic social change" in every important institution from the family to the government.[7]

And Lewis Mumford, who first charted the collision course of technics and civilization more than forty years ago, now summons us all—while the opportunity for choice remains—to overcome the regnant myth of the machine and overturn the pentagon of power through a collective act of willful self-transfiguration: "For its effective salvation mankind will need to undergo something like a spontaneous religious conversion: one that will replace the mechanical world picture with an organic world picture, and give to the human personality, as the highest known manifestation of life, the precedence it now gives to its machines and computers."[8] No technical adjustments or piecemeal reforms will suffice to meet the crisis of humanity: "nothing will produce an effective change but the fresh transformation that has already begun in the human mind."[9]

Common to all of these prophetic texts, and many more like them, is the apprehension of a cultural malaise so historic as to portend—and require—a revolutionary transformation. And in nearly all of them that transformation is seen to rest upon the emergence and successful nurture of a new idea of man. Nowhere have these issues been more boldly drawn, and their resolution more dramatically affirmed, than in Charles A. Reich's *The Greening of America*, one of the first and still among the most comprehensive expressions of the new doctrine of countercultural revolution. Whatever its excesses of enthusiastic rhetoric and premature certitude—surely the greening of American soil has not occurred on schedule, and the evident grayness of the landscape more nearly resembles dusk than dawn—Reich's book contains a powerful critique of the consequences of technological society (the "Corporate State") and an intuition of transforming possibilities no more visionary than a host of subsequent studies which, following at a prudent distance, have profited from Reich's miscalculations and have secured a broader base of critical and popular support. In its forthright statement of the cultural and moral issues, as well as in its sweeping proclamation of the new and better society to come, *The Greening of America* remains an important expression of the emerging paradigmatic world view which has come to characterize the academic counterculture.

There is a revolution coming. It will not be like revolutions of the past. It will originate with the individual and with culture, and it will change the political structure only as its final act. . . . It promises a higher reason, a more human community, and a new and liberated individual. . . .

The revolution is a movement to bring man's thinking, his society, and his life to terms with the revolution of technology and science that has already taken place. Technology demands of man a new mind—a higher, transcendent reason—if it is to be controlled and guided rather than to become an unthinking monster. It demands a new individual responsibility for values, or it will dictate all values. And it promises a life that is more liberated and more beautiful than any man has known, if man has the courage and the imagination to seize that life. . . .

At the heart of everything is what we shall call a

change of consciousness. This means a "new head"
—a new way of living—a new man. . . . Industrial-
ism produced a new man, too—one adapted to the
demands of the machine. In contrast, today's emerging consciousness seeks a new knowledge of what
it means to be human, in order that the machine,
having been built, may now be turned to human
ends; in order that man once more can become a
creative force, renewing and creating his own life
and thus giving life back to his society.[10]

Obviously, this is no detached and judicious observation of the contemporary conflict of cultures but a passionate critical assault upon the old culture and an
equally ardent endorsement of the new one struggling
to be born. Doubtless much of the bad press that Reich's
essay has received is due to its deliberate violation of the
conventions of scholarly discourse and its willing suspen-
sion of disinterest as well as of disbelief. To be sure, if
this departure from tradition also extends to defiance of
the ordinary rules of evidence and empiricism—if it seeks
only to sway the feelings rather than to convince the
mind—then it deserves to be rejected. But that is not
transparently the case with *The Greening of America*,
which is the work of an experienced legal scholar with a
record of substantial contribution to political and constitutional theory.[11] It is not despite its partisanship and
passion, but because of it, that Reich's book deserves to be
taken seriously; it is in the demonstrated courage of its
convictions, in its display of reason in the service of
commitment, that it is most valuable as an example of
the new style of scholarship in the social sciences—
embracing a distinctive methodology as well as an alternative ideology—which may be designated as *radical
humanism*. This new approach, openly rejecting the "non-
intervention policy" of traditional social research, seeks

nothing less than to change the image of man as well as
the institutions of society; more simply, it seeks to create
a new man, a new society, and a new culture.

The broad differences between these two perspectives
on culture, both inside and outside the academy, have
been summarized by the sociologist Philip Slater, whose
analysis of the "two cultures" is based upon the premise
that "each is in fact a total system with an internal logic
and consistency: each is built upon a set of assumptions
which hangs together and is viable under some conditions."[12] Certain of the polarities by virtue of which the
competing perspectives may be differentiated are listed
by Slater as follows:

> The old culture, when forced to choose, tends to
> give preference to property rights over personal
> rights, technological requirements over human
> needs, competition over cooperation, violence over
> sexuality, concentration over distribution, the pro-
> ducer over the consumer, means over ends, secrecy
> over openness, social forms over personal expression,
> striving over gratification, Oedipal love over com-
> munal love, and so on. The new counterculture tends
> to reverse all of these priorities.[13]

Another spokesman for the "cultural revolution," William Braden, has been prepared to concede that much of
the youthful impetus behind the new movement is more
romantic than revolutionary, more appearance than reality; but he contends that the actions and gestures of the
young represent only a single aspect of

> . . . a much more fundamental phenomenon: namely,
> a humanistic revolt against technology, against the
> debatable forms of affluence that technology has so
> far produced in this country, and indeed against the

basic psychological, philosophical and theological assumptions that underlie the technological impulse to manipulate the environment and thereby to dominate the universe. In a real sense, what is called into question is no less than the whole thrust of Western civilization since at least the Renaissance and Reformation.[14]

These various statements of the case should be sufficient to demonstrate that, in the minds of its advocates, a primary characteristic of the countercultural revolution is a *new humanism*: that is, an emphasis upon "people not personnel,"[15] upon man regarded as an end (subject) rather than a means (object), upon the "whole" man as an integration of love and will as well as of reason, and upon the affiliative concept of man-with-man as against the competitive assumption of man-against-man. The central point of this new humanism may be identified by describing it as *person-centered*.

There is also a second characteristic of the intellectual counterculture which is complementary to its humanism but distinct in important ways: namely, a *new radicalism*. This more familiar dimension of the counterculture has been thoroughly explored and chronicled over recent years by participant-observers of such differing experience and interest as Paul Goodman, Herbert Marcuse, Charles Hampden-Turner, Paul Jacobs, and Theodore Roszak.[16] Where the new humanism of the cultural countermovement is person-centered, the new radicalism is *problem*-centered; but its conspicuous differentiation from the old Left is that its approach is problematic without being programmatic. In its characteristic expressions and actions it is defined by morality more than by doctrine, by protest more than by program, and by spontaneity and impulse more than by organization and planning. This is not to say that the new radicalism is no longer centered upon social action in the cause of fundamental change, or that it lacks recognition of the need for coherent strategies and policies; but these objective requirements are regarded as secondary to the higher purpose of raising—even of altering—the consciousness of victims and victimizers alike, and so making possible a new form of "liberation" (embracing mind and spirit as well as body) from what are felt to be the subtle oppressions and ingenious coercions of the technocratic power structure. Thus Emile Capouya writes:

> The idea that much can be accomplished by changing "conditions" is useful only insofar as we remember that we are our conditions, that we embody them in our thoughts and our actions. Customary movements of reform proceed on the assumption that conditions are objective and persons subjective, which amounts to regarding things as real and people as fictitious. For that reason the usual patterns of reform, insofar as they are effective, achieve more ingeniously tyrannical forms of the abuses they set out to correct.[17]

The complementary themes of humanism and radicalism—initiated in the youthful phase of the counterculture and reconfirmed in its maturity—make plausible the designation of the ideology of this movement as that of radical humanism. A succinct statement of its guiding faith has been presented by Erich Fromm (who himself prefers the alternative designation of "humanist radicalism"):

> The position taken . . . is one of rational faith in man's capacity to extricate himself from what seems the fatal web of circumstances that he has created. It is the position of those who are neither "optimists"

nor "pessimists," but radicals who have rational faith in man's capacity to avoid the ultimate catastrophe. This humanist radicalism goes to the roots, and thus to the causes; it seeks to liberate man from the chains of illusions; it postulates that fundamental changes are necessary, not only in our economic and political structure but also in our values, in our concept of man's aims, and in our personal conduct.[18]

CHAPTER 9

MAN IN HISTORY:
Beyond Consensus

To those who still believe in the feasibility of a cumulative "scientific history"—one that will present the Facts of the human adventure, and nothing but the Facts, unless it is also the Laws which those hard data inescapably illuminate—the behavior of American historians in the present century must seem irrational in the extreme. Far from moving in a straight empirical line, these arbiters of the national past have shifted back and forth between opposite poles of ideological commitment: those of "consensus" and "conflict." To be sure, for most of the first half-century, until roughly the end of World War II, there was broad agreement within the craft upon a set of fundamental principles or guidelines concerning the general character of the American past and the proper ways of approaching and interpreting it. That paradigm has been aptly called "Progressive history" because it was conceived in an age of progressive reform, because its major exemplars were themselves ardent Progressives, and most of all because its central thrust was the commitment to an idea of progress through change—and more exactly through conflict. As John Higham has summarized their collective contribution:

Change, these scholars said, takes place through struggle, and progress occurs when the more popular and democratic forces overcome the resistance to change offered by vested interests. And so American history became a story of epic conflict between over- and underprivileged groups. Whether this strife was chiefly between sections, as with Frederick Jackson Turner, or between opposing economic groups, as with Charles Beard, or between Hamiltonian and Jeffersonian ideologies, as with Vernon Parrington, a fundamental dualism cut through the course of American history.[1]

Unlike their predecessors of scientific historiography, and still more unlike those who were to succeed and displace them, the Progressive historians were under no illusion regarding their biased perspective on the past and their immersion in the present. Written history, as Charles A. Beard was to declare in the twilight of his career, is always "an act of faith," and the historian—far from being above the battle—is "in the position of a statesman dealing with public affairs; in writing he acts and in acting he makes choices, large or small, timid or bold, with respect to some conception of the nature of things."[2] The conception which the Progressivists held of the nature of things was dynamic rather than static, grounded in the old revolutionary faith in the indefinite perfectibility both of men and institutions, inspired by the experiments and interventions of the age of reform, and reinforced by the pragmatic and activist spirit of other fields of thought and scholarship (notably the philosophy and psychology of James and Dewey, the jurisprudence of Holmes and Pound, the sociology of Veblen and Ward, and the investigative journalism of Steffens and Tarbell). As Richard Hofstadter put it in his reappraisal of *The Progressive Historians*:

Progressive historical writing did for history what pragmatism did for philosophy, sociological jurisprudence for law, the muckraking spirit for journalism, and what Parrington called "critical realism" for letters. If pragmatism, as someone has said, provided American liberalism with its philosophical nerve, Progressive historiography gave it memory and myth, and naturalized it within the whole framework of American historical experience.[3]

As this suggests, the Progressive historians were not merely reacting to the climate of opinion in their time; they were also acting upon it. In changing the shape of historiography, they were changing the shape of "history": creating a usable past in the service of the present—its needs, urgencies, and aspirations. And in so doing they were affecting the shape of things to come. Their version of the past—their committed history—contained a vision of the future, a vision not so much predictive as prophetic: The future was seen as open and contingent, a matter of choices and challenges, conflicts and crises, to which (as in the Progressive past) men might respond nobly or meanly, through either a triumph of will or a failure of nerve. The emphasis upon conflict was not a brooding apprehension of disaster but an exhilarating sense of opportunity. It is important to recognize that the theme of conflict, in the hands of the Progressive scholars, conveyed none of the pessimism and historical determinism of the European conflict theorists such as Gumplowicz and Ratzenhofer, or, for that matter, Marx.[4] For the Progressive historians, reflecting on the American experience, periods of conflict were climactic moments of active and volitional struggle, illustrating not the tyranny of cosmic forces or invisible hosts but the contending wills and interests—and, not least of all, the ideas and ideologies—of resourceful human beings. "Through revolution and counterrevolution," as Higham has said of their viewpoint, "through reform and reaction, beat the rhythm of an exciting and meaningful history."[5]

This view from the tower of the American panorama, with its positive idea of progress through conscious struggle and its affirmative idea of man as the responsible agent of that progress, reached its zenith in the 1920s and 1930s (the New Deal surely seemed then the conclusive proof and vindication of its claims), and continued to hold the field through the long hiatus of World War II. But then, abruptly, it was overthrown. Within the space of a few years, the conceptual foundations of Progressive history were undermined, its major theses repudiated, and its master builders (Beard, Turner, Parrington, Becker) one by one discredited.[6] By 1950 the grand design of what James Harvey Robinson called the New History, which lately had appeared so monumental and permanent, had come to look (in Higham's phrase) more like a grand illusion.

It is not enough to say, in explanation of the ideological counterrevolution which came so suddenly upon the scene of American historiography, that the times had changed and the climate of opinion had undergone a seasonal turn. The climate of opinion, the spirit of the times, the mood of the nation, were virtually transformed; and in the vanguard of that sea change, at once faithfully reflecting and consciously influencing it, was a new school of interpreters of the American past and the American character. The master theme of conflict—epochal change, class struggle, sectional rivalry, social activism—disappeared from view in a welter of qualifications, equivocations, and outright refutations. In its place there arose the new master metaphor of *consensus* (though, to be sure, the term itself only came to be applied some years later in critical retrospect).[7] All the sharp-edged images of crisis, change, reaction, rivalry, and revolution became blurred and softened into a haze of new pieties and ambiguities; among them "the rediscovery of complexity in American history" (as Hofstadter has called it), along with an appreciation of pervasive continuity in American traditions underlying and overriding all change, a wry sense of the irony of American history (contributed by the neo-Calvinist theologian Reinhold Niebuhr), and a general emphasis on "the enduring uniformities of American life, the stability of institutions, the persistence of a national character."[8]

In a word, the new mood was conservative. The revisionist historians who dominated the decade of the fifties articulated and validated the battle fatigue of the postwar generation: its retreat from liberalism, its farewell to reform, its contentment with Eisenhower ("the bland lead the bland," said Arthur Schlesinger, Jr.), its complacent self-image of the other-directed organization man moving up and making out in the affluent society, its quest for a unifying national purpose within a national character defined by a peculiar political genius. That is not to say that the right turn away from progressivism toward conservatism was, among historians at any rate, merely an unconsidered reaction or revulsion against great ideas and high ideals; on the contrary, much of the original and influential scholarship of the period was more concerned than ever with thought and theory, myths and metaphors, ideas and intellectual images. Indeed, the "consensus history" of the fifties was largely intellectual history, and its characteristic tone (despite Niebuhr and a coterie of literary existentialists) was affirmative and even jubilant in celebration of the singular triumph of American democracy as it was now at last discerned: that is, its harmony, stability, equanimity, and simple unity. The motto of the conservative historian was, as Higham has remarked: "e pluribus unum."[9] Even the "end of ideology," as it was proclaimed by Daniel Bell, signified not the decline of thought or the eclipse of mind but the superannuation of stale dogma and factious disputation, and a recovery of that dynamic equilibrium of thought and action which was there under our noses all along (but until now obscured from vision by the fog of Progressive rhetoric).

The interest of consensus historians in the American national character—a concept implying distinctiveness if not uniqueness—was in part an outgrowth of the wartime hagiography undertaken by scholars and writers as a patriotic duty. Two different kinds of national-character studies emerged from the war effort: those dealing with other nations, chiefly actual or potential enemies, intended to expose the sources of their wickedness[10]—and those dealing with America, intended to illuminate the sources of her greatness. Following the war, as a logical spinoff of all that concentrated energy and talent, explorations of the American character abounded.[11] Also contributing to the new interest in unitary patterns and consensual themes was the adoption by historians of the concept of *culture*, which by the mid-forties had spread far beyond its home base in anthropology and was coming to be accepted (in the words of Alfred Kroeber and Clyde Kluckhohn) as "one of the key notions of contemporary thought."[12] The culture concept, as it was generally if vaguely understood, encompassed all the man-made works of a given community from arts to artifacts, but its central focus was on the felt values, symbols, myths, and ideologies which gave those works coherence and meaning. Invigorated by a heavy injection of psychoanalytic thought in the form of culture-personality studies; dignified by the incorporation of traditional literary and aesthetic connotations (and the subsequent enlistment of T. S. Eliot and Lionel Trilling in the ranks of cultural historians); reinforced by the enthusiastic endorsement of sociology, which treated "culture" as conceptually equiv-

alent to "society" itself; validated by the popular consciousness in the postwar period of the rise and fall (and
hence the reality) of whole cultures—for all of these
reasons the culture concept (or more precisely the culture
theory advanced by spokesmen like Kroeber and Kluckhohn) made rapid headway in both academic and general
thought. Reviewing this development in the sixties,
Jacques Barzun, himself a pioneer cultural historian,
observed:

> Today, therefore, anyone who thinks at all is some-
> thing of a cultural historian. He thinks with the no-
> tions of cultural force, cultural crisis, cultural trend
> perpetually in mind. Newspapers and magazines are
> one mass of cultural "analysis," and books of every
> kind, not excepting fiction, make a large place for
> "the cultural context" as something far more inti-
> mate and compelling than the old economic base,
> the physical environment, or the still older "manners
> and morals."[13]

The concept of culture, like that of national character,
contributed to the new conservatism in American historiography in more than one way. First was its all-
inclusiveness, its totality; it contained everything and
explained everything, or so it seemed to those who believed
the culture concept to be, as Stuart Chase heralded it,
"the foundation stone of the social sciences."[14] If the idea
of culture was the source of explanation of everything
human (and nothing human was alien to it), then the
phenomenon called culture was the source of causation
of everything human. Implicit in the concept was the
principle of cultural determinism. In fact that principle
had long since emerged in anthropology and become the
subject of extended controversy. It was an anthropologist,

Marvin Harris, reflecting on the "culturology" of colleagues such as Leslie White, who said of the culture concept that it "is potentially, if not inherently, deterministic and antidemocratic in its own right."[15] Harris set forth the basis for this charge in two short questions:

If the enculturation experience determines for life how the individual is to conduct the entire pattern of his affairs, from sex to art, what then becomes of the vaunted freedom of the individual? To push to the furthest wall at once, if culture determines how we behave, then what difference is there between a democratic and totalitarian regime other than the illusion to which the actors in the democratic milieu have been enculturated that they are "freer" to choose their individual and collective destinies?[16]

The concept of culture, as it was embraced by historians and others in the fifties, represented an "organic" equivalent of the cybernetic concept of "system" which came to dominate sociology and political science in the same period. Whether the frame of reference chosen was that of the national culture or the social system, the consequence was much the same: an emphasis on "social statics" rather than dynamics, on determinism rather than volition or choice, on stability and harmony rather than conflict and change. The metaphors might vary, but the message was invariable (as it appeared at least to those who remained unbelievers):

All Nature is but Art, unknown to thee;
All Chance, Direction, which thou canst not see;
All Discord, Harmony not understood;
All partial Evil, universal Good:
And, spite of Pride, in erring Reason's spite,
One truth is clear, WHATEVER IS, IS RIGHT.[17]

However unfair that may be as an assessment of the heavenly world of the mid-twentieth-century historians, it is safe to say that their world view and their idea of human possibilities were responsive to the general climate of opinion which prevailed in America during the period roughly bounded by the end of World War II and the involvement of the nation in the Vietnam War. In his significant discussion of the relationship of historians to the "climate of opinion," Robert Allen Skotheim defines his weathervane metaphor as embracing "the fundamental assumptions and attitudes shared by significant elements of a population at a given time"—and including, more specifically and immediately, "recent common assumptions concerning God, nature, reason, and the possibility of man's progress through control of his environment."[18] The historian, in this view, derives his intellectual standpoint and his value orientation—"his sense of what is meaningful and important" in life both past and present—from his climate of opinion. At the base of this assumptive framework of values and commitments is the historian's *idea of man*—his "understanding of human nature and of what constitutes social significance."[19] The contrast between the ideas of man held respectively by Progressive and conservative historians is indicated by Skotheim in this appraisal of alternating moods:

> For example, the progressive climate of the earlier twentieth century refers to the pervasive belief in man's ability to reform society. By contrast, the years following World War II brought an intellectual temper which was more pessimistic about the possibility of significantly improving the human condition, and which instead emphasized the value of traditional American society.[20]

The placid climate of opinion which characterized the nation and its historiography during the fifties had, as it now appears, a remarkably short season. Even before the decade was out, storm signals were appearing on the horizon. In a prescient article published in 1959, "The Cult of the 'American Consensus': Homogenizing our History," John Higham severely criticized the prevailing paradigm as not merely conservative and complacent but stultifying and deadening in its effect upon historical thought. Recognizing the contributions of the consensus school in modifying the simple dualisms of the Progressives, Higham nevertheless concluded that "the conservative frame of reference . . . creates a paralyzing incapacity to deal with the elements of spontaneity, effervescence, and violence in American history. . . . the fog of complacency, flecked with anxiety, spreads backward over the American past."[21] And he expressed the hope that future scholarship would restore the deeper values of the neglected Progressive tradition: "an appreciation of the crusading spirit, a responsiveness to indignation, a sense of injustice."[22]

That hope was to be fulfilled, and then some, more swiftly than Higham or anyone immobilized by the temperate climate of the Eisenhower years could have anticipated. The portents of change were available, for those few attuned to them, even in the midst of plenty and the generation of silence. The civil rights movement, inspirited by the landmark decision of the Supreme Court in 1954 and galvanized by the ascendancy of Martin Luther King via the buses of Montgomery, Alabama, was well under way. The Beat phenomenon flourished and flickered out in the latter half of the decade, leaving behind a significant legacy of literary expression (richer by far, as it turned out, than the artistic residue of the later Hip counterculture). In fact, of course, the major theme of art and literature in the fifties was not cultural affirmation but cultural alienation—specifically, alienation from the air-conditioned nightmare of life in the crystal palace.[23] The academic cult of consensus had its counterpoint, however insubstantial, in an underground cult of dissensus which (following in a venerable tradition) masked its subversive intent in the clown's costume of satiric comedy; Mort Sahl and Lenny Bruce lectured at night to the same youthful audiences who had taken notes from Clinton Rossiter and Daniel Boorstin during the day. And if there was not yet a New Left in the history department, there was a formidable dissenting sociology—notably in the work of C. Wright Mills, whose most influential study (*The Power Elite*) was published in 1956.

All these developments were mere early warning signals, foretelling a change in the climate of opinion. Within a year or two of the new decade, the storm broke over America, the center could not hold, and the bubble of consensus burst. Barton J. Bernstein has described the scene:

> During the early sixties the conservative consensus began to break down. For many, the rediscovery of poverty and racism, the commitment to civil rights for Negroes, the criticism of intervention in Cuba and Vietnam, shattered many of the assumptions of the fifties and compelled intellectuals to re-examine the American past. From historians, and particularly from younger historians, there began to emerge a vigorous criticism of the historical consensus.[24]

What shortly came to be called "New Left" history—alternatively known as neo-Progressive, neo-Beardian, or simply revisionist history—had a positive as well as a critical dimension. Its central purpose was to reestablish the notion of conflict as the dominant theme of our past; but, just as in the case of their Progressive ancestors, it was not struggle for the sake of struggle that aroused the loyalty of the academic New Left. Their interest was in constructing an historical theory of action: a view of history as the clash of active forces, of the ordinary individual in history as himself an actor (rather than the victim-spectator of cosmic events), and of the historian as an active participant in his own narrative.

The New Look in historiography, and its new look at history, were not the exclusive property of younger historians caught up in the wave of protest which swept the campuses in the second half of the decade. Among the senior scholars who were brought to reconsider their standpoint—whether by the dialogue within the academy or by the clamorous events outside it—was the late Richard Hofstadter, whose main work (especially *The American Political Tradition* and *The Age of Reform*) had been identified with the consensus approach. In an essay entitled "Conflict and Consensus in American History," published as the concluding chapter of *The Progressive Historians* (1968), Hofstadter described the shift in his own thinking which led him to recognize the limits of consensus history (while appreciating its contributions) and to reemphasize the centrality of conflict in the American experience. His judgment was summed up in the statement that "in one form or another conflict finally does remain, and ought to remain, somewhat near the center of our focus of attention. . . . History deals with change, and in change conflict is a necessary, and indeed a functional, ingredient."[25] More specifically and pointedly, he concluded:

> There are three major areas in which a history of the United States organized around the guiding idea of consensus breaks down: first, I believe it cannot do justice to the genuinely revolutionary aspects of the American Revolution; second, it is quite helpless and irrelevant on the Civil War and the issues related

to it; and finally, it disposes us to turn away from one
of the most significant facts of American social life
—the racial, ethnic, and religious conflict with
which our history is saturated.[26]

Hofstadter's attention to racial and social conflict as
"one of the most significant facts of American social life"
attests to the impact of the successive confrontations,
riots, and revolts of the sixties which were rooted in the
upward struggle of various minority groups. For some
younger historians, sympathetic identification with (and
participation in) these struggles has led to an interest
in the activities and oppressions of other disadvantaged
and deviant groups in the American past. An example is
the effort of Jesse Lemisch to appraise the American
Revolution "from the bottom up," on the supposition that
"The history of the powerless, the inarticulate, the poor
has not yet begun to be written because they have been
treated no more fairly by historians than they have been
treated by their contemporaries."[27]
     This sympathetic role-taking on the part of the con-
flict historian points to a salient feature of his paradigm
of history—namely, his positive conception of human
nature. Common to virtually all the expressions and explorations of the new school is its repudiation of the
passive image of man implicit in much of postwar history,
and its espousal of an affirmative view of man which
emphasizes his resourcefulness, rationality, and responsibility. Thus, Lemisch has interpreted the American Revolution as an ideological battleground between contesting
assumptions of the nature of human nature:

     While the Loyalists themselves may not have too
     many friends, their accents—manipulation, propa-
     ganda, and the mindlessness of the people—reign
     largely unchallenged, albeit in somewhat different

language, in the recent historiography of the American Revolution. Perhaps underlying this remarkable congruence is a modern lack of faith in man, echoing the Loyalists' dim view of human nature. . . .

The American Revolution can best be re-examined from a point of view which assumes that all men are created equal and rational, and that since they can think and reason they can make their own history. These assumptions are nothing more nor less than the democratic credo.[28]

Another "engaged" historian of the new generation, Norman Pollock, has made a similar charge regarding the psychological pessimism of historians and others in the Cold War period: "As I see it, the essence of the Enlightenment heritage, the affirmation of the rationality of man and the confidence in his ability to make the world over, is being desiccated under the glaring sun of Cold War stresses. . . . the chief casualty in this ambivalent process has been our faith in human potentiality."[29]

As these remarks suggest, the philosophical commitment of historians of the New Left is to a version of radical humanism—one which emphasizes the classic themes of freedom, equality, and human dignity, and interprets the historian's role as that of a moral critic performing what Beard called an act of faith. In this perspective the issue is not *whether* writers of history import a point of view or "bias" into their work—that issue is taken as settled—but rather *what* assumptions and beliefs about the human possibility are contained in the point of view. Thus, one of the leading exponents of conflict history, Staughton Lynd, has protested against the traditional deterministic treatment of the past which "made man an object of history rather than a maker of it," and has called attention to the capacities of "human energy and striving" in the efforts of men to accomplish self-determined goals. "How would the work of the historian be different," he asks, "if man's existential freedom to choose became the historian's point of departure?"[30]

If in this view the central theme of human history is conflict, the central theme of human behavior is *freedom*. Man as the subject of history is a responsible moral agent, free within the boundaries of biology and culture to shape his own career and make his future; and his history is therefore properly the story of liberty, as Croce maintained a generation ago and Hegel proclaimed a century before.[31] Moreover, it is not only the subject of history who is an actor; so also is the "creator" of history, the historian himself—in the sense of seeking and interpreting, questioning and questing in the graveyards of the past, motivated by involvement in the present and concern for the future. As Lynd writes, "The past is ransacked, not for its own sake, but as a source of alternative models of what the future might become."[32]

In two influential essays of the sixties on the subject of historiography—one, by John Higham, written early in the decade, and the other, by Richard Hofstadter, written toward its end—the same conclusion was drawn as to the highest calling of the professional historian: It is that of "moral critic." Higham, observing that with the subsidence of the progressive impulse and the ascendancy of the conservative frame of reference "scholarship is threatened with a moral vacuum," maintained that the time was at hand for a new and more disciplined ethical imperative—"a scholarship engaged in a more widely ranging and a subtler moral criticism than American professional historians have yet undertaken."[33] The new moral history would take seriously the values men have lived by and died for in the course of history, and would not shrink from critical judgment but accept its own considered "moral insight" as a positive advantage to scholarship rather than an irrelevant bias to be neutralized or expunged. "In the simplest sense," wrote Higham, "the historian commits to moral criticism all the resources of his human condition. He derives from moral criticism an enlarged and disciplined sensitivity to what men ought to have done, what they might have done, and what they achieved."[34]

Like Higham, Hofstadter was aware of the risks of activism and engagement on the part of the historian—especially the cardinal sin of losing "respect for the integrity, the independence, the pastness, of the past." But he concluded that the case for the "historian *engagé*" was, on the record, strong enough to outweigh the risks of partisanship and passion.

> But the leading interpreters of America have also been, in this extended sense of the word, *engagé*—they have been committed to the historical realization of certain civic values, even in some cases to specific ends. . . . At their best, the interpretative historians have gone to the past with some passionate concern for the future; and somehow—the examples of Tocqueville and Henry Adams may encourage us—they have produced from the inner tensions of their minds an equipoise that enables them to superimpose upon their commitment a measure of detachment about the past, even to reconcile themselves to having knowledge without power.[35]

The case for the historian as moral critic, presented by these two seasoned professionals, was not intended to encourage a rush to judgment in the portrayal of past events and personalities. In fact, it was addressed not so much to the true believers of the New Left (or the Old Right) as to the more numerous unbelievers of the devitalized Center, whose overweening concern to neutralize passions, to rationalize conflict, to psychoanalyze motives, and to demythologize movements was leading them to homogenize history itself. In so doing, of course, far from escaping a moral posture, they were forcefully if unwittingly imposing one: namely, the amoral morality of complacency.

The appeal for a moral history was, and is, an argument for the relevance of instructed judgment and what Bruno Bettelheim called "the informed heart." It represents an implicit acceptance, not of the entire fervent manifesto of the New Left, but of the central tenet of the conflict school of historiography: its conviction that the past, like the present, is a panorama of issues confronted and of critical choices made or declined by men who were pulled by conscious purposes as well as pushed by exterior or ulterior forces. In assessing the clash of interests and values, the moral historian becomes himself a participant as well as an observer: He is *engaged.* If he cannot affect the outcome of events in history, he can affect their consequences *as* history: the history he composes as an act of faith in the present.

CHAPTER 10

MAN IN SOCIETY:
Beyond Utopia

The competition between contrasting ideological and theoretical frameworks which has characterized the study of American history in recent decades finds a remarkably close parallel in the neighboring terrain of sociology. In both cases a dominant paradigm emphasizing continuity, coherence, and consensus came of age after World War II and held the field almost uncontested until the sixties— when it came immediately and powerfully under challenge by an alternative paradigm centered upon the phenomenon of conflict. In both cases, also, the former framework (known as "system" in sociology) was attacked for its alleged conservatism and neutrality toward values, as well as for its failure to account for and accommodate the forces of change. In both cases, finally, the former model has been held mainly by older scholars while the latter model has been championed predominantly (but not at all exclusively) by younger ones.

The similarities—in substance, language, and tone— between the two simultaneous debates suggest that the two fields of scholarship have been arguing about the same things—with almost exactly the same results. Although the disputants in neither discipline have seemed to notice (or perhaps have not wished to notice) the existence of a parallel controversy in the other, the issues have been drawn in terms so similar as to make many of the arguments virtually interchangeable from one field to the other. Thus, Irving Louis Horowitz, defining the sociological framework of the debate in 1962, entitled his article "Consensus, Conflict, and Co-operation," and wrote in terms that would have needed little translation for contemporary historians:

> Few words in the vocabulary of contemporary sociology appear as soothing or as reassuring as consensus. The chain of agreeable associations of the term symbolize the final mating of the science of sociology and a theory of social equilibrium. . . . Specifically it must be asked whether the movement away from traditional theories of conflict and conflict resolution represents a genuinely new stage in the secularization of social science or is in fact a narrowing down of the field brought about by social pressures.[1]

The term "consensus," as used by sociologists, has its origin in a distinctive body of theory (indeed of "Grand Theory," as C. Wright Mills was to label it[2]) which made its first appearance in the thirties and grew to be the dominant framework of sociological thought in the decade of the fifties. It is the theory of *functionalism,* or structural-functionalism, and its central metaphor is that of *system.* The image of system (derived from the sciences) and the concept of functionalism (borrowed from the toolbox of anthropology) both designate a school of thought associated primarily with the magisterial work of Talcott Parsons, and in particular with two of his major studies, published in 1951, *The Social System* and *Toward a General Theory of Action.*[3] In brief, the functionalist view of society portrays it as a system of interacting roles and interlocking institutions functionally related and geared to the maintenance of stability or equilibrium. The dominant concern is with order, an order based on the conformity of men to shared values; change and conflict, where recognized at all, tend to be perceived as deviations or breakdowns rather than as inherent social processes.

Although functionalism had been around for many years and had no particularly dramatic resonance for sociologists, it was the introduction of the image of *system*—and its sophisticated articulation by Parsons— that provided the nucleus or common denominator which could draw together a wide scattering of researches and speculations and bring about what Robert W. Friedrichs has termed the "paradigmatic consolidation" of sociology in the fifties. The concept brought with it the prestige, bordering on magic, accorded at the time to the development of cybernetics and computer science; thus it not only fulfilled the need felt by many sociologists for a unifying theoretical framework, but it promised a degree of precision, rigor, and respectability hitherto achieved only by the hard sciences and sorely missed by those intent upon the construction of an objective and complete science of society.

There was also something more: The coincidence of the idea and the climate of opinion. As with the similar notion of consensus in the field of history, the image of the system in sociology—intricately equilibrated and ultimately harmonious—was bred and nurtured in the postwar atmosphere of general retreat from conflict and return to "normalcy" discussed in earlier pages. The relevance of the spirit of the age to the rise of the new sociology has been well described by Friedrichs:

A combination of factors—the startlingly smooth transition from a wartime economy to the material

reconstruction of Europe . . . open-ended prosperity
and the return to the homilies of family, education,
and Eisenhower—all united to underwrite an era of
unparalleled conformity and commitment to the
status quo. . . . It was a period in the life history of
the American intellectual that provided every kind of
subtle support the system advocate might wish for a
paradigm whose point of return was dictated by the
relative equilibrium that was the image's unstated
premise. An increasingly prosperous stability—professional as well as civic—conditioned the sociological as well as the lay mind, tempting the former to
perceive in system and its operative theoretical
model, functionalism, an image and a posture that
might justify the new faith in an ordered transition
from one equilibrium to another.[4]

The Parsonian model of the social system—formal,
abstract, coherent, and all-embracing in a manner not
encountered since the era of metaphysical cosmologies
(Hegel, Comte, Spencer) a century before—swept the
field of sociology almost without opposition. By 1959
Kingsley Davis, in his presidential address to the American Sociological Association, felt secure in announcing
that functionalism and Academic Sociology had virtually
become one and the same thing, and a few years later a
national survey of American sociologists revealed that
an overwhelming majority (some 80 percent) might be
counted as believers.[5] To be sure, there were countervailing forces and disparate approaches in the field all
along—prominent among them the Marxist and the sym-
bolic-interactionist[6]—but the impression is irresistible
that the temper of the times and the power of the paradigm combined to elevate the system-functionalist theory
of society to a position of undoubted, if not quite unchallenged, predominance. Like psychological behavior-

ism in the twenties, sociological functionalism in the fifties was an idea whose time had come.

Like classical behaviorism, also, the functionalist portrait of the social system contained within it, unacknowledged and possibly unintended, a distinctly conservative ideology providing theoretical validation for the institutions of social control and constraint, along with a kind of academic absolution (to use Peter Odegard's phrase) for the operations and manipulations of the corporate society. To be sure, this was a latent rather than a manifest function of the theory; the peculiarly high level of abstraction of the analysis (so high as to be arcane to specialists and impenetrable to outsiders) precluded any reference to actual societies, living or dead; and while "values" and "actions" were described and catalogued at length, they were never judged. The Parsonian theory, declaring itself value-free and ethically neutral, played no favorites. But in fact the ideal-typical model of the social system, as a host of critics were to point out, was not chastely descriptive but normative as well; it was not value-free but value-drenched. Its homeostatic model of the efficient social-cybernetic system (which seemed to many to enact Herbert Spencer's Social Statics) presented a standard of societal health, and accordingly of unhealth—one of normality and harmony versus abnormality and deviance—by virtue of its equation of the goals of the system with the good of its human components. Like his Harvard colleague B. F. Skinner, Parsons focused his attention upon the questions of stability and survival of the systematic society—never facing the question of whether or when it might better be scuttled. Like Skinner, also, Parsons adumbrated a utopia in which the imperatives of the society (whoever might assign them or whatever their policy content might be) were internalized as "shared values" by all of its members, thereby obviating conflict and assuring the permanence of the regime. In this empyrean of automatic consensus and conditioned spontaneity, where freedom is the recognition of functional necessities, the customary political issues of liberty and power, democracy and despotism, have been somehow transcended. As Horowitz has written:

> Consensus theory has led to such a stress on continuities and similarities in the life of an industrial complex that all real differences between democracy and autocracy, ruling and being ruled, exploiting and being exploited, are eliminated—in theory at least. . . . Consensus becomes the ideological celebration of the corporate personality, possessing a reality that transcends human society as such.[7]

The idea of man which underlies this vision of systematic society is not difficult to make out; it is what Dennis Wrong has termed the "oversocialized view of man" within an "overintegrated view of society."[8] Although Parsons' social construct is predicated on a theory of "action," and the individuals who inhabit his universe are designated as "actors," the springs of their action are located outside them; they are capable, at least when behaving normally and properly, only of acting with (never against) the system. Once again functionalist sociology parallels behaviorist psychology; it was Skinner, but it may as well have been Parsons, who said that man never acts upon his world: his world acts upon him. Alvin W. Gouldner's judgment on the Parsonian psychology is pointed: "Man is a hollowed-out, empty being filled with substance only by society. Man thus is seen as an entirely *social* being, and the possibility of conflict between man and society is thereby reduced. Man now has and is nothing of his own that need be counterposed to society."[9]

Given the accent of this theory on the needs of the overarching system rather than of the humans who inhabit it—and, indeed, given the one-dimensional view of man which limits his existence to the shadowy performance of "roles"—it is not surprising that there is no consideration of the values of the *person*: freedom, dignity, privacy, responsibility, even rationality itself. On the other hand, there is vast and favorable discussion of agencies and devices of "social control" and "adjustment" organized for the purpose of transforming deviance into conformity. In the Parsonian utopia, as Wayne Hield has observed, "Man is a helpless creature to be adapted and adjusted to the *status quo* or what is called 'social control.' Evidence of conflict or tension or anything which might be considered 'compulsive' and motivated by a sense of inadequacy prompts the social scientist to fit him into the ubiquitous 'social equilibrium.' "[10]

Hield's critical essay, published originally in 1954 in Britain under the title "The Study of Change in Social Science," was perhaps the first shot in the counterattack upon the functionalist consensus theory in sociology. But it was a shot heard round the professional world; for it struck forcefully at the soft underbelly of the system model: namely, its inability to come to terms with the stubborn fact of *change*—not just technical readjustment and self-correction, but fundamental change in society. Before the decade was out—even before the redignification of social change and conflict in the atmosphere of the sixties—other formidable critiques took up the work of undermining the theoretical foundations of the social system. One of the earliest was Ralf Dahrendorf's assertion of its utopian unreality;[11] another was Barrington Moore's attack upon its "new scholasticism";[12] still another, perhaps the most influential, was C. Wright Mills's vivid and provocative assault upon its "Grand Theory." Mills's volume of 1959, *The Sociological Imagination*, stands out as the forerunner of numerous radical-humanistic critiques of Establishment Sociology which were to emerge with increasing frequency and ferocity during the sixties. Indeed, two of the major critiques—Irving L. Horowitz's *The New Sociology* and Maurice Stein and Arthur Vidich's *Sociology on Trial*—were dedicated to, and plainly inspired by, Mills. Both his critical content, directed at the conservative implications of system theory, and his slashing polemical style set the pattern for much subsequent dissent from the consensual society as ordained by Parsons.

Mills's radical humanism was grounded in a definite idea of man—one which conveyed respect for the human person and appreciation for the human possibility, and accordingly was alert to those institutions and arrangements of power which tended toward the domination and diminution of personality. This humanistic commitment found expression in a set of questions which Mills believed to be fundamental to sociological inquiry:

> . . . What varieties of men and women now prevail in this society and in this period? And what varieties are coming to prevail? In what ways are they selected and formed, liberated and repressed, made sensitive and blunted? What kinds of "human nature" are revealed in the conduct and character we observe in this society in this period? And what is the meaning for "human nature" of each and every feature of the society we are examining?[13]

Recognizing that men often feel trapped and driven by coercive forces working through them, Mills repudiated the dictum of Freudians like Ernest Jones that man's chief danger is his own unruly nature and the dark forces pent up within him. "On the contrary: 'man's chief danger' today lies in the unruly forces of contemporary society itself, with its alienating methods of production, its enveloping techniques of political domination, its international anarchy—in a word, its pervasive transformations of the very 'nature' of man and the conditions and aims of his life."[14]

Mills's engaged sociology, demonstrated during the fifties in such trenchant analyses of American institutions as *White Collar* and *The Power Elite*,[15] represented the primary model and precedent for the proliferation of radical studies in the next decade. The immediate trigger for these studies, of course, was the abruptly altered mood of the nation, with its across-the-board challenge to applied sociology: the rediscovery of poverty and the inauguration of community action programs; the radicalization of the civil rights movement and the emergence of a variety of militant liberationist groups; the rise of the youth counterculture and the reappraisal of delinquency, dropping out, and drug use; the feminist revolution; and, above and beneath everything else, the repercussions of the Vietnam War. Within a few years' time, more was happening of social and political significance than had occurred before in the space of a full generation. The effect of it all, in the minds of younger scholars at least, was to put sociology on trial—and to indict the consensus theory of functionalism as irrelevant, incompetent, and irresponsible.

The New Left that rose swiftly and spread widely throughout the field took a variety of forms, mainly centered on the practical side in programs of action and advocacy, and on the theoretical side in a general reinstatement of conflict as the fundamental fact of social life. A typical statement of the radical case was this proclamation of the Sociology Liberation Front in 1968:

The liberal conservative bias of our "theory" exaggerates consensus, ignores conflict, and assumes that

everything can be settled with a little communication, a little patience, and a lot of good will. There
is more of a prayer than a theory, reflecting not
reality but the hopes of our own social class. In the
illusion that we can be responsible members of
society and yet above its petty quarrels, we have
abstained from our moral duty to speak out against
the forces of repression in our society. The reactionary nature of our government becomes "beyond the
scope of our field." But silence means consent, and
by not speaking out we are speaking up for the
status quo.[16]

If Mills was the prophet of the new radicalism in
sociology, Herbert Marcuse has been its major philosophical spirit on the basis of his formidable critique of
the postmodern technological society in *One-Dimensional
Man*, published in 1964.[17] Although Marcuse's idiosyncratic amalgam of Marx and Freud produced a social
analysis which was forbiddingly pessimistic (and composed in a Teutonic terminology of Hegelian dialectics
almost as dense as the prose of Parsons), it also provided
an ingenious foundation for a genuinely critical alternative—a standpoint of "negation" which could not be confused with liberal reformism. (This critical posture, dramatized by Marcuse as the "Great Refusal," was subsequently
reinforced by Theodore Roszak as the hallmark of the Dissenting Academy.[18]) Moreover, the pall of pessimism
which hung over Marcuse's earlier book was transformed
within a few years into an almost ecstatic affirmation of
an impending revolution based on the new sensibility and
liberated consciousness of the radical youth movement.[19]
  The restoration of conflict theory and the resurgence
of radical thought in sociology took other and less militant, but potentially more enduring, forms of expression
during the sixties and early seventies. Not only was there

a revival of interest in the Marxian tradition, stimulated by the predominantly Marxist orientation of the academic left in Europe; interest was also renewed in another distinctive tradition of conflict theory associated with the name of Georg Simmel, much of whose pioneering work at the turn of the century had not become available in English until 1955.[20] Still another approach to conflict which made new converts was that of Lewis Coser, whose *The Functions of Social Conflict* was first published in 1956.

What all these varied perspectives held in common—and shared with their kindred spirits of conflict history—was the conviction that tension and change rather than order and continuity are the fundamental realities of social life. And the keynote of their concerted attack upon consensus sociology was that it fostered a conservative ideology all too ready to market its services to the highest commercial bidder, and so to make of sociology the legitimating and sanctioning agency of the new industrial state. (Particularly effective in driving home this charge was the work of Irving Louis Horowitz, notably in such articles as "Establishment Sociology" and "Sociology for Sale."[21])

If the emphasis on conflict and change characterizes the radical wing of the new sociology, its equally pronounced emphasis on the individual in society characterizes its humanistic commitment. Although it cannot be claimed that this recognition of the person—of man for himself—was an original discovery of the sixties, it is possible to argue that the occupational bias of "sociologism" has traditionally been the tendency to lose sight of the individual human being in the shadowy thicket of his social roles, associations, interactions, reference groups, cultures, systems, institutions, and a host of other hypostatized abstractions all larger than his life. It is not only the historical sense that, as critics often

remark, is chronically absent in sociology; it is the biographical sense as well—the feel for the idiographic
dimension of human existence along with the nomothetic,
the element of personal experience as distinguished from
collective behavior. Something of what (or who) is missing in conventional sociology is indicated by a comment
of Gouldner in reference to one such conceptual scheme:

> It is as if Parsons' social world consists of a series
> of partially overlapping circles of light; when the
> embodied person leaves one circle or social system
> he disappears, becoming visible again only after he
> enters and is "plugged into" the next circle. Parsons
> thus totally inverts the entire world of everyday
> experience. For, in that everyday world it is the em-
> bodied individual that is most continuously in evi-
> dence, and not the social systems in which he par-
> ticipates. Paradoxically, then, Parsons transforms
> the embodied individual from the most to the least
> visible. It is as if the obvious existence of people is
> an embarrassment; as his theoretical system devel-
> ops, . . . the embodied and socialized individual is
> lost from sight.[22]

What is remarkable, then, in the sociological literature
of the sixties is the simultaneous rediscovery of the
missing person (sometimes, one suspects, as an exercise
in serendipity) on the part of numerous investigators
representing widely varying perspectives. The young
radicals have found him in the clothing of the underdog,
the oppressed victim or excluded scapegoat; so, in a
somewhat different manner, have the exponents of the
informal sociology and ethnomethodology of everyday
encounter, such as Erving Goffman and Harold Garfinkel.[23] A new generation of symbolic interactionists,
made aware of this neglected tradition of social psychol-

ogy by the long-awaited publication of Herbert Blumer's definitive study,[24] have discerned the human individual in the form of the dialogical "self" as introduced generations earlier by G. H. Mead.

It is not difficult to perceive, in this convergence of perspectives upon the phenomenon of man, a general reaction among sociologists against the "oversocialized" conception of him contained in the reigning functionalist paradigm. But the reaction of the sixties had another side —against the "overscientific" formulation of theory and research, not only in the shape of Grand Theory, but in the numberless minuscule monographs of what Mills labeled "abstracted empiricism."[25] In the spreading mood of disenchantment with a technology gone pathogenic, science itself (or more properly scientism) was coming under attack as a "sacred cow."[26] Its infallibility was virtually demolished, and its authority seriously eroded, by a concatenation of events both practical and philosophical; and in particular its relevance to the understanding of human nature and conduct, at least as the sole reliable path to that understanding, had begun to be openly and effectively challenged.

The defection from Science opened the door of sociology to the return of humanism. During the decade a remarkable succession of writings appeared under the common rubric of humanistic sociology—ranging from Peter Berger's appeal for the incorporation of history and philosophy as intrinsic dimensions of sociology,[27] to Lewis A. Coser's and Leo Lowenthal's arguments for the relevance of the literary imagination,[28] to Robert A. Nisbet's eloquent case for "Sociology as an Art Form,"[29] to Stanford M. Lyman's and Marvin B. Scott's *Sociology of the Absurd*,[30] and, most powerfully and influentially of all, to the new school of "phenomenological sociology" with its sweeping assault upon the traditional rules of sociological method and its insistent respect for the common sense

and ordinary language (the popular culture) of everyday
life.[31]

The definitions of "humanism" in these diverse formulations of the proper study of society are varied in detail;
but the common thread running through all of them is an
appreciation of the "human imperative"[32] in sociological
inquiry—the inescapable presence of man himself at both
ends of the observation. With respect to the *subject* of
investigation, this means, as John R. Staude has put it,
that "humanistic sociology restores the individual person
to his rightful place as the principal agent of action.
[It sees] man as the creator of his own acts, with all the
uncertainty, ambiguity, dread, anxiety, and responsibility
that such freedom, choice, and decision imply."[33] With
respect to the investigator, the sociologist at work, this
implies an awareness of himself as a participant in the
process, a partner in the dialogue of inquiry—seen not
as a means to the neutralization of "anthropomorphic
subjectivity" but as a step toward more honest and therefore more effective engagement with his subject. It is in
this spirit that Gouldner has issued his famous appeal
for the creation of a "Reflexive Sociology": "The historical
mission of a Reflexive Sociology as I conceive it . . .
would be to *transform* the sociologist, to penetrate deeply
into his daily life and work, enriching them with new
sensitivities, and to raise the sociologist's self-awareness
to a new historical level."[34]

It is also Gouldner, appropriately, who has perceived
the further and higher step in the evolution of a humane
sociology: namely, that it will be a "moral sociology."[35]
For, in this view—more and more widely shared among
sociologists reflecting on the debates and directives of the
last decade—the higher calling of the science is not that
of indiscriminately describing all things social that are,
but rather that of selectively appraising *some* things social
which carry portent for what may be. Recognizing an

obligation not only to advance scientific knowledge but to advance human well-being, the moral sociologist—like his colleague the moral historian—will not fear to make choices and take sides, to venture judgments and assert positions. He will believe, with Gouldner, that his committed sociology "has, as a central part of its historical mission, the task of helping men in their struggle to take possession of what *is* theirs—society and culture—and of aiding them to know who they are and what they may want."[36]

What it comes down to, in the end, is an idea of man —an idea worth holding as an ideal.

At the conclusion of his comprehensive survey of the contemporary contest of ideologies and paradigms in sociology—and in the course of affirming that the field has begun to move forward from the neutral "priestly" mode of discourse to an openly engaged and "prophetic" posture—Robert W. Friedrichs puts the entire matter in perspective with this observation:

> The activities of sociologists as scientists, however, are always and in principle nested in a larger frame that includes the intrasubjective, the unique, and the existential. And it is because we are never able to extricate ourselves from that context, even when we take on the "role" of sociologist as scientist, that the image of man resident within the rhetoric of science may serve as a powerful tool in the service of a more fundamentally realistic and humane paradigm.[37]

CHAPTER 11

MAN IN PSYCHOLOGY:
Beyond Determinism

Both in history and sociology, as the preceding chapters have shown, there has occurred in recent years a progressive polarization of perspectives surrounding the interpretation of the American experience, past and present. In both disciplines a conservative pluralism or consensualism—what C. Wright Mills called the "theory of balance"[1]—has sought unsuccessfully to hold the field against an insurgent radical humanism: a theory of tension, change, and growth. Underlying the competition of viewpoints has been a fundamental if largely unacknowledged disagreement over the nature of man himself —his abilities, responsibilities, and possibilities. In short, the questions at issue in this great debate are not only historical and sociological, nor even ideological, but *psychological* as well.

If that is the case in the most social of the human studies, it would be surprising if there were not a parallel division and dispute at work in the most personal of the sciences of man. In fact, the division of opinion in psychology—of ideology and methodology, theory and therapy, assumption and aspiration—has, if anything, cut deeper and persisted longer than in other fields of study.

And in psychology, more explicitly than anywhere else, what is at issue is the nature and future of man.

If the main effort of nineteenth-century psychology can be characterized as the study of consciousness (experimentally in the tradition of Wundt and his heirs, philosophically in the tradition of James and Dewey[2]), the central feature of twentieth-century psychology may be defined as a "revolt against consciousness."[3] In actuality that revolt has taken two very different forms: those of behaviorism and Freudianism. We have already followed, in Chapter 6, the adventurous career of the behaviorist "psychology without a soul" from its classical beginnings as a businessman's psychology (Watson) to its contemporary apotheosis as psychotechnocracy (Skinner); and we have seen that, in all of its successive stages and variations—"through eras," as Sigmund Koch has labeled them, "of 'classical' behaviorism, neo-behaviorism, deflated neo-behaviorism, 'liberalized' neo-behaviorism, 'subjective' neo-behaviorism," and finally "neo-neo-behaviorism."[4]—there has been no recantation or retreat from the original dogma which asserts that, for the purposes of a scientific psychology, human consciousness is as irrelevant and incompetent as it is immaterial.

Freud, to be sure, came at the subject from the other end—from the inside rather than the outside. In the orthodox theory of psychoanalysis, consciousness was not so much repudiated as depleted and downgraded, both in scope and content; it was portrayed metaphorically as a small and precarious bastion in the realm of mind (Ego), perennially under attack on two separate fronts: from the unconscious and hostile forces of the Superego (depicted by Freud as a kind of enemy garrison or "fifth column" infiltrated into the mind by the surrounding culture), and from the equally unconscious and still more powerful forces of the Id (that "cauldron of seething excitements"[5]). We have examined, in Chapter 2, one aspect of Freud's theory of psychogenetic determinism: the conception of Thanatos, the aggression instinct, as "an innate, independent, instinctual disposition in man." Even aside from that dark vision, there was little in the Freudian scheme of things to support a view of man as, potentially and consciously, the master of himself and the maker of his destiny. Indeed, man was defined by Freud not in the active but in the passive mode: He was not master but mastered, not determining but determined. Man is "lived by the unconscious," said Freud (in agreement with Groddeck): "The deeply rooted belief in psychic freedom and choice . . . is quite unscientific and must give ground before the claims of a determinism which governs mental life."[6]

That quotation from Freud, virtually interchangeable with similar statements by Watson and Skinner, indicates the common denominator underlying the vast differences of the Freudian and behaviorist psychologies: namely, the idea of man as essentially passive and reactive, as the "victim-spectator" of blind forces beyond his control which shape his character and determine his conduct. It is not wholly coincidental that there should have emerged within a few years of one another, in the same climate of opinion, the two most popular and influential schools of psychology in the twentieth century—one which was to dominate the academy and the laboratory, the other which was to dominate the clinic and consulting room. Both were responsive to the scientific *Zeitgeist* of the period with its demands for objectivity, causal analysis, and at least a pretense of ethical neutrality. And both, as it now appears in retrospect, were symptomatic of that general decline of confidence in the personal powers of rationality and responsibility which, after World War I if not earlier, came to characterize the modern temper.

Rollo May, in a section of *Love and Will* headed "The Undermining of Personal Responsibility," delineates the way in which Freud "formulated a new image of man that shook to the very foundations Western man's emotional, moral, and intellectual self-image . . . [through] an unavoidable undermining of will and decision and an undercutting of the individual's sense of responsibility." The great practical significance of this new theory of human nature, according to May, is that "It reflected, rationalized, and played into the hands of modern man's most pervasive tendency—which has became almost an endemic disease in the middle of the twentieth century—to see himself as passive, the willy-nilly product of the powerful juggernaut of psychological drives." And he adds: "Great men . . . *reflect* what is emerging from the depths of their culture and, having reflected, then interpret and mold what they find." Freud, for all his genius, was a child of his time; but, with his genius, he was also a shaker of his time and a shaper of times to come. After him and because of him, as May concludes, "man's image of himself will never be the same again. . . ."[7]

That image—nurtured and conditioned in the behaviorist's laboratory at the same time as it was inculcated on the analyst's couch—has been, until very recently, so completely predominant throughout the field as to gain consensual endorsement as the true and abiding image of "Psychological Man." Nor is that all; those who make this claim often go on to stake a grander claim: namely, that the image of Psychological Man is the authentic representation of twentieth-century humanity, the appropriate model and "character ideal" for our time. Thus, Philip Rieff, in his admiring study of Freud, heralds the emergence of "the psychological man" as the worthy successor of the three ideal-typical character models which are seen as symbolizing respective stages of Western civilization: political man, the product of classical antiquity; religious man, spawn of the Judeo-Christian tradition; and economic man, child of the Enlightenment and incarnation of modern liberalism. It would seem to be an occasion for celebration; but the announcement of the birth of this new man—the reproduction of ourselves and the personification of the future—is uttered more in resignation than rejoicing. Here is no new "Song of Myself": no hope of self-healing, no support of reason, no affirmation of the meaning of human existence, no encouragement to human ideals and aspirations. To embrace Psychological Man, we are told by Rieff in uncompromising terms, is to accept the fact that the human condition is incurable.

Freudianism closes off the long-established quarrel of Western man with his own spirit. It marks the archaism of the classical legacy of political man, for the new man must live beyond reason—reason having proved no adequate guide to his safe conduct through the meaningless experience of life. It marks the repudiation of the Christian legacy of the religious man, for the new man is taught to live a little beyond conscience—conscience having proved no adequate guide to his safe conduct through life, and furthermore to have added absurd burdens of meaning to the experience of life. Finally, psychoanalysis marks the exhaustion of the liberal legacy represented historically in economic man, for now men must live with the knowledge that their dreams are by function optimistic and cannot be fulfilled. Aware at last that he is chronically ill, psychological man may nevertheless end the ancient quest of his predecessors for a healing doctrine. His experience with the latest one, Freud's, may finally teach him that every cure must expose him to new illness.[8]

It may be so. The twentieth century may in truth be the "Age of Psychology,"[9] and its appropriate paradigm therefore that of Psychological Man. But now a new doubt arises: *Who is Psychological Man?* For the classical image propounded by the psychoanalytic and behaviorist schools alike—the image of Manipulated Man, the passive victim of mindless forces working through him, whether from without or from within—no longer holds the field uncontested. An alternative idea of man, not merely different from, but deliberately opposed to, the classical image, has been emerging in psychology over recent years with increasing clarity and mounting support. It is the counterpart of that radical humanism whose insurgent career we have traced in the neighboring fields of sociology and history; and it travels, appropriately enough, under the banner of humanistic psychology.

The term "humanistic psychology" refers to an intramural orientation which first made its appearance in the fifties as a loose assembly of like-minded psychologists and has since evolved into an academic movement at once interdisciplinary in range and international in membership. For all its diverse and ambiguous accretions over subsequent years (some of which, in the excitement of exploring the farther reaches of the "human potential," have confused its purpose and diluted its intellectual content), humanistic psychology still rests centrally upon the conceptual foundation laid down by Abraham H. Maslow and a handful of colleagues under the rhetorical title of the "Third Force."[10] That label has the virtue of pinpointing the essential distinction of the humanistic approach from the two prevailing "forces" of the psychological Establishment—behaviorism and Freudianism. Although these two orthodoxies differ profoundly from each other in most respects, they are perceived by humanists as equivalent in their portrayal of man as a fundamentally helpless agent of ulterior or exterior circumstances beyond his control. Against this deterministic assumption, the deepest convictions and commitments of those who style themselves humanists hold out for an active center or "proprium" within the human organism, an element of resourcefulness and creativity— whether given in direct experience, discovered in empirical experiment, deduced from the logic of emergent evolution (self-consciousness), or grounded in an act of faith. They are convinced, in Mortimer Adler's phrase, of "the difference of man and the difference it makes."[11] In short, humanistic psychology has proposed a conception of human nature as active rather than reactive, and of human conduct as normally conscious and responsible rather than unconscious and involuntary.

Another way to put the issue is that in contrast to the two prevalent forms of determinism in psychology—the environmental and the instinctual—humanistic psychology has advanced the existentialist hypothesis of *self-determinism*. For while there is no single body of theory which clearly predominates in the humanist persuasion, but rather a convergence of various traditions and schools of thought, the movement owes a crucial debt to existentialist psychology and philosophy—as well as to the "ex-Freudians" (Adler, Jung, Rank) and the "neo-Freudians" (Fromm, Horney, Sullivan) in psychoanalysis, the "non-Freudians" in psychotherapy (Rogers, May), the "personalists" in personality theory (Maslow, Allport, Murray, Kelley), and the "interpersonalists" in social psychology (Dewey, Cooley, Mead).[12] The common denominator of these and other contributory sources is the postulate of the purposive (existential) self, of the responsible human person conceived in terms both of his uniqueness and his wholeness—in a word, his *presence*. This recognition of man-in-person, as distinguished from man-in-general, goes to the heart of the difference between the humanistic perspective and the various mechanistic and positivistic psychologies which have traditionally held the field. And it is this personalism—conveyed with particular force and grace by Allport[13]—which has found increasing acceptance among the new generation of psychologists and social scientists for whom the categorical imperatives of alienation, other-directedness, mass society, cybernetics, technocracy, and the like have had existential as well as intellectual meaning. In short, it has been the resistance of humanistic psychology to the challenge of the corporate state and the technological society —its therapeutic response to "eco-spasm" and "future shock"—which has brought it within the ambience of the new academic counterculture; and in turn it has instructed and disciplined that new consciousness with its spirited defense of responsibility and intentionality.

In doing so, it has acted as the psychology of *humanism*—the appropriate expression for the Age of Anxiety of an ancient tradition in the history of human thought. The fact that humanism has had diverse and inconsistent interpretations over the centuries does not diminish its legitimacy, for the very meaning of the term varies necessarily and properly with sea changes in cultural consciousness and moral sensibility. Thus, without laboring the point, it is not implausible that Renaissance humanism, for example, should have found its focus in attention to the conditions and characteristics of man *qua* man, in contradistinction to the religious humanism of the medieval synthesis (which regarded humanity as the highest order of created things but subordinate to the Divine Purpose); and that scientific humanism, carrying on the warfare between science and theology in the Age of Progress, should have augmented this distinction to the point of becoming all but indistinguishable from atheism. To attempt to define "humanism," in other words, is to seek to identify the particular features of the human form and the human spirit which at a given moment appear most prominent and precious. The act of definition (which in this case is also one of self-definition) is therefore normative as well as descriptive; it not only points to something real, it points with pride and views with alarm. That which is deemed most definitive of man —hence central to humanism—is that which is felt to be most valuable and vulnerable, as well as venerable, in the human condition.[14]

Something of the contemporary currency of humanism has been indicated by Joseph Wood Krutch in an essay entitled "Meaning for 'Humanism' ":

> In this sense, a humanist is anyone who rejects the attempt to describe or account for man wholly on the basis of physics, chemistry, and animal behavior. He is anyone who believes that will, reason, and purpose are real and significant; that value and justice are aspects of a reality called good and evil and rest upon some foundation other than custom; that consciousness is so far from being a mere epiphenomenon that it is the most tremendous of actualities; that the unmeasurable may be significant; or, to sum it all up, that those human realities which sometimes seem to exist only in the human mind are the perceptions, rather than merely the creations, of the mind. He is, in other words, anyone who says that there are more things in heaven and earth than are dreamed of in the positivist attitude.[15]

That interpretation makes clear how far the new humanism in psychology and the social studies has moved from the doctrinaire posture of the older humanism which was founded upon the rock of positivist science and technological progress. The priorities have not only been reshuffled but virtually reversed at crucial points. Thus, the values which were chiefly incorporated (not to say enshrined) in the old scientific humanism—objectivity, ethical neutrality, reductive causal analysis, prediction, and control—have been critically challenged and relegated to the periphery of attention, when they have not been rejected outright, by the new psychological humanism. Still more significantly, those aspects of the human experience which were systematically devalued and discredited by the old dispensation—such as consciousness, commitment, choice, spontaneity, responsibility, love and will, freedom and dignity—have been rediscovered, refurbished, and restored to a central position in the vocabulary of humanistic psychology. The preliminary and general task is seen to be that of "discovering man in psychology" (to use Frank Severin's title);[16] more specifically, it implies an attitude of regard—"unconditional regard," in Carl Rogers' famous phrase—for the human person as a *subject* rather than object (as end rather than means), and as an irreducible organic *whole* rather than a mechanical assemblage of parts. This recovery of the missing person in psychology—the return of the human actor to the stage of his own drama—carries with it other commitments and consequences. The concept of the whole man conveys a recognition of "full-humanness," of the affective and conative dimensions of everyday life as constructive rather than destructive powers, indivisible components of the total process of *minding*: that is, choosing, responding, relating, and acting upon the world.

Related to the concept of holism are two other dimensions of humanistic psychology—its twin emphases upon what may be called the *normal* and the *sociable*. The first distinguishes the humanistic alternative from the Freudian tradition with its heavy stress upon the "abnormal"; whereas the phenomena of everyday life constituted for Freud the domain of psychopathology, for the humanistic psychologist they are valued in themselves as authentic samples of individual experience in all its rich diversity—its peaks and nadirs, ordinary pleasures and extraordinary yearnings, predictable routines and unpredictable contingencies. The universal experiences of suffering and dread, grief and loss, anxiety and loneliness, are not ignored or eliminated but reappraised and re-presented within a wider definition of what it means to be fully and *normally* human. "The basic message," as Clark Moustakas (a pioneer of the humanist movement) has put it, "is that loneliness is a condition of human life, an experience of being human which enables the individual to sustain, extend and deepen his humanity."[17]

But it is not only the depths and valleys of the existential terrain that are accommodated within the new portrait of the humanly normal; more sharply and distinctively, the peaks and "pluses" of personal experience are —almost for the first time in modern behavioral science —recognized as real and studied as significant. More than any other single spokesman, it was Abraham Maslow who, in a succession of highly original and provocative writings, laid bare the morbid preoccupation of psychology with "pessimistic, negative and limited conceptions" of human nature along with its attendant neglect of such equally human experiences as love, ecstasy, gaiety, exuberance, the joy of creativity, and the happiness of pursuit. Where psychology in its positivist and Freudian phases had "voluntarily restricted itself to only half of its rightful jurisdiction, and that the darker, meaner half," Maslow undertook (as Calvin S. Hall and Gardner Lindzey were to summarize his work) "to supply the other half of the picture, the brighter, better half, and to give a portrait of the whole man."[18] Like Jung before him, Maslow wondered why we should have come to regard as psychological realism an obsession with the "shadow" side of human nature while denying the circumambience of light: "This is not a call for optimism. Rather it is a demand for realism in the best sense of the word. It is ridiculous to identify realism with darkness, misery, pathology and breakdown, as so many contemporary novelists have done. Happiness is as real as unhappiness; gratification is as real as frustration; love is as real as hostility."[19]

There is an important consequence to this affirmation of the normality of ordinary existence. If consciousness is as real as unconsciousness; if the light of reason is as important in the conduct of life as the dark at the top of the stairs; if the pull of purpose is no less motivational than the push of subterranean drives—if, in short, man is at some time a conscious actor and moral agent in the working out of his destiny—then a remarkable about-face is in order in psychology. The science of man, to paraphrase Kurt Riezler, must begin with respect for the subject matter. In place of the behaviorist axiom that the causes of man's conduct are to be found in his environment, and of the Freudian axiom that those causes are to be found in his unconscious, the new psychology of humanism proposes the outrageous hypothesis that man may have a directive hand in his own life, that he may know something about what he is doing and seeking, and that (in Allport's phrase) he has a "right to be believed."[20] This shift of focus from object to subject, from causal analysis to reasonable dialogue, constitutes a shock of recognition; for now the human person, emerging from the shadows at last, advances to be recognized.

An important corollary of the humanistic commitment to normality is the affirmation of sociability as an intrinsic, almost a defining, characteristic of man's nature. While this is not a novel notion in the history of thought, neither is it the dominant motif in modern scholarship with its recurrent themes of aggression and competition, alienation and mutual aversion. Even where man is regarded as a "social animal," it is less often his *sociability* —i.e., his capacity to love, to enter into dialogue, to enhance personal growth through significant relationships—than his vulnerability to *socialization*, defined as the internalizing of cultural norms, that receives major attention. (Hence the "oversocialized" view of man which Dennis Wrong and other critics have identified as the persisting bias of sociologists from Durkheim to Parsons.) The distinction is not merely terminological but conceptual. Nearly all creatures great and small, from coral to cattle, from ants to anthropoids, are "social" animals; but human sociability is mediated by the unique capacity for symbolic interaction: for the meeting of minds. What this difference implies is that the product of that human intercourse is not *less* individuality but *more*—not the melding of I and Thou into an undifferentiated mass or collectivity but the enhancement of each as a distinctive identity ("the rediscovery," in Dilthey's phrase, "of the I in the Thou").

The theoretical sources of this recognition of the sociable dimension of human experience, ranging from biology to philosophy, represent a striking integration of perspectives. Primary among them is the interactionist or transactionalist school in American social psychology, first developed by Dewey and Mead and introduced into psychiatry (as "the science of interpersonal relations") by Sullivan.[21] In European psychoanalysis, the theme was originally emphasized by Adler (under the rubric of "social feeling"), further elaborated by Rank (as "relationship"), and subsequently amplified by the neo-Freudians Fromm and Horney into a comprehensive theory of personal growth through "relatedness" and "productive love."[22] Another influential contribution has been Cassirer's philosophy of symbolic forms, first published in three volumes and later popularized in *An Essay on Man*. (Cassirer's essential thesis is summed up in his comment on Socrates: "We may epitomize the thought of Socrates by saying that man is defined by him as that being who, when asked a rational question, can give a rational answer. Both his knowledge and his morality are comprehended in this circle. It is by this fundamental faculty, by this faculty of giving a response to himself and others, that man becomes a 'responsible' being, a moral subject."[23]) But perhaps the profoundest philosophical impact upon the thought of humanistic psychology has emanated from that large body of existential thinkers (Buber, Binswanger, Berdyaev, and Boss, to mention only the B's) who have defined the condition of man as "being-in-the-world" and "being-with-others." The existential psychology of Binswanger, Straus, Frankl, and others has had a direct influence upon humanistic psychotherapy, especially as interpreted by Rollo May;[24] and the existential philosophy of dialogue formulated by Buber in particular—with important variations on the part of Marcel, Tillich, Jaspers, and the later Camus—has had still wider and deeper reverberations in the work of American psychologists of humanism (notably that of Carl R. Rogers).[25]

The largest significance of these and other convergent streams of influence has been their clarification and fortification of the humanist idea of man as not just the socializing but the *caring* animal—the creature that not only talks but listens, not only commands but communes. It is in the expression of his inborn ability to *love*, as Fromm in particular has made us aware, that man is most fully and normally human; and the basic elements of mature love are "care, responsibility, respect, and knowledge."[26] In his affections and affiliations, his movement toward commitment and concern, man recovers his highest potentialities and therein discovers himself.

And, in much the same way, man is discovered in psychology. Like its humanistic counterparts in sociology and history, the new psychology begins and ends in an act of faith. Its starting point is a conception of human nature—an idea of man—not as a fully determinate and predictable "given" but as an open system of shifting parameters, live options, and indefinite possibilities of becoming; the fundamental faith of the humanist is that there is a self worthy of actualizing and a consciousness worthy of the task. Psychological Man as newly reconstructed is neither doomed by inner perversity to reenact the ritual murder of himself and others, nor damned by outer circumstances to react compulsively and "robopathically" to the operant cues of grand conditioners. To be sure, he may—individually or collectively—yet choose the damnation or the doom; for the freedom which is held out to him by the psychology of humanism carries no built-in guarantee of results, no insurance against failure of nerve. That is the fearful part of it. But there is a prayerful part as well: For among his options, we are just now ready to believe, man may choose himself. The final act of faith of the humanist is that, informed of the alternatives and aware of the consequences, he will.

NOTES

PREFACE

1. Bruno Bettelheim, "Joey: A Mechanical Boy," *Scientific American* (March 1959). Reprinted in Eric and Mary Josephson, eds., *Man Alone: Alienation in Modern Society* (New York: Dell, 1962), pp. 437–38.
2. John B. Watson, *Behaviorism* (Chicago: University of Chicago Press, 1958), p. 269.
3. Franz Kafka, "The Metamorphosis." Published in Franz Kafka, *The Penal Colony* (New York: Schocken Books, 1961), p. 67.
4. Ernest G. Schachtel, *Metamorphosis* (New York: Basic Books, 1959), p. 248.
5. B. F. Skinner, *Science and Human Behavior* (New York: Macmillan, 1953), p. 447.
6. William Faulkner (Nobel Prize award speech, 1950), in *Saturday Review* (February 3, 1951): 5–6.

INTRODUCTION

1. Arthur O. Lovejoy, *Reflections on Human Nature* (Baltimore: Johns Hopkins Press, 1961), p. 13.
2. *Ibid.*
3. For details on these and other opponents of the idea of mind, and the mind of ideas, see my *The Broken Image* (New York: Braziller, 1964), chaps. 1–3.

4. Pierre Teilhard de Chardin, *The Phenomenon of Man* (New York: Harper, 1959), p. 53.

5. H. J. Eysenck, *The Psychology of Politics* (New York: Praeger, 1954), p. 2.

6. Clark L. Hull, *Principles of Behavior: An Introduction to Behavior Theory* (New York: Appleton-Century, 1943), p. 25.

7. Robert O'Brien, Clarence C. Schrag, and Walter T. Martin, eds., *Readings in General Sociology* (Boston: Houghton Mifflin, 3d ed., 1964), p. 15. Cited in Robert W. Friedrichs, *A Sociology of Sociology* (New York: Free Press, 1970), p. 226.

8. *Ibid.*

9. *Ibid.*

10. H. Richard Niebuhr, *Radical Monotheism in Western Culture* (New York: Harper, 1960), pp. 139–40. Quoted in Friedrichs, *A Sociology of Sociology*, pp. 229–30.

11. See Matson, *The Broken Image*, pp. 251–56.

12. Peter L. Berger and Thomas Luckmann, *The Social Construction of Reality* (Garden City: Doubleday Anchor, 1967).

13. Cf. Michael Polanyi, *Personal Knowledge: Towards a Post-Critical Philosophy* (Chicago: University of Chicago Press, 1958).

14. Stewart E. Perry, *The Human Nature of Science* (New York: Free Press, 1966).

15. Louis Wirth, Preface to Karl Mannheim, *Ideology and Utopia* (New York: Harcourt, Brace, 1949), p. xxii.

16. Richard L. Means, *The Ethical Imperative: The Crisis in American Values* (Garden City: Doubleday, 1969).

17. Polanyi, *Personal Knowledge*, pp. 142f.; Arthur Koestler, *The Sleepwalkers* (New York: Macmillan, 1959).

18. Abraham H. Maslow, *The Psychology of Science* (New York: Harper and Row, 1966), p. 122.

19. Alvin W. Gouldner, *The Coming Crisis of Western Sociology* (New York: Basic Books, 1970).

20. Abraham H. Maslow, *Toward a Psychology of Being* (New York: Van Nostrand, 2d ed., 1968), p. iii.

21. Willis Harman, "The New Copernican Revolution," in

John F. Glass and John R. Staude, eds., *Humanistic Society* (Pacific Palisades, Calif.: Goodyear, 1972), pp. 99–105.

22. Friedrichs, *A Sociology of Sociology*, chap. 6.
23. Charles A. Reich, *The Greening of America* (New York: Random House, 1970); Philip Slater, *The Pursuit of Loneliness* (Boston: Beacon Press, 1970); Theodore Roszak, *The Making of a Counter Culture* (Garden City: Doubleday Anchor, 1968); Theodore Roszak, *Where the Wasteland Ends* (Garden City: Doubleday, 1972).
24. Maurice Friedman, *The Hidden Human Image* (New York: Delacorte, 1974).
25. Thomas Kuhn, *The Structure of Scientific Revolutions* (Chicago: University of Chicago, 1962). Cf. E. A. Burtt, *The Metaphysical Foundations of Modern Science* (Garden City: Doubleday Anchor, 1955).
26. Gouldner, *The Coming Crisis of Western Sociology*, p. 29.
27. Teilhard de Chardin, *The Phenomenon of Man*, p. 56.
28. Charles Horton Cooley, *Human Nature and the Social Order* (New York: Scribner's, 1902).
29. Means, *The Ethical Imperative*, p. 76.
30. Gouldner, *The Coming Crisis of Western Sociology*, p. 12.
31. See Karl Mannheim, *Ideology and Utopia* (New York: Harcourt, Brace, 1949); Erving Goffman, *The Presentation of Self in Everyday Life* (New York: Doubleday Anchor, 1959); Erving Goffman, *Relations in Public: Microstudies of the Public Order* (New York: Basic Books, 1971).
32. Lewis Mumford, *In the Name of Sanity* (New York: Harcourt, Brace, 1954), p. 60.

CHAPTER 1

1. J. Arthur Thomson, *Darwinism and Human Life* (1910), quoted in R. E. Park and E. W. Burgess, eds., *Introduction to the Science of Sociology* (Chicago: University of Chicago, 1921), pp. 512–13.
2. Marvin Harris, *The Rise of Anthropological Theory* (New York: Crowell, 1968), pp. 122–23.

3. Garrett Hardin, *Nature and Man's Fate* (New York: Mentor, 1959), p. 56.
4. Loren Eiseley, *Darwin's Century* (Garden City: Doubleday Anchor, 1961), p. 182.
5. Harris, *The Rise of Anthropological Theory*, pp. 125, 129.
6. Stanley Edgar Hyman, *The Tangled Bank: Darwin, Marx, Frazer and Freud as Imaginative Writers* (New York: Atheneum, 1962), p. 29.
7. *Ibid.*, p. 27.
8. *Ibid.*, p. 28. Emphasis added.
9. *Ibid.*, p. 26.
10. Harris, *The Rise of Anthropological Theory*, p. 117.
11. Henry D. Aiken, *The Age of Ideology* (New York: Mentor, 1956), p. 166.
12. Richard Hofstadter, "Discussion" (of an article by Erik Erikson), *American Journal of Psychiatry* (September 1965): 251.
13. *Ibid.* Emphasis added.
14. *Ibid.*, p. 252.
15. Eiseley, *Darwin's Century*, p. 335.
16. *Ibid.*, p. 336.
17. *Ibid.*, pp. 345–46.
18. Hofstadter, "Discussion," p. 251.
19. Richard Hofstadter, *Social Darwinism in American Thought* (New York: Braziller, 1959), p. 125.
20. Julian Huxley, Introduction, in Charles Darwin, *The Origin of Species* (New York: Mentor, 1958), p. xv.
21. G. Murray McKinley, *Evolution: Today and Tomorrow* (New York: Ronald, 1956), p. 69.
22. P. B. Medawar, *The Future of Man* (New York: New American Library, 1959), p. 92.
23. George Gaylord Simpson, *The Meaning of Evolution* (New York: Mentor, 1951), pp. 141–42.
24. Theodosius Dobzhansky, *Mankind Evolving* (New Haven: Yale, 1962), pp. 346–47.
25. Medawar, *The Future of Man*, pp. 94–95.
26. Margaret Mead, *Continuities in Cultural Evolution* (New Haven: Yale, 1964), p. 12.

27. C. H. Waddington, *The Nature of Life* (London: Allen & Unwin, 1961), p. 103.
28. E. A. Burtt, *The Metaphysical Foundations of Modern Science* (Garden City: Doubleday Anchor, 1955), p. 17.
29. R. G. Collingwood, *The Idea of Nature* (New York: Oxford, 1960), p. 1.
30. *Ibid.*, p. 9.
31. *Ibid.*, p. 10.
32. *Ibid.*
33. *Ibid.*, p. 13. Emphasis added.
34. Cf. Dobzhansky, *Mankind Evolving, passim.*
35. Theodosius Dobzhansky, *The Biological Basis of Human Freedom* (New York: Columbia, 1956).

CHAPTER 2

1. Sigmund Freud, *Civilization and Its Discontents* (London: Hogarth, 1930), pp. 102–103.
2. Sigmund Freud, *An Outline of Psychoanalysis* (New York: Norton, 1949), p. 20.
3. Sigmund Freud, *Beyond the Pleasure Principle* (London: Hogarth, 1920), p. 60.
4. Marthe Robert, *The Psychoanalytic Revolution: Sigmund Freud's Life and Achievement* (New York: Harcourt, Brace, and World, 1966), p. 329.
5. Freud, *Civilization and Its Discontents*, pp. 98–99.
6. *Ibid.*, pp. 85–86.
7. Otto Fenichel, "A Critique of the Death Instinct," in *Collected Papers*, 1st Series (New York: Norton, 1953). Cf. Clara Thompson, *Psychoanalysis: Evolution and Development* (New York: Grove, 1957), p. 191.
8. Leonard Berkowitz, *Aggression: A Social-Psychological Analysis* (New York: McGraw-Hill, 1962), p. 8.
9. John Dollard, et al., *Frustration and Aggression* (New Haven: Yale, 1939).
10. Abraham H. Maslow, *Motivation and Personality* (New York: Harper, 1954), p. 176.

11. Erich Fromm, *Man For Himself* (New York: Rinehart, 1947), p. 218. Cf. Fromm, *The Anatomy of Human Destructiveness* (New York: Holt, Rinehart and Winston, 1973), Appendix.

12. Harry Stack Sullivan, *The Interpersonal Theory of Psychiatry* (New York: Norton, 1953), pp. 213–14.

13. Thompson, *Psychoanalysis: Evolution and Development*, p. 54.

14. Floyd W. Matson, *The Broken Image* (New York: Braziller, 1964), p. 202.

15. John Seeley, *The Americanization of the Unconscious* (New York: Science House, 1967).

16. Norman O. Brown, *Love Against Death* (Wesleyan, 1959); Herbert Marcuse, *Eros and Civilization* (New York: Vintage, 1955); Lionel Trilling, *Freud and the Crisis of Our Culture* (Boston, 1955); Stanley Edgar Hyman, "Psychoanalysis and the Climate of Tragedy," in Benjamin Nelson, ed., *Freud and the Twentieth Century* (New York: Meridian, 1957), pp. 167–85; John Schaar, *Escape From Authority* (New York: Basic Books, 1961); Paul Roazen, *Freud: Political and Social Thought* (New York: Knopf, 1968).

17. Trilling, *Freud and the Crisis of Our Culture*.

18. Brown, *Love Against Death*, pp. ix–x.

19. *Ibid.*, p. xi.

20. Herbert Marcuse, *One-Dimensional Man* (Boston: Beacon, 1964).

21. Marcuse, *Eros and Civilization*, p. 216.

22. Philip Rieff, *Freud: The Mind of the Moralist* (New York: Viking, 1959), pp. 342–44.

23. Herbert Marcuse, *Negations* (Boston: Beacon, 1968), p. 257.

24. Roazen, *Freud*, p. 210.

25. Schaar, *Escape From Authority*, cited above.

26. Roazan, *Freud*, p. 203.

27. *Ibid.*, p. 205.

28. *Ibid.*, p. 207.

29. *Ibid.*, p. 209.

30. Morris Opler, "Culture and the Human Potential," in

Herbert Otto, ed., *Explorations in Human Potentialities* (Springfield, Ill.: Thomas, 1966), Chap. 3.
31. Frederic Wertham, *A Sign for Cain* (New York: Macmillan, 1966), p. 9.
32. *Ibid.*, pp. 364–65.
33. Richard L. Means, *The Ethical Imperative* (Garden City: Doubleday, 1969), p. 160.

CHAPTER 3

1. William McDougall, *An Introduction to Social Psychology* (Boston: John W. Luce, 1908); Wilfred Trotter, *Instincts of the Herd in War and Peace* (London: Ernest Benn, 1915).
2. L. L. Bernard, *Instinct: A Study in Social Psychology* (New York: Holt, 1924); Knight Dunlop, "Are There Any Instincts?" *Journal of Abnormal and Social Psychology*, 14 (1919–20): 307–11. Cf. Ashley Montagu, *Man and Aggression* (New York: Oxford University Press, 2d ed., 1973), Introduction.
3. See Lionel Tiger, *Men in Groups* (New York: Random House, 1969); Robert Ardrey, *The Territorial Imperative* (New York: Atheneum, 1966); Arthur R. Jensen, "Social Class, Race, and Genetics: Implications for Education," *American Educational Research Journal*, 5 (January 1968): 1–42.
4. Cf. Montagu, *Man and Aggression*, pp. 4–5.
5. Konrad Lorenz, *On Aggression* (New York: Harcourt, Brace, and World, 1966). Another proponent of Lorenz's views is the psychologist Anthony Storr, principally in his *Human Aggression* (New York: Atheneum, 1968).
6. Desmond Morris, *The Naked Ape* (New York: McGraw-Hill, 1968); Morris, *The Human Zoo* (New York: Dell, 1969).
7. John Hurrell Crook, "The Nature and Function of Territorial Aggression," in Montagu, *Man and Aggression*, pp. 189–90.
8. Lorenz, *On Aggression*, p. ix.

9. *Ibid.*, p. 229.
10. Morris, *The Naked Ape*, p. 176.
11. *Ibid.*, pp. 176–77.
12. Ardrey, *The Territorial Imperative*, p. 116.
13. *Ibid.*, p. 236.
14. Lorenz, *On Aggression*, p. 46.
15. *Ibid.*, p. 265.
16. Morris, *The Naked Ape*, p. 176.
17. Lorenz, *Oh Aggression*, p. 48.
18. Ardrey, *The Territorial Imperative*, pp. 291f.; Tiger, *Men in Groups*, pp. 9f.
19. T. C. Schneirla, "Instinct and Aggression," in Montagu, *Man and Aggression*, p. 146.
20. J. P. Scott, "That Old-Time Aggression," *The Nation* (January 9, 1967): 53–54.
21. Sir Solly Zuckerman, "The Human Beast," *Nature* (November 5, 1966): 563–64.
22. Crook, in *Man and Aggression*, pp. 172–73.
23. Lorenz, *On Aggression*, p. 47.
24. Schneirla, in *Man and Aggression*, p. 149.
25. Ralph Holloway, "Territory and Aggression in Man: A Look at Ardrey's *Territorial Imperative*," in *Man and Aggression*, pp. 181–82.
26. Kenneth Boulding, "Am I a Man or a Mouse—or Both?" *War/Peace Report* (March 1967): 14–17; reprinted in Montagu, *Man and Aggression*, p. 175. Direct evidence of a racist tinge in Lorenz's early work, notably a 1940 article favoring the Nazi principle of eugenics, is adduced by Leon Eisenberg, "The *Human* Nature of Human Nature," *Science*, 176 (April 1972): 123–28. Cf. Erich Fromm, *The Anatomy of Human Destructiveness* (New York: Holt, Rinehart and Winston, 1973), p. 21.
27. Ardrey, *The Territorial Imperative*, pp. 316–17.
28. Sally Carrighar, "War Is Not in Our Genes," *New York Times Magazine* (September 10, 1967); reprinted in Montagu, *Man and Aggression*, p. 125.
29. Crook, in *Man and Aggression*, p. 217. Eisenberg writes similarly: "What we believe of man affects the behavior of men, for it determines what each expects of the

other. Theories of education, of political science, of economics, and the very policies of governments are based on implicit concepts of the nature of man. . . . What we choose to believe about the nature of man has social consequences. Those consequences should be weighed in assessing the belief we choose to hold, even provisionally, given the lack of compelling proof for any of the currently fashionable theories." "The *Human Nature of Human Nature*," pp. 124–25.

CHAPTER 4

1. Victor C. Ferkiss, *Technological Man* (New York: Braziller, 1969), pp. 17–18.
2. Emanuel G. Mesthene, quoted in Ferkiss, p. 20. See also Emanuel G. Mesthene, *Technological Change* (New York: New American Library, 1970).
3. Dwight D. Eisenhower, "Farewell Address" (1961); reprinted in Floyd W. Matson, ed., *Voices of Crisis* (New York: Odyssey Press, 1967), pp. 137–38.
4. Lynn White, Jr., "On Intellectual Gloom," *American Scholar*, 35 (Spring 1966): 223.
5. Friedrich Juenger, *The Failure of Technology* (Chicago: Regnery, 1956).
6. Jacques Ellul, *The Technological Society* (New York: Knopf, 1964).
7. Herbert J. Muller, *The Children of Frankenstein: A Primer on Modern Technology and Human Values* (Bloomington: Indiana University Press, 1970).
8. Erich Fromm, *The Revolution of Hope* (New York: Bantam Books, 1968), p. 34.
9. *Ibid.*, p. 40.
10. Lewis Yablonsky, *Robopaths: People as Machines* (Baltimore: Penguin Books, 1972), p. 6–7.
11. Zbigniew Brezinski, "America in the Technotronic Age," *Encounter*, 30 (January 1968): 16–26; Herman Kahn and Anthony J. Wiener, *The Year 2000* (New York: Macmillan, 1967); Marshall McLuhan, *Understanding*

Media (New York: McGraw-Hill, 1964); Alvin Toffler, *Future Shock* (New York: Random House, 1970).

12. Lewis Mumford, *The Myth of the Machine* (New York: Harcourt, Brace, and World, 1967), p. 4.
13. Jerry H. Rosenberg, *The Death of Privacy* (New York: Random House, 1969), pp. 27f.
14. Quoted in Rosenberg, *Death of Privacy*, p. 38.
15. *Ibid.*, p. 205.
16. Arthur R. Miller, "The National Data Center and Personal Privacy," *Atlantic Monthly* (November 1967): 55.
17. Quoted in Rosenberg, *The Death of Privacy*, p. 20.
18. In addition to Rosenberg, cited above, see also Alan F. Westin, *Privacy and Freedom* (New York: Atheneum, 1967).
19. Rosenberg, *The Death of Privacy*, p. 17.
20. *Ibid.*, p. 20. See also Kahn and Wiener, *The Year* 2000, p. 352.
21. W. H. Ferry, "Must We Rewrite the Constitution to Control Technology?" *Saturday Review*, 51 (March 2, 1968): 50–54.
22. Walter Lippmann, *The Public Philosophy* (New York: New American Library, 1955), p. 76.
23. Roderick Seidenberg, *Posthistoric Man* (Chapel Hill: University of North Carolina Press, 1950).

CHAPTER 5

1. Gordon Rattray Taylor, *The Biological Time Bomb* (New York: World, 1968); Alvin Toffler, *Future Shock* (New York: Random House, 1970).
2. James D. Watson, *The Double Helix* (New York: New American Library, 1968).
3. R. Michael Davidson, "And Now: The Evolution Revolution," *Avant-Garde* (January–February, 1969).
4. See, in addition to Toffler and Rattray Taylor, David Rorvik, *As Man Becomes Machine* (New York: Doubleday, 1971); Arthur C. Clarke, *Profiles of the Future*

(New York: Harper and Row, 1963); Albert Rosenfeld, *The Second Genesis: The Coming Control of Life* (Englewood Cliffs, N.J.: Prentice Hall, 1969).

5. Quoted in Rattray Taylor, *The Biological Time Bomb*, p. 223.
6. Jean Rostand, *Can Man Be Modified?* (New York: Basic Books, 1959).
7. Quoted in Rattray Taylor, *The Biological Time Bomb*, p. 225.
8. Donald Fleming, "On Living in a Biological Revolution," *Atlantic Monthly* (February, 1969).
9. *Ibid.*
10. Cf. Joshua Lederberg, "Experimental Genetics and Human Evolution," *Bulletin of the Atomic Scientists*, 22 (1966): 4–11, Herman G. Muller, "What Genetic Course Will Man Steer?" *Bulletin of the Atomic Scientists*, 24 (1968): 6–12.
11. See Herbert J. Muller, *The Uses of the Future* (Bloomington: Indiana University Press, 1974).
12. Charles Reich, *The Greening of America* (New York: Random House, 1970).
13. W. H. Ferry, "Must We Rewrite the Constitution to Control Technology?" *Saturday Review*, 51 (March 2, 1968): 50–54.
14. Anatol Rapoport, *Strategy and Conscience* (New York: Harper and Row, 1964).
15. Lewis Mumford, *In the Name of Sanity* (New York: Harcourt, Brace, 1954), p. 60.
16. See Nicholas Anastasiow, "Educational Relevance and Jensen's Conclusions," *Phi Delta Kappan* (September, 1969): 32–35.
17. See especially Arthur R. Jensen, "Social Class, Race, and Genetics; Implications for Education," *American Educational Research Journal*, 5 (January, 1968): 1–42.
18. Arthur R. Jensen, "How Much Can We Boost IQ and Scholastic Achievement?" *Harvard Educational Review*, 39, No. 1 (Winter, 1969): 2–123.
19. Juan Comas, " 'Scientific' Racism Again?" *Current Anthropology*, 2 (October, 1961): 303–14.

20. Manning Nash, "Race and the Ideology of Race," *Current Anthropology*, 3 (June, 1962): 285–88.
21. Comas, " 'Scientific' Racism Again?"
22. Audrey M. Shuey, *The Testing of Negro Intelligence* (Lynchburg, Va.: J. P. Bell Co., 1958); Carleton Putnam, *Race and Reason, a Yankee View* (Washington, D.C.: 1961).
23. For discussion, see R. W. Pugh, *Psychology and the Black Experience* (Monterey, Cal.: Brooks/Cole, 1972).
24. Lionel Tiger, *Men in Groups* (New York: Random House, 1969), p. 11.
25. Bruce Eckland, "Genetics and Sociology: A Reconsideration," *American Sociological Review*, 32 (April, 1967): 173–194.
26. Gardner Murphy, "Psychology in the Year 2000," *American Psychologist*, 24, No. 5 (May, 1969): 527.
27. Thomas F. Pettigrew, "Race, Mental Illness, and Intelligence: A Social Psychological View," *Eugenics Quarterly*, 11, No. 4 (December, 1964): 189–215.
28. James McVicker Hunt, *Intelligence and Experience* (New York: Ronald 1961); cited in Pettigrew, "Race, Mental Illness, and Intelligence."
29. *Ibid.*
30. James McVicker Hunt, "Black Genes—White Environment," *Trans-Action*, 6, No. 18 (June, 1969): 12–22.
31. Davidson, "And Now: The Evolution Revolution."
32. Rostand, *Can Man Be Modified?*
33. Davidson, "And Now: The Evolution Revolution."
34. *The Biological Time Bomb*, p. 44.
35. Davidson, "And Now: The Evolution Revolution."
36. *Ibid.*
37. James Bonner, "The Next New Biology," *Plant Science Bulletin*, 11, No. 3 (December, 1965): 1–7.
38. David Krech, "Psychoneurobiochemeducation," *California Monthly* (June-July, 1969); reprinted in *Current*, no. 110 (September, 1969): 55–64.
39. *Ibid.*
40. Alexander G. Wesman, "Intelligent Testing," *American Psychologist*, 24 (1968): 267–274.

41. O. D. Duncan, D. L. Featherman and B. Duncan, *Socio-economic Background and Occupational Achievement: Extensions of a Basic Model*. Final Report, Project No. 5-0074 (EO-101). U.S. Department of Health, Education, and Welfare, Office of Education, Bureau of Research, May, 1968. Quoted in Jensen, "How Much Can We Boost IQ and Scholastic Achievement?"

42. *Ibid.*

43. Manning Nash, "Race and the Ideology of Race," *Current Anthropology*, 3 (June, 1962): 285.

44. *Ibid.*, p. 288.

45. Anastasiow, "Educational Relevance and Jensen's Conclusions."

46. One example, which appears to be due to simple error (but error of a remarkably convenient kind), is worthy of note. In his discussion of heritability estimates, referring to his tabulated figures, Jensen writes (p. 50 of the article): "For example we see that the correlation between identical or monozygotic (MZ) twins reared apart is .75. Since MZ twins develop from a single fertilized ovum and thus have exactly the same genes, any difference between the twins must be due to nongenetic factors. And if they are reared apart in uncorrelated environments, the difference between a perfect correlation (1.00) and the obtained correlation (.75) gives an estimate of the proportion of the variance in IQs attributable to environmental differences. $1.00 - 0.75 = 0.25$. Thus 75 percent of the variance can be said to be due to genetic variation (this is the heritability) and 25 percent to environmental variation." However, variance is *not* calculated by the formula of 1.00 minus the correlation, but the correlation squared. Thus the proportion of variance in MZ twins should be 0.75×0.75, or 55 percent. This means that the *most* that could be attributed to genetic factors would be 55 percent— and this figure does not exclude pre-natal or uterine events of an "environmental" (nurtural) sort. This apparent statistical error also skews the results elsewhere in the course of the paper.

47. Jensen, "Social Class, Race, and Genetics," pp. 23, 30.
48. Gordon M. Harrington, "Genetics and Education; Comments on the Jensen and Caspari Addresses," *American Educational Research Journal*, 5, No. 4 (November, 1968): 717.
49. Ernest Caspari, "Genetic Endowment and Environment in the Determination of Human Behavior; Biological Viewpoint," *American Educational Research Journal*, 5 (January, 1968): 54.
50. Stanley M. Garn, "Cultural Factors Affecting the Study of Human Biology," *Human Biology*, 26, No. 2 (1954): 50.
51. *Ibid.*, p. 53.
52. Harrington, "Genetics and Education," p. 716.
53. Norbert Wiener, *The Human Use of Human Beings* (Garden City: Doubleday Anchor, 1954), p. 186.

CHAPTER 6

1. B. F. Skinner, *The Behavior of Organisms: An Experimental Analysis* (New York: Appleton-Century, 1938), p. 5.
2. John B. Watson, *Behavior: An Introduction to Comparative Psychology* (New York: Holt, 1914), p. 27.
3. Gardner Murphy, *Historical Introduction to Modern Psychology* (New York: Harcourt, Brace, rev. ed., 1951), p. 253.
4. John B. Watson, *Behaviorism* (Chicago: University of Chicago, 1958), pp. 5–6.
5. B. F. Skinner, *Beyond Freedom and Dignity* (New York: Knopf, 1971), p. 15.
6. Paul G. Creelan, "Religion, Language, and Sexuality in J. B. Watson," *Journal of Humanistic Psychology*, 15, No. 4 (Fall, 1975): 57.
7. David Bakan, "Behaviorism and American Urbanization," *Journal of the History of the Behavioral Sciences*, 2 (1968), quoted in Creelan, p. 57.

8. E. A. Burtt, *The Metaphysical Foundations of Modern Science* (Garden City, N.Y.: Doubleday Anchor, 1955).

9. Gordon W. Allport, *Becoming: Basic Considerations for a Psychology of Personality* (New Haven: Yale, 1955), p. 8.

10. Elie Halévy, *The Growth of Philosophic Radicalism* (Boston: Beacon, 1955), p. 458.

11. Watson, *Behaviorism*, p. 11.

12. John B. Watson, *Psychology from the Standpoint of a Behaviorist* (Philadelphia: Lippincott, 3d ed., 1929), p. 7.

13. John B. Watson, *The Ways of Behaviorism* (New York: Harper, 1926), p. 9.

14. James McConnell, quoted in Lewis M. Andrews and Marvin Karlins, *Requiem for Democracy? An Inquiry into the Limits of Behavioral Control* (New York: Holt, Rinehart and Winston, 1971), p. 3.

15. Watson, *Behaviorism*, p. 303.

16. *Ibid.*

17. *Ibid.*

18. *Ibid.*

19. Edna Heidbreder, *Seven Psychologies* (New York: Appleton-Century, 1935), p. 257.

20. Ludwig Gumplowicz, *The Outlines of Sociology* (Philadelphia: American Academy of Political and Social Science, 1899), p. 148.

21. Skinner, *Beyond Freedom and Dignity*, p. 205.

22. *Ibid.*, p. 211. Emphasis added.

23. Edwin G. Boring, *A History of Experimental Psychology* (New York: Appleton-Crofts, 2d ed., 1950), p. 645.

24. Quoted in Robert S. Woodworth, *Contemporary Schools of Psychology* (New York: Ronald, rev. ed., 1948), p. 92.

25. *Ibid.*, p. 93.

26. See Jean Meynaud, *Technocracy* (New York: Free Press, 1970); Friedrich Juenger, *The Failure of Technology* (Chicago: Regnery, 1956).

27. Sigmund Koch, "Psychology and Emerging Conceptions of Knowledge as Unitary," in T. W. Wann, ed., *Behavior-*

ism and Phenomenology (Chicago: University of Chicago, 1964), p. 19.

28. Skinner, *The Behavior of Organisms*, p. 5.
29. B. F. Skinner, *Science and Human Behavior* (New York: Macmillan, 1953), p. 5.
30. *Ibid.*, p. 6.
31. *Ibid.*
32. B. F. Skinner, *Walden Two* (New York: Macmillan, 1948), p. 214.
33. Skinner, *Science and Human Behavior*, p. 436.
34. *Ibid.*, p. 9.
35. *Ibid.*, p. 10.
36. *Ibid.*, p. 29.
37. *Ibid.*, *pp.* 447–48.
38. Paul Kurtz, "Democracy and the Technology of Control," *The Humanist* (November 1971), reprinted in Floyd W. Matson, ed., *Without/Within: Behaviorism and Humanism* (Monterey, Calif.: Brooks/Cole, 1973), p. 56.
39. Skinner, *Walden Two*, p. 289.
40. *Time* (September 20, 1971): 43–44.
41. Skinner, *Walden Two*, p. 260.
42. *Ibid.*, p. 225.
43. *Ibid.*, p. 145.
44. See, among other writings by Skinner, "The Control of Human Behavior," *Transactions of the New York Academy of Sciences*, 2d ser., 17 (May 1955); "Freedom and the Control of Men," *American Scholar*, 25 (1955–56): 47–65; "Contingencies of Reinforcement in the Design of a Culture," *Behavioral Science* 11 (1966): 159–66.
45. *The Center Magazine*, 5 (March–April 1972): 63–65.
46. Skinner, *Beyond Freedom and Dignity*, pp. 200–201.
47. Quoted in Theodore Roszak, *Where the Wasteland Ends* (Garden City: Doubleday, 1972), p. 454.
48. Skinner, *Science and Human Behavior*, p. 448.
49. Kenneth B. Clark, *Pathos of Power* (New York: Harper & Row, 1974), pp. 172–177.

50. Quoted in Jerry Rosenberg, *The Death of Privacy* (New York: Random House, 1969), p. 15.
51. Aldous Huxley, quoted in Andrews and Karlins, *Requiem for Democracy?*, p. 1.
52. Lewis Mumford, *The Pentagon of Power* (New York: Harcourt Brace Jovanovich, 1970), p. 435.

CHAPTER 7

1. Gunnar Myrdal, *An American Dilemma: The Negro Problem and Modern Democracy* (New York: Harper, 1944), p. 3. Emphasis in original.
2. *Ibid.*, pp. 4–5.
3. *Ibid.*, p. 8. Emphasis added.
4. Carl Becker, *Freedom and Responsibility in the American Way of Life* (New York: Knopf, 1951), p. 31.
5. Bernard Bailyn, *The Ideological Origins of the American Revolution* (Cambridge, Mass.: Harvard, 1967), p. 35.
6. Jean de Crèvecoeur, "Letters from an American Farmer," in Henry Steele Commager, ed., *Living in America* (New York: Harper, 1951), pp. 20–21.
7. Don M. Wolfe, *The Image of Man in America* (New York: McGraw-Hill, 1957), p. 16.
8. Quoted in Wolfe, *ibid.*, p. 17.
9. *Ibid.*, pp. 17–18.
10. Hans J. Morgenthau, *The Purpose of American Politics* (New York: Knopf, 1960), pp. 22–23.
11. See Bailyn, *Ideological Origins of the American Revolution*, chap. 3.
12. Saul K. Padover, ed., *The World of the Founding Fathers* (New York: Thomas Yoseloff, 1960), p. 40.
13. *Ibid.*, p. 39.
14. *Ibid.*, p. 40. Cf. Arthur O. Lovejoy, *Reflections on Human Nature* (Baltimore: Johns Hopkins, 1961), Lecture 2.
15. Padover, *World of the Founding Fathers*, p. 41.
16. *Ibid.*, pp. 41–42.
17. For a more detailed discussion of the Madisonian view,

see Floyd W. Matson, "Party and Faction," *Antioch Review*, 18 (Fall 1958): 331–42.

18. *The Federalist* (New York: Modern Library, n.d.), "The Federalist Number Ten," p. 56.

19. Bailyn, *Ideological Origins of the American Revolution*, p. 319.

20. Myrdal, *An American Dilemma*, p. 7.

CHAPTER 8

1. Theodore Roszak, *The Making of a Counter Culture* (New York: Doubleday Anchor, 1969).

2. Lewis Mumford, *The Pentagon of Power* (New York: Harcourt Brace Jovanovich, 1970), chap. 11, pp. 300f.

3. George B. Leonard, *The Transformation* (New York: Delacorte, 1972), pp. 2–3.

4. William Irwin Thompson, *At the Edge of History: Speculations on the Transformation of Culture* (New York: Harper and Row, 1971).

5. Theodore Roszak, *Where the Wasteland Ends* (Garden City, N.Y.: Doubleday, 1972), pp. xxi–xxii.

6. Eugene S. Schwartz, *Overskill: The Decline of Technology in Modern Civilization* (New York: Ballantine Books, 1971), p. 274.

7. Lewis Yablonsky, *Robopaths: People as Machines* (Baltimore: Penguin, 1972), p. 188.

8. *The Pentagon of Power*, p. 413.

9. *Ibid.*, p. 434.

10. Charles A. Reich, *The Greening of America* (New York: Random House, 1970), pp. 13–15.

11. See especially his influential contribution to welfare law and theory, "The New Property," *Yale Law Journal*, 73 (1964): 733–87.

12. Philip Slater, *The Pursuit of Loneliness: American Culture at the Breaking Point* (Boston: Beacon, 1970), p. 97.

13. *Ibid.*, p. 100.

14. William Braden, *The Age of Aquarius: Technology and*

the Cultural Revolution (Chicago: Quadrangle, 1970), p. 5.

15. Paul Goodman, *People or Personnel: Decentralizing and the Mixed System* (New York: Random House, 1965).

16. Herbert Marcuse, *One-Dimensional Man* (Boston: Beacon, 1964); Charles Hampden-Turner, *Radical Man* (Cambridge, Mass.: Schenkman, 1970); Paul Jacobs and Saul Landau, eds., *The New Radicals* (New York: Vintage, 1966).

17. Emile Capouya, quoted in Ted Clark and Dennis T. Jaffe, *Toward a Radical Therapy* (New York: Gordon and Breach, 1973), p. 55.

18. Erich Fromm, *The Anatomy of Human Destructiveness* (New York: Holt, Rinehart, and Winston, 1973), p. 438.

CHAPTER 9

1. John Higham, "Beyond Consensus: The Historian as Moral Critic," *American Historical Review*, 67 (April 1962); reprinted in Robert Allen Skotheim, ed., *The Historian and the Climate of Opinion* (Reading, Mass.: Addison-Wesley, 1969), p. 199.

2. Charles A. Beard, "Written History as an Act of Faith," *American Historical Review*, 29 (January 1934): 219–31.

3. Richard Hofstadter, *The Progressive Historians* (New York: Vintage, 1970), p. xii.

4. See Robert Flint, *The Philosophy of History in France and Germany* (Edinburgh: 1874); Harry Elmer Barnes, *Introduction to the History of Sociology* (Chicago: University of Chicago, 1947), chap. 19.

5. Higham, "Beyond Consensus," p. 199.

6. Hofstadter, *The Progressive Historians*, pp. xiiif.

7. See, for example, John Higham, "The Cult of the 'American Consensus,'" *Commentary*, 27 (1959): 93–100; J. Rogers Hollingsworth, "Consensus and Continuity in Recent American Historical Writing," *South Atlantic Quarterly*, 61 (1962): 40–50.

8. Higham, "Beyond Consensus," p. 200.

9. *Ibid.*, p. 201.

10. Representative studies include Ruth Benedict, *The Chrys-anthemum and the Sword* (Boston: Houghton Mifflin, 1946); Geoffrey Gorer and J. Rickman, *The People of Great Russia* (London: Cresset, 1949); Margaret Mead, "The Study of National Character," in Daniel Lerner and Harold D. Lasswell, eds., *The Policy Sciences* (Stanford: Stanford University, 1951).

11. The most influential study, originally written in connection with a projected multivolume series on national character, is David Riesman, Nathan Glazer, and Reuel Denney, *The Lonely Crowd: A Study of the Changing American Character* (New Haven: Yale, 1950). See also David Potter, *People of Plenty: Economic Abundance and American Character* (Chicago: University of Chicago, 1954). For a general survey, see Thomas L. Hartshorne, *The Distorted Image: Changing Conceptions of the American Character Since Turner* (Cleveland: Case Western Reserve University, 1968).

12. Alfred Kroeber and Clyde Kluckhohn, *Culture: A Critical Review of Concepts and Definitions* (New York: Vintage, 1963), p. 357.

13. Jacques Barzun, "Cultural History as Synthesis," in Fritz Stern, ed., *The Varieties of History from Voltaire to the Present* (New York: Meridian, 1956), pp. 392–93. See also Robert F. Berkhofer, Jr., "Clio and the Culture Concept: Some Impressions of a Changing Relationship in American Historiography," *Social Science Quarterly*, 53 (September 1972): 297–320.

14. Stuart Chase, *The Proper Study of Mankind* (New York: Harper, 1948), p. 59.

15. Marvin Harris, *The Rise of Anthropological Theory* (New York: Crowell, 1968), p. 298.

16. *Ibid.*

17. Alexander Pope, *An Essay on Man*, in W. H. Auden and Norman Holmes Pearson, eds., *Poets of the English Language* (New York: Viking, 1950), vol. 3, p. 394.

18. Skotheim, *The Historian and the Climate of Opinion*, pp. 1–2. See also Robert Allen Skotheim, *American Intellectual Histories and Historians* (Princeton: Princeton University, 1966), pp. viii, 118, *passim*.

19. Skotheim, *The Historian and the Climate of Opinion*, p. 3.

20. *Ibid.*, p. 2.

21. Higham, "The Cult of the 'American Consensus,'" pp. 708–709.

22. *Ibid.*, p. 709.

23. See Eric and Mary Josephson, eds., *Man Alone: Alienation in Modern Society* (New York: Dell, 1962), Introduction.

24. Barton J. Bernstein, ed., *Towards a New Past: Dissenting Essays in American History* (New York: Vintage, 1969), pp. ix–x.

25. Hofstadter, *The Progressive Historians*, p. 458.

26. *Ibid.*, p. 459.

27. Jesse Lemisch, "The American Revolution Seen From the Bottom Up," in Bernstein, *Towards a New Past*, p. 29. For a variety of "New Left" perspectives, juxtaposed with "consensus" interpretations of the same events, see Allen F. Davis and Harold D. Woodman, eds., *Conflict and Consensus in Modern American History* (Lexington, Mass.: Heath, 3d ed., 1972).

28. Lemisch, "The American Revolution Seen From the Bottom Up," p. 29.

29. Norman Pollock, "Populism, Authoritarianism, and the Historian," in Skotheim, *The Historian and the Climate of Opinion*, p. 129.

30. Staughton Lynd, "Historical Past and Existential Present," in Theodore Roszak, ed., *The Dissenting Academy* (New York: Pantheon, 1967), pp. 98, 102.

31. Benedetto Croce, *History as the Story of Liberty* (New York: Norton, 1941), p. 59.

32. Lynd, "Historical Past and Existential Present," p. 107.

33. Higham, "Beyond Consensus," p. 205.

34. *Ibid.*, p. 210.

35. Hofstadter, *The Progressive Historians*, p. 465.

CHAPTER 10

1. Irving Louis Horowitz, *Professing Sociology: Studies in the Life Cycle of Social Science* (Chicago: Aldine, 1968), p. 3.
2. C. Wright Mills, *The Sociological Imagination* (New York: Oxford University, 1959), p. 256.
3. Talcott Parsons, *The Social System* (Glencoe, Ill.: Free Press, 1951); Talcott Parsons and Edward Shils, eds., *Toward a General Theory of Action* (Cambridge, Mass.: Harvard, 1951).
4. Robert W. Friedrichs, *A Sociology of Sociology* (New York: Free Press, 1970), p. 17.
5. Alvin W. Gouldner and J. Timothy Sprehe, "The Study of Man 4: Sociologists Look at Themselves," *Trans-Action*, 2 (May–June, 1965): 42–44.
6. See Friedrichs, *A Sociology of Sociology*, chap. 11, "The Marxist Analogue"; Herbert Blumer, *Symbolic Interactionism: Perspective and Method* (Englewood Cliffs, N.J.: Prentice-Hall, 1969).
7. Horowitz, *Professing Sociology*, pp. 10–11.
8. Dennis Wrong, "The Oversocialized Conception of Man in Modern Sociology," *American Sociological Review*, 26 (April 1961): 183–93.
9. Alvin W. Gouldner, *The Coming Crisis of Western Sociology* (New York: Basic Books, 1970), p. 206.
10. Wayne Hield, "The Study of Change in Social Science," *The British Journal of Sociology* (March 1964); reprinted in N.J. Demerath III and Richard A. Peterson, eds., *System, Change, and Conflict* (New York: Free Press, 1967), pp. 258–59.
11. Ralf Dahrendorf, "Out of Utopia: Toward a Reorientation of Sociological Analysis," *American Journal of Sociology*, 64 (September 1958): 115–27.
12. Barrington Moore, Jr., "The New Scholasticism and the Study of Politics," *World Politics* (October 1953); reprinted in Barrington Moore, Jr., *Political Power and Social Theory* (Cambridge, Mass.: Harvard, 1958).
13. Mills, *The Sociological Imagination*, p. 7.

14. *Ibid.*, p. 13.
15. C. Wright Mills, *White Collar* (New York: Oxford University, 1951); C. Wright Mills, *The Power Elite* (New York: Oxford University, 1956).
16. Quoted in Steven E. Deutsch, "The Radical Perspective in Sociology," in John F. Glass and John R. Stande, eds., *Humanistic Society* (Pacific Palisades, Calif.: Goodyear, 1972), p. 208.
17. Herbert Marcuse, *One-Dimensional Man* (Boston: Beacon, 1964).
18. Theodore Roszak, ed., *The Dissenting Academy* (New York: Pantheon, 1967), Introduction.
19. Herbert Marcuse, *An Essay on Liberation* (Boston: Beacon, 1969).
20. Georg Simmel, *The Sociology of Georg Simmel*, trans. K. H. Wolff (New York: Free Press, 1950).
21. Irving Louis Horowitz, "Establishment Sociology: The Value of Being Value-Free," *Inquiry: Journal of Interdisciplinary Research*, 6 (Spring 1963); Irving Louis Horowitz, "Sociology for Sale," *Studies on the Left*, 3 (Winter 1963). Both articles are reprinted in Horowitz, *Professing Sociology*, pp. 159–73.
22. Gouldner, *The Coming Crisis of Western Sociology*, p. 224.
23. Representative of Goffman's numerous writings are: *The Presentation of Self in Everyday Life* (New York: Doubleday Anchor, 1959); *Relations in Public: Microstudies of the Public Order* (New York: Basic Books, 1971); *Frame Analysis: An Essay on the Organization of Experience* (New York: Harper and Row, 1974). See also Harold Garfinkel, *Studies in Ethnomethodology* (Englewood Cliffs, N.J.: Prentice-Hall, 1967); Jack D. Douglas, *Understanding Everyday Life: Toward the Reconstruction of Sociological Knowledge* (Chicago: Aldine, 1970).
24. Blumer, *Symbolic Interactionism*. See also Tamotsu Shibutani, ed., *Human Nature and Collective Behavior: Papers in Honor of Herbert Blumer* (Englewood Cliffs, N.J.: Prentice-Hall, 1970); George Herbert Mead, *Mind, Self, and Society* (Chicago: University of Chicago, 1934).

234   NOTES

25. Mills, *The Sociological Imagination*, chap. 3, "Abstracted Empiricism."
26. Anthony Standen, *Science Is a Sacred Cow* (New York: Dutton, 1958). For a comprehensive review of these developments, see Eugene S. Schwartz, *Overskill: The Decline of Technology in Modern Civilization* (New York: Ballantine, 1971).
27. Peter L. Berger, *Invitation to Sociology: A Humanistic Interpretation* (New York: Doubleday Anchor, 1963).
28. Lewis A. Coser, ed., *Sociology Through Literature* (Englewood Cliffs, N.J.: Prentice-Hall, 1963); Leo Lowenthal, *Literature and the Image of Man* (Boston: Beacon, 1957).
29. Robert A. Nisbet, "Sociology as an Art Form," in Maurice Stein and Arthur Vidich, eds., *Sociology on Trial* (Englewood Cliffs, N.J.: Prentice-Hall, 1963).
30. Stanford M. Lyman and Marvin B. Scott, *A Sociology of the Absurd* (New York: Appleton-Century, 1970).
31. See John Glass, "The Humanistic Challenge to Sociology," in Glass and Staude, *Humanistic Society*, pp. 1–11.
32. The phrase is that of an anthropologist, Alexander Alland, Jr., *The Human Imperative* (New York: Columbia University, 1972). See also Richard L. Means, *The Ethical Imperative* (Garden City, N.Y.: Doubleday, 1969).
33. John R. Staude, "The Theoretical Foundations of Humanistic Sociology," in Glass and Staude, *Humanistic Society*, p. 263.
34. Gouldner, *The Coming Crisis of Western Sociology*, p. 489.
35. *Ibid.*, p. 491.
36. *Ibid.*, p. 509. See, in this connection, Amitai Etzioni's conception of sociology as an agency of social activation in pursuit of the creation of an active society of "active actors." Amitai Etzioni, *The Active Society* (New York: Free Press, 1968), pp. 4, 15, *passim*.
37. Friedrichs, *A Sociology of Sociology*, pp. 299–300.

CHAPTER 11

1. C. Wright Mills, *The Power Elite* (New York: Oxford University, Galaxy Edition, 1959), chap. 11, "The Theory of Balance."
2. On these and other early psychologists, see Floyd W. Matson, ed., *Being, Becoming, and Behavior* (New York: Braziller, 1967), parts 1 and 2.
3. On the rise and fall of consciousness in psychology, see James J. Dagenais, *Models of Man: A Phenomenological Critique of Some Paradigms in the Human Sciences* (The Hague: Martinus Nijhoff, 1972), pp. 6f.
4. Sigmund Koch, "Psychology Cannot Be a Coherent Science," *Psychology Today* (September 1969); reprinted in Floyd W. Matson, ed., *Without/Within* (Monterey, Calif.: Brooks/Cole, 1973), p. 84.
5. The phrase is in Sigmund Freud, *New Introductory Lectures on Psychoanalysis* (New York: Norton, 1933), p. 103.
6. Quoted in Rollo May, *Love and Will* (New York: Norton, 1969), p. 183.
7. *Ibid.*, pp. 182–183.
8. Philip Rieff, *Freud: The Mind of the Moralist* (New York: Viking, 1959), p. 357.
9. Ernest Havemann, *The Age of Psychology* (New York: Grove, 1957).
10. See Abraham H. Maslow, *Toward a Psychology of Being* (Princeton: Van Nostrand, 1962).
11. Mortimer J. Adler, *The Difference of Man and the Difference It Makes* (New York: Holt, Rinehart and Winston, 1967).
12. See Floyd W. Matson, "Humanistic Theory: The Third Revolution in Psychology," *The Humanist* (March–April 1971); reprinted in Thomas J. Greening, ed., *Existential Humanistic Psychology* (Monterey, Calif.: Brooks/Cole, 1971), pp. 43–53.
13. Gordon W. Allport, *Becoming* (New Haven: Yale, 1955); Gordon W. Allport, *Personality and Social Encounter* (Boston: Beacon, 1960).

14. For this discussion of humanism, I have drawn on my essay, "Toward a New Humanism," in Paul Kurtz, ed., *The Humanist Alternative* (Buffalo, N.Y.: Prometheus Books, 1973).

15. Quoted in Frank T. Severin, ed., *Humanistic Viewpoints in Psychology* (New York: McGraw-Hill, 1965), p. 3.

16. Frank T. Severin, *Discovering Man in Psychology: A Humanistic Approach* (New York: McGraw-Hill, 1973), pp. 93–97.

17. Clark Moustakas, *Loneliness* (Englewood Cliffs, N.J.: Prentice-Hall, 1961), p. ix. See also James F. T. Bugental, *The Search for Authenticity* (New York: Holt, Rinehart and Winston, 1965).

18. Calvin S. Hall and Gardner Lindzey, eds., *Theories of Personality* (New York: Wiley, 1957), p. 325. See also Abraham H. Maslow, *The Farther Reaches of Human Nature* (New York: Viking, 1971), esp. part 1.

19. Abraham H. Maslow, "A Philosophy of Psychology: The Need for a Mature Science of Human Nature," *Main Currents in Modern Thought*, 13 (1957): 27–32; reprinted in John J. Mitchell, ed., *Human Nature: Theories, Conjectures, and Descriptions* (Metuchen, N.J.: Scarecrow Press, 1972), p. 10.

20. Allport, *Personality and Social Encounter*, p. 97.

21. See John Dewey and Arthur F. Bentley, *Knowing and the Known* (Boston: Beacon, 1949); G. H. Mead, *Mind, Self, and Society* (Chicago: University of Chicago, 1934); Harry Stack Sullivan, *The Interpersonal Theory of Psychiatry* (New York: Norton, 1953).

22. See Heinz and Rowena Ansbacher, *The Individual Psychology of Alfred Adler* (New York: Basic Books, 1956); Otto Rank, *Will Therapy and Truth and Reality* (New York: Knopf, 1945), p. 155, *passim*; Erich Fromm, *Man for Himself* (New York: Rinehart, 1947); Karen Horney, *Neurosis and Human Growth* (New York: Norton, 1950).

23. Ernst Cassirer, *An Essay on Man* (Garden City, N.Y.: Doubleday Anchor, 1953), p. 21.

24. Rollo May, ed., *Existence: A New Dimension in Psy-*

chiatry and Psychology (New York: Basic Books, 1958). See also Adrian Van Kaam, *Existential Foundations of Psychology* (Garden City, N.Y.: Doubleday, 1969).

25. See Maurice S. Friedman, *Martin Buber: The Life of Dialogue* (New York: Harper Torchbooks, 1960), pp. 184f.; Floyd W. Matson and Ashley Montagu, eds., *The Human Dialogue: Perspectives on Communication* (New York: Free Press, 1967), pp. 6f.; Carl R. Rogers, *On Becoming a Person* (Boston: Houghton Mifflin, 1961).

26. Erich Fromm, *The Art of Loving* (New York: Harper and Row, 1957), pp. 7–32, "The Theory of Love." See also Izette de Forrest, *The Leaven of Love: A Development of the Psychoanalytic Theory and Technique of Sandor Ferenczi* (New York: Harper, 1954).

INDEX

Academic Counterculture, 154–163
  cultural revolution and, 156–163
  technological revolution and, 156–163
Acetylcholinesterase, 99
Adams, John, 150–151
Adams, Samuel, 150
Adler, Mortimer J., xx, 202, 208
African Genesis (Ardrey), 56
Age of Reform, The (Hofstadter), 175
Aggression, 51–54
  Ardrey on, 56–61, 64–66
  children and, 51–52
  defined, 58
  education and, 63
  instinctual (biological), 24–25, 28–29, 55-67
  Lorenz on, 57–67
  social (cultural), 55, 61–67
Aiken, Henry D., 23–24
Air Crib, 124
Allport, Gordon W., 50, 109, 113–114, 202, 203, 207

American Creed, 137–153
American Dilemma, An (Myrdal), 137–138
American Economic Association, 78
American Political Tradition, The (Hofstadter), 175
American Psychological Association, 129
American Revolution, humanism and, 138, 140, 142, 145, 147, 151, 175–177
American Sociological Association, 184
Analysis of the Phenomena of the Human Mind (Mill), 114
Anastasiow, Nicholas, 105
Ardrey, Robert, 36
  on aggression, 56–61, 64–66
Associationism, 113, 114

Bailyn, Bernard, 140, 152
Bakan, David, 113
Barzun, Jacques, 170

Beard, Charles A., 14, 165, 167, 177
Beat phenomenon, 173–174
Beccaria, Marchese di, 140
Bechterev, Vladimir M., 114
Becker, Carl, 139–140, 167
Behavior of Organisms, The (Skinner), 119
Behaviorism, 56
　psychological revolution, 110–133
Bell, Daniel, 168–169
Bennett, E. L., 99
Bentley, A. F., 2
Berdyaev, Nikoli A., 209
Berger, Peter, 193
Berkowitz, Leonard, 41
Bernard, L. L., 56
Bernstein, Barton J., 174
Bettelheim, Bruno, xv, 180
Beyond Freedom and Dignity (Skinner), 111, 120, 121, 126
Beyond the Pleasure Principle (Freud), 36, 38–39
Bhagavad Gita, 2
Bible, the, 2
Biological revolution, 84–109
　biological intervention, 98–101
　control and, 85–89
　determinism and, 84–85, 92–109
　education and, 92, 99–100, 104–105
　Evolution Revolution, 98–101
　freedom and, 84–85, 91–92
　futurists and, 89–90
　heredity-environment interactions, 96–109
　humanism and, 29–30, 90
　IQ, 94, 97, 101–109
　new consciousness and, 90

religion and, 88
technological revolution and, 73
Biological Time Bomb, The (Taylor), 84
Blumer, Herbert, 193
Bonner, James, 99
Boorstin, Daniel J., 149–150, 174
Boring, E. G., 118
Boulding, Kenneth, 64–65
Braden, William, 160–161
Brain biology, 99–100
Brave New World (Huxley), 132
Bridgman, P. W., 3, 7
Brown, Norman O., 41, 44-49
Browne, Sir Thomas, xiii
Bruce, Lenny, 174
Brzezinski, Zbigniew, 76
Buber, Martin, 209
Burnet, Sir Macfarlane, 86–87
Burtt, E. A., 32, 34, 113

Cabanis, Pierre, 114
Callicles, 146
Camus, Albert, 209
Can Man Be Modified? (Rostand), 87
Capouya, Emile, 162
Carrighar, Sally, 66
Caspari, Ernest, 106, 107
Cassirer, Ernst, 3, 208–209
Center for the Study of Democratic Institutions, 126
Chamberlain, Houston, 29
Chase, Stuart, 170
Children, aggression and, 51–52
Children of Frankenstein, The (Muller), 74
Cholinesterase, 99
Chomsky, Noam, 132

Church, Francis, xiii
Cicero, Marcus Tullius, 146
Civil rights movement, 173
Civil War, 175–176
Civilization and Its Discontents (Freud), 36–40
Clark, Kenneth B., 129–131
Cold War, 177
Collingwood, R. G., 32–35
Comas, Juan, 93, 94
Coming Crisis of Western Sociology, The (Gouldner), 9
Computer privacy, 80–83
Comte, Auguste, 184
Conditioned reflex, the, 114
Consensus history, 167–174
Consensus sociology, 182, 186, 191
Conservatism
  in history, 167–174
  in humanism, 167–174, 181
  in sociology, 181
Cooley, Charles Horton, 11, 202
Coser, Lewis, 191, 193
Cosmology, 33–34
Creelan, Paul G., 112–113
Crèvecoeur, Michel Guillaume St. Jean de, 141
Croce, Benedetto, 178
Crook, John Hurrell, 57–58, 62–63, 66–67
"Cult of the 'American Consensus,' The: Homogenizing our History" (Highman), 173
Cultural evolution, 29–35
"Cultural Factors Affecting the Study of Human Biology" (Garn), 107
Cultural revolution, 156–163
  history and, 169–174
  humanism and, 169–174

Dahrendorf, Ralf, 187
Dart, Raymond, 56
Darwin, Charles, xviii, 9, 20–29
  images of struggle and conflict, 22, 26
  as a product of his culture, 20–21
Darwinism, 19–35
  compared to Social Darwinism, 19–20
  conflict as a law of nature, 25
  ideology and, 24
  Nature and, 20, 27
  sociology and, 24
Darwinism and Human Life (Thomson), 20
Davidson, R. Michael, 84–85, 98
Davis, Kingsley, 184
Death instinct concept, 36–41, 44–46, 56
Death of Privacy, The (Rosenberg), 81
Democracy, humanism and, 145–146
Democratic man, 137–153
Destructiveness
  Freud on, 36–41, 44–46
  Fromm on, 42
  Maslow on, 41–42
Determinism, 50
  biological revolution and, 84–85, 92–109
  genetic, 92–109
  history and, 170–171
  humanism and, 170–171
  psychological revolution and, 121–123
  psychology and, 202
  technological revolution and, 76

Dewey, John, 50, 165, 197, 202, 208
Dilthey, Wilhelm, 6, 8, 208
DNA, 91, 95, 98
Dobzhansky, Theodosius, 30, 35
Double Helix, The (Watson), 84
Dubos, René, 26
Duncan, O. D., 102–103
Dunlop, Knight, 56

Eckland, Bruce, 95
Education
  aggression and, 63
  biological revolution and, 92, 99–100, 104–105
  compensatory, 92, 104–105
Einstein, Albert, 9
Eiseley, Loren, 25–26
Eisenhower, Dwight D., 71–73, 132, 168, 173
Eliot, T. S., 169
Ellul, Jacques, 74, 76
Enlightenment, the, 137–153, 177
Environment-heredity interactions, 96–109
Equalitarianism, 140
Erasmus, Desiderius, 146
Escape From Authority (Schaar), 51
Essay on Man, An (Cassirer), 208–209
Essay on the Principle of Population, An (Malthus), 21
"Establishment Sociology" (Horowitz), 191
Ethology, 55–67
Evolution, 19–53
  cultural, 29–35
  doctrine of, 23–24
Evolution Revolution, 98–101

Existentialism, 168, 209
Eysenck, H. J., 3, 95

Failure of Technology, The (Juenger), 74
Faulkner, William, xxi–xxii
Federalist, The, 148, 149, 151
Fenichel, Otto, 41
Ferkiss, Victor, 71–72
Ferry, W. H., 82, 90
Fleming, Donald, 87–89
Freedom, xvii, xx–xxi
  biological revolution and, 84–85, 91–92
  humanism and, 137, 141–144, 178
  psychological revolution and, 119, 121–123, 125–128
Freud, Sigmund, xviii–xix, 9, 36–52, 190, 197–199, 205
  biological orientation of, 43
  death instinct concept, 36–41, 44–46, 56
  on destructiveness, 36–41, 44–46
  Marx and, 48–49
  as a product of his culture, 37–38, 44–45, 199
Freud, Sophie, 38
Friedman, Maurice, 10
Friedrichs, Robert W., 4, 9, 183–184, 195
Fromm, Erich, 43, 50, 51, 162–163, 202, 208
  on destructiveness, 42
  on individuality, 74–75
Fulbright, J. William, 110
Functionalism
  humanism and, 182–187
  in sociology, 182–187
Functions of Social Conflict, The (Coser), 191

Future Shock (Toffler), 84
Futurists
   biological revolution and, 88–
      90
   technological revolution and,
      90

Galileo, 9
Gallagher, Cornelius J., 132
Garfinkel, Harold, 192
Garn, Stanley, 107–108
Genetic determinism, 92–109
Goffman, Erving, 14, 192
Goodman, Paul, 161
Gouldner, Alvin W., 9, 10, 13,
      186, 192, 194–195
Grant, Madison, 29
Greening of America, The
      (Reich), 157–160
Grotius, Hugo, 140
Gumplowicz, Ludwig, 2, 117,
      166

Halévy, Elie, 114
Hall, Calvin S., 206
Hamilton, Alexander, 146–148
Hampden-Turner, Charles, 161
Hardin, Garrett, 20
Harman, Willis, 9
Harrington, Gordon M., 106–
      108
Harris, Marvin, 20–23, 171
Hartley, David, 114
Haydn, Hiram, 146
Hegel, Georg Wilhelm, 178, 184
Heidbreder, Edna, 116
Heilbroner, Robert L., 71
Heredity
   -environment interactions,
      96–109

intelligence and, 92–96, 104–
      106
Hield, Wayne, 187
Higham, John, 164–168, 173,
      178–179
History
   consensus, 167–174
   conservatism and, 167–174
   culture and, 169–174
   determinism and, 170–171
   humanism and, 164–180
   the New Left, 174–180
   Progressives, 164–167, 172–
      173
Hobbes, Thomas, 2, 113, 144,
      146, 148
Hofstadter, Richard, 24–25, 27–
      28, 165–168, 175–176, 178,
      179
Holbach, Baron Paul Henri, 114
Holloway, Ralph, 64
Holmes, Oliver Wendell, 150,
      165
Hooker, Sir Joseph, 23
Horney, Karen, 43, 202, 208
Horowitz, Irving Louis, 182,
      186, 188, 191
Hull, Clark L., 4, 119
*Human Use of Human Beings,
   The* (Wiener), 109
Humanism, 137–210
   Academic Counterculture,
      154–163
   the American Creed, 137–
      153
   American Revolution and,
      138, 140, 142, 145, 147,
      151, 175–177
   biological revolution and, 29–
      30, 90
   consensus history, 167–174
   conservatism and, 167–174,
      181

Humanism (*cont'd*)
   cultural revolution and, 156–163
   culture and, 169–174
   defined, 194, 203–204
   democracy and, 145–146
   democratic man, 137–153
   determinism and, 170–171
   the Enlightenment, 137–153, 177
   equalitarianism and, 140
   freedom and, 137, 141–144, 178
   functionalism and, 182–187
   history and, 164–180
   human nature and, 138, 140, 146, 150, 154, 176–177
   individuality and, 140
   natural rights and, 143–145
   the New Left, 174–180, 189–190
   person-centered, 161–163
   populism and, 140
   Progressives and, 164–167, 172–173
   psychology and, 196–210
   Puritanism and, 141, 143
   radical, 154–163, 188–189
   the social contract and, 145
   sociology and, 181–195
   technological revolution and, 90, 156–160, 183
   utopianism and, 140–141, 185–187
Humanistic indeterminism, 76
Hunt, J. M., 96, 97
Huxley, Aldous, 132
Huxley, Julian, 26, 29
Huxley, Thomas, 23
Hyman, Stanley Edgar, 22, 44

Individuality
   Fromm on, 74–75

   humanism and, 140
   psychological revolution and, 110–133
   technological revolution and, 75–83
Instinctual (biological) aggression theory, 24–25, 28–29, 55–67
Intelligence
   defined, 103
   genetically fixed and predetermined, 93–94
   heredity and, 92–96, 104–106
   racial differences in, 92–96, 104–106
Intelligence and Experience (Hunt), 96
IQ, 94, 97, 101–109

Jacobs, Paul, 161
James, William, 165, 197
Jaspers, Karl, 209
Jefferson, Thomas, 146, 147, 150
Jensen, Arthur R., 92–94, 101–107
Jones, Ernest, 188
Juenger, Friedrich, 74
Jung, Carl Gustav, 202, 206

Kafka, Franz, xvii–xviii
Kahn, Herman, 76
Keith, Sir Arthur, 56
Keynes, John Maynard, 21
King, Martin Luther, 173
Kipling, Rudyard, xiii
Klein, Melanie, 51, 52
Kluckhohn, Clyde, 169, 170
Knowledge, self-observing, 9–10
Koch, Sigmund, 119, 127, 197

Koestler, Arthur, 8
Krech, David, 99–100
Kroeber, Alfred, 169, 170
Kropotkin, Prince Pëtr Aleksee-
    vich, 27
Krutch, Joseph Wood, 204
Kuhn, Thomas, 10

La Mettrie, Julien Offroy de,
    xvi, 114
Lederberg, Joshua, 89, 98–99
Lemisch, Jesse, 176–177
Leonard, George B., 156
Life Against Death (Brown),
    45–46
Lindzey, Gardner, 206
Lippmann, Walter, 82
Locke, John, 113, 140, 144–146
LOGIC (Local Government In-
    formation Control), 81
Lorenz, Konrad, 36, 57–67, 95
    on aggression, 57–67
Love and Will (May), 198–199
Lovejoy, Arthur O., 1, 146
Lowenthal, Leo, 193
Lyell, Charles, 23
Lyman, Stanford M., 193
Lynd, Staughton, 177–178

McConnell, James, 115
McDougall, William, 56
Machiavelli, Niccolò, 65, 144,
    146
McLuhan, Marshall, 76
Macy, John, 78–79
Madison, James, 147–151
Magna Carta, 151
Malthus, Thomas Robert, 21
Man
    as a beast, xiv, xvi–xx
    as a free agent, xiv, xx–xxii
    as a machine, xiv–xvi
    as the self-conscious animal,
        xiv
Mankind Quarterly, The, 94
Mannheim, Karl, 6, 7, 14
Marcuse, Herbert, xxi, 41, 44,
    47–49, 161, 190
Marx, Karl, 6, 9, 75, 190
    Freud and, 48–49
Maslow, Abraham, xiv, 8, 201,
    202, 206–207
    on destructiveness, 41–42
Materialism, psychological revo-
    lution and, 112–113
May, Rollo, 198–199, 202, 209
Mead, G. H., 193, 202, 208
Mead, Margaret, 31
"Meaning for 'Humanism' "
    (Krutch), 204
Means, Richard L., 8, 12, 54
Medawar, P. B., 30
Mesthene, Emanuel G., 72
"Metamorphosis, The" (Kafka),
    xvii–xviii
Mill, James, 114
Mill, John Stuart, 8
Miller, Arthur R., 79
Mills, C. Wright, 174, 182, 187–
    190, 193, 196
Minority unrest, 176
Molecular biology, 86–87
Montagu, Ashley, 63
Montaigne, Michel Eyquem de,
    xiii
Montesquieu, 140, 147–148
Moore, Barrington, 187
More, Thomas, 146
Morgenthau, Hans, 142–143
Morris, Desmond, 57–61, 95
Moustakas, Clark, 206
Muller, Herbert J., 74
Muller, Herman G., 89

Mumford, Lewis, 13, 15, 74, 90, 109, 133, 157
  indeterministic view of, 76
Murphy, Gardner, 95–96
Mutual Aid (Kropotkin), 27
Myrdal, Gunnar, 137–138, 140, 153
Myth of the Machine, The (Mumford), 76

Nash, Manning, 93, 104, 105
National Academy of Sciences, 94
National data bank, 77–83
Natural rights, 143–145
Nature-nurture controversy, 90–92
Negro-white intelligence difference, 92–94, 104–106
Neo-Darwinism, 26, 28
Neo-Freudianism, 47–49, 52
  revisionists, 43–44
New Deal, 167
New Left, the, 174–180, 189–190
New Sociology, The (Horowitz), 188
Newton, Sir Isaac, xvi
Niebuhr, H. Richard, 4–6, 168
Nisbet, Robert A., 193
Nixon, Richard M., 77

Odegard, Peter, 185
On Aggression (Lorenz), 57–58
One-Dimensional Man (Marcuse), 190
Opler, Morris, 53
Origin of Species (Darwin), 21–23

Padover, Saul K., 145, 148
Paine, Tom, 141–142, 150
Parrington, Vernon, 165–167
Parsons, Talcott, 182–192
Pavlov, Ivan Petrovich, 114, 115
Pentagon of Power, The (Mumford), 76, 133
Percy, Thomas, xiii
Personalism, 9, 202–203
Person-centered humanism, 161–163
Pettigrew, Thomas F., 96–97
Pickering, Sir George, 87
Plato, xiii, 149
Polanyi, Michael, 8
Pollock, Norman, 177
Populism, 140
Posthistoric Man (Seidenberg), 83
Pound, Roscoe, 165
Power Elite, The (Mills), 174, 189
Pragmatism, Social Darwinism and, 28
Privacy, technological revolution and, 79–83
Progressive Historians, The (Hofstadter), 165–166, 175
Progressives
  history and, 164–167, 172–173
  humanism and, 164–167, 172–173
Psychological revolution, 110–133
  behaviorism and, 110–133
  the conditioned reflex, 114
  determinism and, 121–123
  freedom and, 119, 121–123, 125–128
  individuality and, 110–133
  materialism and, 112–113

Psychological revolution (cont'd)
technological revolution and,
73
Psychology, 196–210
determinism and, 202
humanism and, 196–210
personalism in, 202–203
technological revolution and,
203
Psychotechnocracy, 110–133
Psychotechnology, 127–131
Pufendorf, Baron Samuel von,
140
Puritanism, humanism and,
141, 143
Putnam, Carleton, 94

Race and Reason (Putnam), 94
Races
genetic differences in intelli-
gence, 92–96, 104–106
Social Darwinism and, 28–29
Radical humanism, 154–163,
188–189
Rapoport, Anatol, 90
Ratzenhofer, Gustav, 166
Reflections on Human Nature
(Lovejoy), 1
Reich, Charles, 9, 90, 157–160
Reich, Wilhelm, 41
Revolution of Hope, The: To-
ward a Humanized Society
(Fromm), 74–75
Rieff, Philip, 48, 199–200
Riesman, David, 50
Riezler, Kurt, 207
Rights of Man, The (Paine),
141–142
RNA, 95
Roazen, Paul, 41, 44, 51–52
Robert, Marthe, 39
Robinson, James Harvey, 167

Robopaths: People as Machines
(Yablonsky), 75, 157
Rogers, Carl, 202, 205, 209
Rosenberg, Jerry M., 81
Rossiter, Clinton, 174
Rostand, Jean, 87, 98
Roszak, Theodore, 8, 9, 156,
161, 190
Rousseau, Jean-Jacques, xiii,
140, 143, 146, 149
Ruggles, Richard, 78
Ruggles Committee, 78

Sahl, Mort, 174
Sartre, Jean-Paul, xx
Schaar, John H., 44, 51
Schachtel, Ernest G., xx
Scheler, Max, 6
Schlesinger, Arthur, Jr., 168
Schneirla, T. C., 62–64
Schwartz, Eugene S., 156–157
Science and Human Behavior
(Skinner), 121
" 'Scientific' Racism Again?"
(Comas), 94
Scott, J. P., 62
Scott, Marvin B., 193
Seeley, John, 43–44
Seidenberg, Roderick, 74, 76,
83
Self-observing knowledge, 9–10
Seneca, Marcus Annaeus, xiii
Sensationalism, 113
Severin, Frank, 205
Shils, Edward W., 80
Shockley, William, 94
Shuey, Audrey M., 94
Simmel, Georg, 191
Simpson, George Gaylord, 29–
30
Skinner, B. F., xxi, 111, 112,
117–128, 185, 186, 197,
198

Skinner Box, 124
Skotheim, Robert Allen, 172
Slater, Philip, 9
Social (cultural) aggression, 55, 61–67
Social contract, the, 145
Social Darwinism, xviii, 27–28, 56, 67
  compared to Darwinism, 19–20
  instinctual aggression theory, 24–25, 28–29
  pragmatism and, 28
  scientific racism and, 28–29
Social Science Research Council, 78
Social System, The (Parsons), 182
Sociological Imagination, The (Mills), 187–188
Sociology, 181–195
  consensus, 182, 186, 191
  conservatism in, 181
  Darwinism and, 24
  functionalism and, 182–187
  humanism and, 181–195
  the New Left, 189–190
  system in, 181, 183–184
  utopianism and, 185–187
Sociology of the Absurd (Lyman and Scott), 193
Sociology Liberation Front, 189–190
"Sociology for Sale" (Horowitz), 191
Sociology on Trial (Stein and Vidich), 188
Socrates, xiv, 13, 146, 208–209
Spencer, Herbert, 21–24, 184, 185
Spencerianism, 22, 28
Spengler, Oswald, 45

Spirit of the Laws (Montesquieu), 147
Spitz, David, 103
Staude, John R., 194
Steffens, Lincoln, 165
Stein, Maurice, 188
Stoddard, Lothrop, 29
Storr, Anthony, 95
Strachey, Lytton, xix
Student activism, 155
"Study of Change in Social Science, The" (Hield), 187
Sullivan, Harry Stack, 42, 43, 202, 208

Tarbell, Ida Minerva, 165
Tatum, Edward L., 98–99
Taylor, Gordon Rattray, 84, 98
Technological ethos, 73–77, 88–89
Technological Man (Ferkiss), 71–72
Technological revolution, 71–83
  Academic Counterculture and, 156–160
  biological revolution and, 73
  control and, 72
  determinism and, 76
  futurists and, 90
  humanism and, 90, 156–160, 183
  individuality and, 75–83
  national data bank, 77–83
  privacy and, 79–83
  psychological revolution and, 73
  psychology and, 203
  technological ethos and, 73–77, 88–89
Teilhard de Chardin, Pierre, 3, 10
Tennyson, Alfred Lord, xiii, 22

Territorial Imperative, The
    (Ardrey), 57–58
Testing of Negro Intelligence,
    The (Shuey), 94
Thompson, Clara, 43
Thompson, William Irwin, 156
Thomson, J. Arthur, 20
Thrasymachus, 146
Tiger, Lionel, 56, 57, 61, 64, 94
Tillich, Paul, 209
Tinbergen, Niko, 57, 95
Toffler, Alvin, 76, 84
Toward a General Theory of
    Action (Parsons), 182
Trilling, Lionel, 41, 44, 45, 169
Trotter, Wilfred, 56
Turgot, Anne Robert Jacques,
    34
Turner, Frederick Jackson, 165,
    167

U.S. Bill of Rights, 138, 151,
    153
U.S. Bureau of Internal Rev-
    enue, 80
U.S. Congress, 80
U.S. Constitution, 77, 81, 138,
    147, 148, 151
U.S. Supreme Court, 173
Untermeyer, Louis, xiii
Utopianism
    humanism and, 140–141,
        185–187
    sociology and, 185–187

Veblen, Thorstein, 165
Vidich, Arthur, 188
Voltaire, 34, 140

Waddington, C. H., 32
Walden Two (Skinner), 111,
    120, 121, 123–125
Wallace, Alfred, 21
Ward, Harry Frederick, 165
Watergate, 14, 77, 82
Watson, James D., 84
Watson, John B., xvi, 2, 110–
    120, 124, 197, 198
Weber, Max, 6
Weltanschauung, 46
Wertham, Frederic, 53–54
Wesman, Alexander G., 101–
    102
White, Leslie, 171
White, Lynn, Jr., 73
White Collar (Mills), 189
Wiener, Norbert, 72, 109
Wirth, Louis, 7
Wolfe, Don M., 141, 142
Wrong, Dennis, 186, 208
Wundt, Wilhelm, 197

Yablonsky, Lewis, 75, 157

Zeitgeist, 56, 66, 198
Zuckerman, Sir Solly, 62

128.3   c.1
M   Matson, F.W.

                The idea of man